Connecting the Isiac Cults

Scientific Studies of Religion: Inquiry and Explanation

Series editors: Luther H. Martin, Donald Wiebe, Radek Kundt, and Dimitris Xygalatas

Scientific Studies of Religion: Inquiry and Explanation publishes cutting-edge research in the new and growing field of scientific studies in religion. Its aim is to publish empirical, experimental, historical, and ethnographic research on religious thought, behaviour, and institutional structures. The series works with a broad notion of scientific that includes innovative work on understanding religion(s), both past and present. With an emphasis on the cognitive science of religion, the series includes complementary approaches to the study of religion, such as psychology and computer modeling of religious data. Titles seek to provide explanatory accounts for the religious behaviors under review, both past and present.

The Attraction of Religion
Edited by D. Jason Slone and James A. Van Slyke

The Cognitive Science of Religion
Edited by D. Jason Slone and William W. McCorkle Jr.

The Construction of the Supernatural in Euro-American Cultures
Benson Saler

Contemporary Evolutionary Theories of Culture and the Study of Religion
Radek Kundt

Death Anxiety and Religious Belief
Jonathan Jong and Jamin Halberstadt

Gnosticism and the History of Religions
David G. Robertson

The Impact of Ritual on Child Cognition
Veronika Rybanska

Language, Cognition, and Biblical Exegesis
Edited by Ronit Nikolsky, Istvan Czachesz, Frederick S. Tappenden and Tamas Biro

The Learned Practice of Religion in the Modern University
Donald Wiebe

The Mind of Mithraists
Luther H. Martin

Naturalism and Protectionism in the Study of Religion
Juraj Franek

New Patterns for Comparative Religion
William E. Paden

Philosophical Foundations of the Cognitive Science of Religion
Robert N. McCauley with E. Thomas Lawson

Religion, Disease, and Immunology
Thomas B. Ellis

Religion Explained?
Edited by Luther H. Martin and Donald Wiebe

Religion in Science Fiction
Steven Hrotic

Religious Evolution and the Axial Age
Stephen K. Sanderson

The Roman Mithras Cult
Olympia Panagiotidou with Roger Beck

Solving the Evolutionary Puzzle of Human Cooperation
Glenn Barenthin

The Study of Greek and Roman Religions
Nickolas P. Roubekas

Understanding Religion Through Artificial Intelligence
Justin E. Lane

Connecting the Isiac Cults

*Formal Modeling in the
Hellenistic Mediterranean*

Tomáš Glomb

BLOOMSBURY ACADEMIC
LONDON • NEW YORK • OXFORD • NEW DELHI • SYDNEY

BLOOMSBURY ACADEMIC
Bloomsbury Publishing Plc
50 Bedford Square, London, WC1B 3DP, UK
1385 Broadway, New York, NY 10018, USA
29 Earlsfort Terrace, Dublin 2, Ireland

BLOOMSBURY, BLOOMSBURY ACADEMIC and the Diana logo are trademarks of Bloomsbury Publishing Plc

First published in Great Britain 2023
This paperback edition published 2024

Copyright © Tomáš Glomb, 2023

Tomáš Glomb has asserted his right under the Copyright, Designs and Patents Act, 1988, to be identified as Author of this work.

For legal purposes the Acknowledgments on pp. x–xi constitute an extension of this copyright page.

All rights reserved. No part of this publication may be reproduced or transmitted in any form or by any means, electronic or mechanical, including photocopying, recording, or any information storage or retrieval system, without prior permission in writing from the publishers.

Bloomsbury Publishing Plc does not have any control over, or responsibility for, any third-party websites referred to or in this book. All internet addresses given in this book were correct at the time of going to press. The author and publisher regret any inconvenience caused if addresses have changed or sites have ceased to exist, but can accept no responsibility for any such changes.

A catalogue record for this book is available from the British Library.

Library of Congress Control Number: 2022940167

ISBN: HB: 978-1-3502-1069-1
PB: 978-1-3502-1073-8
ePDF: 978-1-3502-1070-7
eBook: 978-1-3502-1071-4

Series: Scientific Studies of Religion: Inquiry and Explanation

Typeset by Newgen KnowledgeWorks Pvt. Ltd., Chennai, India

To find out more about our authors and books visit www.bloomsbury.com and sign up for our newsletters.

To my Mom, Dad, Kateřina, and all the good dogs …

Contents

List of Figures	viii
List of Tables	ix
Acknowledgments	x
List of Abbreviations	xii

1	Introduction	1
2	Development of the Isiac Cults	7
3	Spread of the Isiac Cults: An Overview	19
4	Case Study 1: Spread of the Isiac Cults across the Aegean Sea	55
5	Case Study 2: Spread of the Isiac Cults on the West Coast of Asia Minor	89
6	Political Activities of the Ptolemaic Dynasty and Their Impact on the Spread of the Isiac Cults Abroad: A Historical Pattern	115

Appendix: Places under Ptolemaic Influence	143
References	157
Index	175

Figures

3.1	Spatial extent of the early and final spread of the Isiac cults outside Egypt	32
3.2	Islands in the Aegean Sea	34
3.3	Greece with relevant ancient cities	37
3.4	Northern Aegean with relevant ancient cities	39
3.5	Western Asia Minor with relevant ancient cities	40
3.6	Eastern Mediterranean with relevant ancient cities	43
3.7	Black Sea region with relevant ancient cities	46
4.1	Area of interest—case study 1	56
4.2	Transportation network of the case study 1	71
4.3	Dissemination of relevant Ptolemaic military garrisons together with temples and artifacts related to the Isiac cults in the area of interest on the transportation network	73
4.4	Average monthly precipitation (mm) in the Aegean Sea between 1960 and 1990	74
4.5	Overall scheme of the famine vulnerability model	75
4.6	Food shortage vulnerability—output from the environmental model	79
4.7	Visualization of the parameters	80
5.1	Area of interest with regions—case study 2	93
5.2	Transportation network on the west coast of Hellenistic Asia Minor	101
5.3	Places under the Ptolemaic influence and the evidence of the Isiac cults on the west coast of Hellenistic Asia Minor in the period of interest	102
5.4	Visualization of the "number of visits" parameter on the west coast of Hellenistic Asia Minor	105
5.5	Dendrogram with groups of similar cities with respect to their parameters	107
A.1	Ptolemaic garrisons and places under Ptolemaic influence incorporated in case studies 1 and 2	156

Table

4.1 Variance in spatial intensity of the Isiac cults explained by selected factors   83

Acknowledgments

The research presented in this book is based on two case studies previously published in *PLOS One*. Chapter 4, Case Study 1—Spread of the Isiac Cults across the Aegean Sea, is an extended and edited version of the research article: Glomb, Tomáš, Adam Mertel, Zdeněk Pospíšil, Zdeněk Stachoň, and Aleš Chalupa. 2018. "Ptolemaic Military Operations Were a Dominant Factor in the Spread of Egyptian Cults across the Early Hellenistic Aegean Sea." *PLOS One* 13 (3): e0193786. Chapter 5, Case Study 2—Spread of the Isiac Cults on the West Coast of Asia Minor, is an expanded version of the research article: Glomb, Tomáš, Adam Mertel, Zdeněk Pospíšil, and Aleš Chalupa. 2020. "Ptolemaic Political Activities on the West Coast of Hellenistic Asia Minor Had a Significant Impact on the Local Spread of the Isiac Cults: A Spatial Network Analysis." *PLOS One* 15 (4): e0230733.

I am very thankful for all the support from my friends and colleagues from the Department for the Study of Religions at Masaryk University in Brno. Specifically, I would like to thank David Zbíral for guidance and ideas, which helped to shape this research, both in my student and postdoctoral years. I would also like to express my gratitude to Aleš Chalupa, who pushed forward the methodology of formalized modeling at the department and taught me how to approach history in innovative ways. I would like to thank the whole interdisciplinary team from the Generative Historiography of Religion (GEHIR) project for a great collaborative environment throughout my doctoral studies and for their friendship. I am especially grateful to Adam Mertel, Zdeněk Pospíšil, and Zdeněk Stachoň for their geographical and mathematical expertise and contribution to the research presented in this book.

I also want to thank the editors and colleagues that made possible the transformation from a book proposal to the present text. Radek Kundt, who first told me that I could write this book with Bloomsbury, deserves my gratitude for this opportunity. I thank to Luther H. Martin and Donald Wiebe for their nice words and comments on my book proposal. I am very grateful to Lalle Pursglove and Lily McMahon from Bloomsbury for providing helping hand with necessities related to making this book and for checking up on me during the writing process.

Finally, I want to thank my friends and colleagues from the University of Bergen, Eivind Heldaas Seland and Francesca Mazzilli, who always provided me with positive energy while I was working on the manuscript.

Abbreviations

IC	Guarducci, Margherita, ed. 1935–1950. *Inscriptiones Creticae*, 4 vols. Rome: Libreria dello Stato.
ID	Roussel, Pierre, and Marcel Launey, eds. 1937. *Inscriptions de Délos: Vol. 4. Décrets postérieurs à 166 av. J.-C. (Nos 1497–1524), Dédicaces postérieures à 166 av. J.-C. (Nos 1525–2219)*. Paris: Champion.
IG II.^{2}	Kirchner, Johannes, ed. 1913–1940. *Inscriptiones Graecae II et III: Inscriptiones Atticae Euclidis anno posteriores*, 2nd edn. Berlin: Reimer.
IG II.^{3}1	Lambert, Steven D., Michael J. Osborne, Sean G. Byrne, Voula N. Bardani, and Stephen V. Tracy, eds. 2012. *Inscriptiones Graecae II et III: Inscriptiones Atticae Euclidis anno posteriores*, 3rd edn. Berlin: De Gruyter.
IG XI.4	Roussel, Pierre, ed. 1914. *Inscriptiones Graecae XI. Inscriptiones Deli*, fasc. 4. Berlin: Reimer.
IG XII.3	Hiller von Gaertringen, Friedrich, ed. 1898. *Inscriptiones Graecae, XII. Inscriptiones Insularum Maris Aegaei Praeter Delum, 3. Inscriptiones Symes, Teutlussae, Teli, Nisyri, Astypalaeae, Anaphes, Therae et Therasiae, Pholegandri, Meli, Cimoli*. Berlin: Reimer—with Hiller von Gaertringen, Friedrich, ed. 1904. *Inscriptiones Graecae, XII,3. Supplementum*. Berlin: Reimer.
IG XII.5	Hiller von Gaertringen, Friedrich, ed. 1903–1909. *Inscriptiones Graecae XII,5. Inscriptiones Cycladum*. Berlin: Reimer.
IG XII.7	Delamarre, Jules, ed. 1908. *Inscriptiones Graecae XII,7. Inscriptiones Amorgi et insularum vicinarum*. Berlin: Reimer.
OGIS	Dittenberger, Wilhelm, ed. 1903–1905. *Orientis Graeci Inscriptiones Selectae*, 2 vols. Lipsiae: S. Hirzel.
P.Eleph.	Rubensohn, Otto, Wilhelm Spiegelberg, Wilhelm Schubart, and American Society of Papyrologists. 1907. *Elephantine-Papyri*. Berlin: Weidmann.

P.Tebt.	Grenfell, Bernard P., Campbell C. Edgar, Edgar J. Goodspeed, Josiah G. Smyly, and Arthur S. Hunt, eds. 1902–1976. *The Tebtunis Papyri*, 4 vols. London: H. Frowde.
RICIS	Bricault, Laurent. 2005. *Recueil des Inscriptions concernant les Cultes Isiaques: RICIS*. Paris: Diffusion de Boccard; Bricault, Laurent. 2008. "RICIS Supplément I." In *Bibliotheca Isiaca I*, edited by L. Bricault, 77–130. Bordeaux: Ausonius; Bricault, Laurent. 2011. "RICIS Supplément II." In *Bibliotheca Isiaca II*, edited by L. Bricault and R. Veymiers, 273–316. Bordeaux: Ausonius; Bricault, Laurent. 2014. "RICIS Supplément III." In *Bibliotheca Isiaca III*, edited by L. Bricault and R. Veymiers, 139–206. Bordeaux: Ausonius; Bricault, Laurent. 2020. "RICIS Supplément IV." In *Bibliotheca Isiaca IV*, edited by L. Bricault and R. Veymiers, 357–82. Bordeaux: Ausonius.
SB	Preisigke, Friedrich, Friedrich Bilabel, Emil Kiessling, and Hans-Albert Rupprecht, eds. 1915–1993. *Sammelbuch griechischer Urkunden aus Ägypten*. Strassburg: K. J. Trübner (vol. 1), Berlin and Leipzig: W. de Gruyter (2–3), Heidelberg: Im Selbstverlag des Verfassers (4), and Wiesbaden: Harrassowitz (5–18).

1

Introduction

After the campaign of Alexander the Great had ended with his death in 323 BCE, the Mediterranean world was bigger and more ethnically mixed than before his time. The *diadochi*, that is, the former generals and companions of Alexander the Great, became rivals and engaged in a power struggle to control parts of the empire that Alexander had left behind. Egypt, where Alexander had been recognized as a pharaoh, came under the rule of Ptolemy, a former Macedonian general of Alexander's army, later known as Ptolemy I Soter. From then on, the Ptolemaic dynasty ruled Egypt for three centuries (Anson 2014; Hölbl 2001). In this context, the Egyptian cults related to the divine couple of Isis and Sarapis (i.e., the Isiac cults) began to spread from Egypt to islands and other coastal regions of the Mediterranean world. In the subsequent centuries, these cults spread further inland, and by the fourth century CE, the Isiac cults had been disseminated across the whole Roman empire (Bricault 2013, 2005b, 2001, 2004). This book focuses on the question of which factors were behind the success of the early spread of the Isiac cults and which of these factors had more impact on the process of the spread than others. The time frame of the early spread covers approximately the first two centuries of the Ptolemaic dynasty (end of the fourth century BCE–second century BCE), before Egypt and its political and economic partners came under Roman influence.

At the time when this book is being written, the academic discussion on the spread of the Isiac cults is already more than a century old. Throughout the years, the discussion yielded several persuasive, but often mutually opposing, hypotheses pointing to different factors behind the success of the early spread of the Isiac cults. The first of such hypotheses shared the assumption that history was a result of important events revolving around intentions of significant historical figures (see e.g., Fraser 1960; Cumont 1911)—a view that was not seriously challenged in the discussion on this topic for a long time. The situation eventually changed, and some of the contemporary researchers hypothesize that the process of the early spread of the Isiac cults is a more complex issue and that factors affecting the spread could be related to the political, economic, and social spheres of the ancient Mediterranean (Bricault 2004). However, a firm consensus is still absent in the debate, and the question of which factors had more weight than others remains unresolved.

So far, research on this topic has been conducted by using established historiographical methods such as critical analysis of archaeological and literary sources. The lack of the firm consensus and the inability to construct more specific hypotheses in the discussion on the early spread of the Isiac cults outside Egypt possibly indicate that this "traditional" historiographical methodology is reaching its limits. This book presents interdisciplinary approaches and results and demonstrates that these limits can be overcome, and the debate pushed forward. More specifically, this book aims to discuss how to supplement the historiographical methodological apparatus by innovative methods used in the study of the dynamics of complex systems (i.e., mathematical and geospatial modeling, network science).

To be able to identify the crucial factors influencing the spread of the Isiac cults outside Egypt and to compare their respective impact on the process of the spread using interdisciplinary and often mathematically oriented methods, the research topic has to be defined systematically and as specifically as possible. This book follows and evaluates the hypothesis of a leading researcher in the Isiac studies, Laurent Bricault, that the early spread of the Isiac cults is a long-term, complex, and multivariate process (Bricault 2004). The book deals with the research problem from the spatial-populational (macro) perspective. Therefore, it does not consider any possible cognitive (Pachis 2014) or micro-social factors in the presented analyses. The epicenter of the spread of the Isiac cults was Hellenistic Egypt and, more specifically, Alexandria, its capital and the main port. The outcome of the early spread is attested by collected and geocoded archaeological evidence (Bricault 2005b). The results of the current discussion are that the spread of the Isiac cults was significantly influenced by the interplay of political, economic, and social factors (Bricault 2004). However, we have to bear in mind that the spread of these cults and the key factors were scrutinized mainly by established historiographical methods. Inviting other disciplines, such as mathematics, geography, and network science, into this research opens the way to (a) proceed into greater detail when selecting and defining the factors of the spread and (b) evaluate quantitatively the interplay between the selected factors and their individual weight in the spreading process. However, the combination of the factors essential for the spread, their individual impact, and mutual interplay could have varied significantly in different regions of the ancient Mediterranean. For example, political, economic, and certainly geographic conditions of the ancient Aegean Islands were very different to the aspects relevant for the ancient Asia Minor or Italy. In other words, it is not possible to perceive the ancient Mediterranean as politically, economically, demographically, or geographically homogenous.

Following that rationale, this book focuses on the specific situation of the early spread of the Isiac cults in two regions—Hellenistic Aegean Sea and western coast of Asia Minor. Each region is covered by its own case study. The case study on the Aegean Sea was previously published as "Ptolemaic Military Operations Were a Dominant Factor in the Spread of Egyptian Cults across the Early Hellenistic Aegean Sea" in *PLOS One* (Glomb et al. 2018). The case study on Asia Minor was published two years later in *PLOS One* as "Ptolemaic Political Activities on the West Coast of Hellenistic Asia Minor Had a Significant Impact on the Local Spread of the Isiac Cults: A Spatial Network Analysis" (Glomb et al. 2020). The selection of the regions in question was based on the historical reality that they were both dramatically influenced by political and economic activities of the Ptolemaic dynasty and thus serve as suitable areas for comparison with respect to factors involved in the early spread of the Isiac cults. Although the case studies were published as standalone analyses and they are separated by two years with respect to the time of their publication, they are meant to be read together as one contribution to the academic debate. Mainly, when read together, they reveal common historical trends and factors involved in both regions despite their significant geographical and political differences. They present to the reader a bigger picture of this particular cultural transmission going beyond individual pieces of historical mosaic of the spread of the Isiac cults discussed in the academic debate. In this book, the two case studies are expanded by providing detailed historical context and theoretical-methodological frame. The results are interpreted in the final chapter as one contribution, and they are thus tied together to represent the ideal form in which they should be read. To sum up, the main task of this book is to present how quantitative approaches are an adequate tool to analyze the potential impact of the individual factors in the process of the early spread of the Isiac cults across the Aegean Sea and on the western coast of Asia Minor and how the results obtained by such an approach contribute to the ongoing academic debate on the topic. The description of the chapters in this book is as follows.

Chapter 2, Development of the Isiac Cults, serves as an introduction to the history of the Isiac cults. It clarifies the cultural, political, and theological background of these cults. This chapter helps to understand the conditions in the homeland of these cults before and during their early spread. In the first part of the chapter, the origins of the divine figures of Isis and Sarapis as well as their attributes are discussed. In the second part of the chapter, the religious policies of the Ptolemaic rulers toward the Isiac cults are described in greater detail.

Chapter 3, Spread of the Isiac Cults—an Overview, describes the spatial dissemination of the Isiac cults from the fourth century BCE to the fourth century CE and puts the process of the spread in the broader historical context of the ancient Mediterranean. This chapter also delineates the most influential hypotheses from the beginning of the academic discussion on this topic, which were presented by Franz Cumont, who stressed the importance of the Ptolemaic political propaganda in the spread of the Isiac cults (Cumont 1911), and Peter M. Fraser, who opposed Cumont and claimed that the Isiac cults spread spontaneously by private initiative of pious worshippers, for example, as a possible by-product of maritime trade and grain export (Fraser 1960). The milestones of the discussion with respect to shifts in conceptualization of the spread as well as the current state of the debate are also discussed in this chapter.

The third chapter is followed by the two case studies demonstrating the potential of interdisciplinary approaches to the topic. Chapter 4, Case Study 1—Spread of the Isiac Cults across the Aegean Sea, presents the first case study oriented on the quantitative exploration of the early spread of the Isiac cults. It deals with this research problem in the area of the Hellenistic Aegean Sea region in detail and is divided into multiple subchapters leading to a quantitative analysis of the research problem. The specific temporal and geographical extent of the research problem is defined in the section 4.1, Area and Period of Interest. The century-old discussion on the topic is revisited in the section 4.2, Academic Discussion on the Early Spread of the Isiac Cults across the Ancient Aegean Sea. The section 4.3, Factors of the Spread, identifies individual factors with a potential impact on the process of the early spread of the Isiac cults across the Aegean Sea. The selection of these factors reflects the spatial-populational (macro) perspective of the book and the current state of the academic discussion on the topic. The most relevant factors in this regard belong to the political and economic (commercial) sphere of the ancient Mediterranean because the Hellenistic Aegean region was significantly impacted by Ptolemaic political and economic activities. The section 4.4, Quantitative Analysis, is the most technical part of the chapter. It focuses on the quantitative evaluation of the possible impact of different factors on the early spread of the Isiac cults across the ancient transportation network in the Aegean Sea region. First, the section introduces the ancient maritime transportation network as a platform for the quantitative analysis. The construction of the transportation network between Egypt and the Aegean Sea region is a crucial step for the analysis because these ancient routes define the relationships between Aegean ports with respect to distance and connectivity—both very important aspects with considerable impact on the spread of the Isiac cults. The second part of this section is focused on the operationalization of the factors involved in the spread of the Isiac cults. This part describes the process of transformation of the selected factors of a potential influence on the spread into geocoded parameters of the network. Subsequently, the chapter introduces a mathematical model that is able to determine which parameters of the network persuasively explain the spatial dissemination of archaeological evidence related to the Isiac cults. Finally, the chapter presents results suggesting that the Ptolemaic military activities during the third century BCE in the Aegean played a significant role in the local spread of the Isiac cults.

Following the results from the previous case study, the case study presented in Chapter 5, Case Study 2—Spread of the Isiac Cults on the West Coast of Asia Minor, aims to contribute to the question if the positive role of the Ptolemaic political activities in the process of the spread of the Isiac cults is a trend that can be revealed in other regions of the ancient Mediterranean. Geographically, this case study focuses on the early spread of the Isiac cults on the west coast of ancient Asia Minor, that is, a region with a very specific political situation related to actions of the first Ptolemaic kings. The chapter proceeds very similarly as the previous one with respect to disclosing individual research procedures. The possible impact of political factors on the spread of the Isiac cults in the west coast of Hellenistic Asia Minor is evaluated through three crucial methodological steps: (1) construction of a model of the ancient transportation network; (2) identification, categorization, and geocoding the cities under the Ptolemaic influence in the area of interest; and finally, (3) statistical analysis of the spatial relationships between the archaeological evidence related to the Isiac cults from the area of interest and the cities under the Ptolemaic influence on the ancient transportation network. The results presented in this chapter suggest that the Ptolemaic political activities in the Hellenistic Asia Minor played a very important role in the process of the spread of the Isiac cults in the region.

Chapter 6, Political Activities of the Ptolemaic Dynasty and Their Impact on the Spread of the Isiac Cults Abroad—a Historical Pattern, is conceptualized as the core of the book. It interprets the results from the two case studies and puts them in a broader historical picture of Ptolemaic policies and actions abroad using the theoretical approaches inspired by the Annales school and especially by the theorizing of Fernand Braudel who approaches history as a dynamic mixture of long-term processes and sets aside the perception of history as a series of important events. In this regard, the chapter discusses how the book relates to the field of cliodynamics, which observes dynamic historical processes and emerging historical patterns by using mathematical models. These theoretical approaches are further supplemented by the perspective of the network theory, which is a suitable tool for defining relationships between selected variables in a research problem. These approaches allow for the conceptualization of the spread of the Isiac cults as (a) a long-term transmission of specific cultic practice from one socio-spatial milieu to another and (b) a transmission happening on a transportation network. While offering explanation of the contribution of these approaches to the academic discussion on the topic of the spread of the Isiac cults, this chapter also aims to generally introduce this type of quantitative research to the audience of historians and to argue that its benefits outweigh the costs. This chapter thus ties together the insights gained by the quantitative approaches and insights derived by the established methodological apparatus of historiography in a synergic manner. It also sketches the possible future directions of research in the topic. Next to theoretical implications, this chapter also deals with the question of how the historiography of ancient Mediterranean and beyond is changing with respect to new interdisciplinary methodologies and which other methods beside those applied in the case studies presented in the book can be a fruitful addition when studying cultural transmission in antiquity. It also discusses the caveats of the quantitative approaches with respect to the validity of the results.

2

Development of the Isiac Cults

2.1 Isis and Sarapis—Historical Introduction

During the reign of the first Ptolemies in Egypt, the cult of the divine couple of Isis and Sarapis, and also their individual cults, became known and established in many coastal cities and islands of the ancient Mediterranean and subsequently spread further into the mainland (Bricault 2004, 2013; Witt 1997: 46–58; Dunand 1973a, 1980). This early phase of the spread is the main focus of the book. However, the history and formation of these cults preceding the process of their spread are also worth exploring because it could help to unveil and understand the theological aspects of the cults of Isis and Sarapis, which possibly played a significant role in the process of the adoption of the Isiac cults both inside and outside Egypt.

The personalities of Isis and Sarapis followed slightly different paths before they emerged as a divine couple under the Ptolemies. It is chronologically accurate to elaborate on the origins and evolution of the goddess Isis first. The first appearances of the goddess Isis, under her older Egyptian name Eset, are attested in the *Pyramid Texts* from the fifth dynasty, ca. 2494–2345 BCE (Witt 1997: 13–15; Münster 1968; Pinch 2002: 9–12; Malek 2014; Allen 2015). According to this literary evidence, her role at that time was to assist the deceased king. This protective aspect of Isis/Eset was in later periods subsequently accessible also to nobles and common people. Although the *Pyramid Texts* cannot be perceived as a collection of complete myths, they do allude to certain mythological scenes. Considering Isis, the *Pyramid Texts* refer to her acts of mourning and searching for her husband Osiris who was murdered by his brother Seth. According to the theology of the Heliopolitan sun cult, Isis and Osiris were children of Geb and Nut, and the goddess Isis became a wife of her brother Osiris and assisted him during his mythological kingship (Witt 1997: 36–45; Pinch 2002: 9–12, 149–52). The myth of Isis and Osiris, which is described most extensively in Plutarch's *De*

Iside et Osiride, continues with Isis reuniting the scattered body parts of dead Osiris and revivifying Osiris's sexual member. Isis then became pregnant and gave birth to her son Horus who later defeated Seth and became the rightful king of Egypt. By the time of the New Kingdom (ca. 1550–1069 BCE), Isis, Osiris, and Horus became a popular and substantially venerated divine family (Pinch 2002: 149–52). During the first millennium BCE, the cult of Isis had developed further and took on a prominent position in Egyptian culture. At that time, the figure of Isis also acquired new attributes, and some of the old ones were more highlighted. For example, she had always been perceived as a giver of life who caused the Nile floods and thus made the soil fertile (Witt 1997: 13–35). This aspect resonated with Greek views identifying her with Demeter, the Greek goddess of fertility (Witt 1997: 38, 67; Pinch 2002: 151). Isis was also venerated as a goddess of the sea, and during the Hellenistic period, sailors prayed to her for safe travels (Bricault 2006, 2020). In summary, Isis was a universal goddess with a number of significant roles such as a mourning protector, giver of life, ideal queen, wife, sister, and mother of the king. In the *Pyramid Texts* (no. 2089), the king is said to be drinking milk from the breasts of his "mother Isis." The relationship between Isis, Osiris, and Horus served as a role model for Egyptian royal families. Queens of the Ptolemaic era often identified themselves with Isis (Fraser 1972: 246–76).

The origin of the god Sarapis is a more complicated issue. The figure of the god Sarapis had suddenly emerged in the cultural context of Hellenistic Egypt, and until fourth century BCE, he had not played any part in any known myth. In the fourth century BCE, only few references relating to his existence were documented. However, in the third century BCE, the god Sarapis became popular across the Mediterranean (Stambaugh 1972; Moyer 2011: 142–207; Fraser 1972, 1960, 1967; Brady, Mitchell, and Mullett 1978). The first discussion on the nature and origins of Sarapis is datable to the Hellenistic period. In the first century BCE, Diodorus Siculus wrote (*Bibliotheca* I.25, translated by Charles H. Oldfather in Diodorus Siculus and Oldfather 1989):

> Osiris has been given the name Sarapis by some, Dionysus by others, Pluto by others, Ammon by others, Zeus by some, and many have considered Pan to be the same god; and some say that Sarapis is the god whom the Greeks call Pluto.

A story of the origins of Sarapis is recorded by Tacitus (*Historiae* IV.83–84) and Plutarch (*De Iside et Osiride* 28). They describe a legend according to which Ptolemy I ordered to bring the statue of Sarapis from Sinope to Egypt based on the instructions he had received from the god Sarapis himself in a dream (Borgeaud and Volokhine 2000). After describing the arrival of the statue of Sarapis and the subsequent construction of the temple of Sarapis in Rhacotis, Tacitus opened further discussion (*Historiae* IV.84, translated by Alfred J. Church, William J. Brodribb, and Sara Bryant 1942):

> A temple, proportioned to the grandeur of the city, was erected in a place called Rhacotis, where there had stood a chapel consecrated in old times to Serapis and Isis. Such is the most popular account of the origin and introduction of the God Serapis. I am aware indeed that there are some who say that he was brought from Seleucia, a city of Syria, in the reign of Ptolemy III., while others assert that it was the act of the same king, but that the place from which he was brought was Memphis, once a famous city and the strength of ancient Egypt. The God himself, because he heals the sick, many identified with Aesculapius; others with Osiris, the deity of the highest antiquity among these nations; not a few with Jupiter, as being supreme ruler of all things; but most people with Pluto, arguing from the emblems which may be seen on his statues, or from conjectures of their own.

Plutarch elaborated on the discussion of the origins of Sarapis as well (*De Iside et Osiride* 28, translated by Frank C. Babbitt in Plutarch 1936):

> It is better to identify Osiris with Dionysus and Serapis with Osiris, who received this appellation at the time when he changed his nature. For this reason Serapis is a god of all peoples in common, even as Osiris is; and this they who have participated in the holy rites well know.

Cyril of Alexandria revisited this discussion in the fourth century CE (*Contra Iulianum* I.13, translated by John E. Stambaugh in Stambaugh 1972: 3–4):

> Some do not think that he is Pluto, but rather Osiris, or according to others Apis; as there was a great deal of contention about this matter, they erected the image, they say, when they had come to agreement, of "Osirapis," as if from a single compound, so that both Osiris and Apis would be thought of in the same deity.

The identification of Sarapis with the Egyptian bull god Apis is also mentioned by Nymphodorus who presumably lived in the third century BCE (Clement of Alexandria, *Stromateis* I.21). The identification with Osiris and Apis is mentioned by Athenodorus of Tarsus (Clement of Alexandria, *Protrepticus* IV.48). Both these references are, however, only secondarily referred to by Clement of Alexandria.

Besides Tacitus's and Plutarch's ancient accounts connecting the introduction of the cult of Sarapis to Ptolemy I, there are other literary sources referring to Sarapis in the time of Ptolemy I. Macrobius states that Nicocreon, the king of Cyprus, received an oracle from Sarapis (Macrobius, *Saturnalia* I.20.16). Nicocreon died in 312/11 BCE, which is the time when Ptolemy I had already consolidated his rule over Egypt (although he assumed the title of the king in 305 BCE). In another source, Menander incorporated the line "How holy is the god Sarapis!" into one of his plays before he died in 290 BCE (Fraser 1967: 41; Stambaugh 1972: 10; Pfeiffer 2008: 390). Moreover, a Greek dedication of the statue found in Alexandrian Serapeum is often dated to the time of Ptolemy I as well—the text is as follows: "Delok[les had it (i.e. the statue) m]ade. Aristodemos, son of Dio[..]os, Athenian, had it (dedicated) to Serapis and to Isis" (Bernand 2001, No. 2; translated in Pfeiffer 2008: 394).

However, there is also literary evidence rendering Alexander the Great as a founder or participant of the cult of Sarapis in Alexandria or in Babylon. This complicated the modern discussion focusing both on the time and place of the origins of Sarapis. The first evidence drawing such a connection is *Historia Alexandri Magni* by Pseudo-Callisthenes. *Historia Alexandri Magni* is a biographical novel narrating legendary deeds of Alexander the Great. The text is most probably a composition of several other texts, and its oldest versions are dated to the third century CE (Stambaugh 1972: 11; Samuel 1986). According to *Historia Alexandri Magni*, Alexander discovered Sarapis to be an ancient Egyptian deity and dedicated a temple in newly founded Alexandria to him. However, the text has only a limited historical value in this regard because it is of a very late date and the acts of Alexander described there have legendary and mythical attributes. More historically accurate accounts of Alexander's campaign (Plutarch, *Alexander* 76; Arrian, *Anabasis* VII.26.2) mention that shortly before his death, Alexander consulted Sarapis in his temple in Babylon. The credibility of these references is often dismissed based on the assumption that the name of a native Babylonian deity in the original royal diaries of Alexander could have been changed to Sarapis by these later authors because Sarapis was a popular deity during their lifetime (cf. e.g., Anson 1996; Pearson 1955; Fraser 1967: 29; Bosworth 1988; Hammond 1988). However, the academic discussion on the credibility of this possibility mentioned by Plutarch and Arrian is still open (Bosworth 1988; Chugg 2005).

The consensus among researchers is that with high probability Sarapis is of Egyptian origins (see e.g., Wilcken 1927; Stambaugh 1972; Fraser 1960, 1967; Moyer 2011; Pfeiffer 2008). The evidence supporting such a hypothesis was most convincingly introduced by the historian and papyrologist Ulrich Wilcken in the first half of the twentieth century (Wilcken 1927). A piece of archeological evidence that supports significantly the hypothesis of Sarapis's Egyptian origins is a fragmentary curse dated to late fourth century BCE and preserved on a papyrus (Wilcken 1927: 77–89, 97–104; Rowlandson and Bagnall 1998: 63; "The Curse of Artemisia" n.d.). A woman named Artemisia, daughter of Amasis, appeals in the text to a god named Oserapis to punish the father of her daughter because the man did not arrange a proper burial for her child. Artemisia is a Greek name; however, Amasis is an Egyptian one. The fragmentary curse of Artemisia points to a specific and ethnically mixed community in Egyptian Memphis, sometimes called Hellenomemphites. A Greek community existed in Memphis as early as the sixth century BCE after Ahmose II brought Greek mercenaries there, and they then intermarried with the native population (Thompson 2012: 14–15). The name Oserapis from the curse and its relation to the city of Memphis clearly refer to the cult of Osiris-Apis practiced there at that time. The bulls sacred to Apis, which were bred in the temple in Memphis, were ritually buried after their death, and according to the theology of this cult, these bulls joined Osiris in death and merged together into a deity called Osiris-Apis (Thompson 2012; Mojsov 2005: 24). Artemisia mentions the god Oserapis in the context of funerary rites, which is a domain of Osiris-Apis, a god related to the underworld and also concerned with fertility (Stambaugh 1972: 36–53). Later, Sarapis had the same attributes clearly incorporated into his iconography—he often wears a *kalathos* on his head as a symbol of fertility and is accompanied by Kerberos, a guardian of the gates to the underworld (Stambaugh 1972: 91–3). Due to these features, he was often identified with the god Pluto by the Greeks. Wilcken found the name Osorapis also in other papyri from Memphis. The name Osorapis or Oserapis seems to be, according to Wilcken and others, a transliteration of Egyptian name for Osiris-Apis (*Wsir-Ḥp*) and is, at the same time, the etymological antecedent of the name Sarapis or Serapis (Wilcken 1927: 18–29, 77–89; Stambaugh 1972: 1–6). That this is the case could be further supported by the fact that the temple in Memphis was later called a Serapeum (Thompson 1987, 2012: 99–246; Stambaugh 1972: 5). The origins of Sarapis in Egyptian Memphis and the relationship of this figure to Osiris-Apis also resonate in the ancient discussion described earlier in this text.

In the academic discussion during the twentieth century, the Egyptian origins of Sarapis were often perceived and interpreted from the position that approaches history as a series of events related to significant individuals. This approach is apparent in the argument of the British historian and classical scholar Peter M. Fraser who introduced his hypothesis about the "creation" of Sarapis in 1960 and then repeated it in 1967. Bearing in mind the etymological development of the name Osiris-Apis into Sarapis laid out by Wilcken, Fraser argued that Sarapis was "created out" from Osiris-Apis by Ptolemy I. After Ptolemy I had "created" Sarapis, he, according to Fraser, immediately established the cult of Sarapis in Alexandria (Fraser 1960, 1967). In 1962, the American classicist and ancient historian Charles B. Welles opposed Fraser and claimed that the origins of Sarapis were closely tied to Alexander the Great. Welles found support for his hypothesis mainly in Pseudo-Callisthenes and Arrian's *Anabasis* (Welles 1962). A recent academic debate, however, reflects the issue of the origins of Sarapis as a long-term process related to the demographical development in ancient Memphis. It is argued that Ptolemy I did not so much "create" the cult of Sarapis but rather gave royal patronage to an already-existing cultural "product" of Hellenomemphites and helped to define a more consistent theology for the cult (see e.g., Legras 2014; Moyer 2011: 147–9).

Both Isis and Sarapis had convenient theological aspects for an unproblematic adaptation outside their country of origin. During the Hellenistic period, they were perceived as universalistic deities with soteriological attributes (Fraser 1972: 255–61), which could have been particularly appealing for people of the ever-changing Hellenistic world. Isis and Sarapis were originally Egyptian deities, but they were presented by the Ptolemaic dynasty in a Greek manner, and their adaptation into the Greek pantheon was thus unconstrained. Due to the matching attributes with other Greek deities, Isis and Sarapis successfully underwent the process of *interpretatio Graeca*. Sarapis was identified with Pluto, Dionysus, or Zeus, and Isis was often identified with Demeter or Aphrodite (Dunand 2007; Stambaugh 1972). Besides the universalistic and soteriological powers, some of the individual aspects of Isis or Sarapis could have played a more significant role in the process of adaptation of their cults abroad than others. For example, Isis was a patron deity of seafarers who could have erected altars or leave a dedication for her after they had successfully arrived in their destination (Bricault 2006). Sarapis was also a healing deity and shared similar healing practices with the very popular Greek god of medicine, Asclepius (Stambaugh 1972: 75–8).

2.2 Isis and Sarapis under the Ptolemies

Inscriptions from Alexandria suggest that Isis and Sarapis became perceived as a divine couple quickly during the rule of the first Ptolemies in Egypt (Fraser 1960, 1972: 246–76; Stambaugh 1972: 30–1; Hölbl 2001: 85–123). Although

Isis, together with Horus and Anubis, were Egyptian deities with a long-lasting tradition, Sarapis fitted naturally into this divine family through his link to Osiris. Accordingly, Sarapis took the role of Osiris as a husband of Isis and father of Horus (or later Harpocrates) (Fraser 1972: 259–60). The family of Isis was a mythical role model for Egyptian kings and queens, which was preserved even after the incorporation of Sarapis into this family during the Ptolemaic era. This is attested particularly for the first two centuries of the Ptolemaic dynasty in dedications addressing Isis and Sarapis alongside the Ptolemaic king and queen (see e.g., SB I 585, 586; OGIS I 62, 63, 82; Pfeiffer 2008: 400–3; Fassa 2015). A title attributed to the divine couple of Isis and Sarapis, which occurs in the historical evidence from the third century BCE, is *Soteres* or *Theoi Soteres* (Savior gods) (Bricault 1999: 337–8). This suggests that together they were venerated as universal deities with far-reaching powers. The title *Soteres* in the royal cult of Isis and Sarapis is also compatible with the self-presentation of the Ptolemaic ruler as a *basileus* (triumphant and charismatic king) whose qualities were expressed in epithets such as *Soter* (Savior) or *Euergetes* (Benefactor) (Hölbl 2001: 90–8). However, the appeal of Sarapis to ethnically diverse population of Egypt is a complicated issue. Researchers often discuss the possibility that Ptolemy I gave royal patronage to the cult of Sarapis in order to unify native Egyptians and Greeks under his rule (Stambaugh 1972: 96; Hölbl 2001: 99). There are, however, a number of voices in the discussion that offer other possible explanations of Ptolemy's intentions. The historian Ian Moyer claims that by promoting the cult of Sarapis, Ptolemy I rather intended "to tie a diverse array of immigrants more closely to the kingdom of Egypt and the Ptolemaic dynasty" (Moyer 2011: 149). Françoise Dunand too expresses the opinion that the Ptolemies did not intend to unify the Greeks and the native Egyptians by a joint cult and claims that the Ptolemaic dynasty kept the status of these ethnic groups apart also by means of fiscal privileges for the Greeks (Dunand 2007: 260–1). Although the consensus regarding this issue has not been reached, researchers agree that whatever were the intentions of Ptolemy I, the god Sarapis was worshiped primarily, and almost exclusively, in the Greek milieu (Moyer 2011: 148; Fraser 1960: 5–20; Stambaugh 1972: 94–6; Borgeaud and Volokhine 2000: 60). The native Egyptians, on the other hand, continued to venerate the probable predecessor of Sarapis, the Memphian Osiris-Apis, and perceived Sarapis as an *interpretatio Graeca* of Osiris-Apis or Osiris alone (Moyer 2011: 148; Thompson 2012: 197–246).

As discussed above, the evidence suggests that the cult of Sarapis was promoted and introduced to the broader, and mainly Greek, audience by

Ptolemy I. In the academic discussion, this royal patronage of the cult of Sarapis is recognized as a significant political statement of the Ptolemaic dynasty. However, it was not the first time Ptolemy I used the religious sphere for a similar action. After Alexander had advanced on Egypt in 332 BCE, he peacefully conquered the country and took it from the Persian rule (Arrian, *Anabasis* III.1; Hölbl 2001: 9–10; Loyd 2011). There, he obtained divine kingship as a pharaoh and was recognized as the son of Ammon (Arrian, *Anabasis* III.1–3; Loyd 2011; Hölbl 2001: 9–11; Worthington 2016: 32–5). After Alexander's death in Babylon, Ptolemy I managed to get hold of Alexander's remains and transported them to Memphis and later to Alexandria (Diodorus, *Bibliotheca Historica* XVIII.28.3; Strabo, *Geographica* XVII.1.8; Curtius Rufus, *Historiae Alexandri Magni* X.10.20; Pausanias, *Descriptio Graeciae* I.7.1; Worthington 2016: 129–46; Hölbl 2001: 15). Ptolemy I did so because he saw himself as the successor of Alexander in Egypt. To further strengthen the legitimacy of his rule, Ptolemy I established a state cult of Alexander and granted the priest of Alexander the position of the highest state priest (Hölbl 2001: 94–5). Moreover, Ptolemy I issued coins depicting either Alexander or himself with attributes of Greek and Egyptian deities such as Ammon and Zeus (Worthington 2016: 162; Hölbl 2001: 93). In summary, Ptolemy I established specific links to the religious sphere in order to present himself and his dynasty as legitimate. The promotion of the cult of Sarapis could have also provided cultural familiarity and legitimacy for the Greeks in Egypt. It needs to be noted here that a temple of Isis, founded by Egyptian merchants, existed in the Athenian port of Piraeus as early as ca. 333/332 BCE (RICIS 101/0101, text in translation in Harland n.d.a). The potential of the cult of Isis to be positively adapted in Greek territories and Greek social milieus was thus apparent in the time of Alexander the Great. Moreover, Alexander is said to have built a sanctuary of Isis in newly founded Alexandria (Arrian, *Anabasis* III.1). This situation could have also supported the religious policy of the first Ptolemies including their ambitions with respect to dedicating temples to Isis and Sarapis in Egypt.

Ptolemy II Philadelphus (reigned 284–246 BCE) approached the development of the ruler cult very actively. He arranged for an official deification of his deceased parents as *Theoi Soteres* (Savior Gods) and also established the festival of *Ptolemaia* to further honor his father (Marquaille 2008: 48–63; Buraselis 2008: 298–9; Hölbl 2001: 94–5). *Ptolemaia* were held at various places across the Mediterranean, and for a time, they were a competition for the Olympic Games with respect to prestige (Reger 1994a: 44–7; Hölbl

2001: 94). Ptolemy II married his sister Arsinoe II, and in 272/1 BCE, they were incorporated into the cult of Alexander as living divine rulers *Theoi Adelphoi* (Sibling Gods) (Buraselis 2008; Pfeiffer 2008: 398–400). This family model meant to be perceived as a *hieros gamos* inspired by the mythic couples of Zeus and Hera, or Isis and Osiris/Sarapis (Pfeiffer 2008: 399; Grimm 1998: 70; Hölbl 2001: 112). Arsinoe II was attributed the epithet *Philadelphos* (brother loving), and her popularity transcended the borders of Egypt. During her lifetime she was identified with Aphrodite and had a temple dedicated to her at Cape of Zephyrion where she was worshiped as Aphrodite-Arsinoe, a patron goddess of seafaring (Hölbl 2001: 101–4). Also, a number of cities in the ancient Mediterranean were renamed after her as a sign of honor (Hölbl 2001: 104; Reger 1994a: 50–1). After Arsinoe II had died, Ptolemy II elevated her posthumously to the position of an individual goddess sharing all the Egyptian temples (Carney 2013: 106–34; Pfeiffer 2008: 399). This subsequently led to the transformation of the Greek divine ruler Arsinoe to an Egyptian goddess depicted as such in the temples (Quaegebeur 1998, 1971; Pfeiffer 2008: 399). Finally, she was identified with Isis by both the Egyptians and the Greeks (Quaegebeur 1971; Pfeiffer 2008: 399–400). The ruler cult of Ptolemy II was also institutionally linked with the cult of Sarapis. This is attested by an altar found in the Alexandrian *temenos* for Sarapis bearing the text: "(Altar) of King Ptolemy and Arsinoe Philadelphus, (descendants) of the savior gods" (Bernand 2001, No. 8; Pfeiffer 2008: 400). The absence of the title *Theoi Adelphoi* suggests that the altar was erected most probably before 272/1 BCE. Moreover, Ptolemy II founded the so-called daughter library at the Alexandrian Serapeum (Stambaugh 1972: 7–8), which does not contradict the possibility that the Serapeum stood in Alexandria also during the lifetime of Ptolemy I as it is mentioned by Tacitus (*Historiae* IV.83–84) and Plutarch (*De Iside et Osiride* 28).

From the time of Ptolemy II, we can see the ruler cult practiced by organized associations called *basilistai* (Dunand 1973a: 125; Pfeiffer 2008: 401–3; Fischer-Bovet 2014: 280–90). Among other purposes, these associations helped to build and maintain common identities for people serving under the Ptolemies especially outside Egypt—on the topic of voluntary associations in the ancient Mediterranean, see Harland (2003). The patrons/leaders of these associations were often Ptolemaic military or administrative officials (Dunand 1973a: 125; Pfeiffer 2008: 401–3; Fischer-Bovet 2014: 280–90). Analyzing this type of cult practice allows us to observe the merging of the ruler cult and the cult of Isis and Sarapis in greater detail. A relevant example comes from the island of

Thera in Cyclades. An inscription found in the sanctuary of Egyptian deities on Thera dated to the first half of the third century BCE (IG XII.3 443; RICIS 202/1202) reads as follows: "Diokles and the royalists (*basilistai*) dedicated the offering receptacle (*thēsaurus*) to Sarapis, Isis, and Anubis" (translation in Harland n.d.b). An inscription from the temple of Egyptian deities on Thera dated to ca. 270 BCE also mentions Arsinoe (II) Philadelphus (IG XII.3 462; RICIS 202/1201). Besides *basilistai*, other associations devoted to worship of Isis and Sarapis are attested in the Aegean Sea region (mainly to the end of the third century BCE). These associations were known under the names of *Sarapiastai* or *Isiastai*, and their activities could be linked to a number of places in the region such as Athens, Rhodos, Kos, Delos, Keos, Limyra, and elsewhere. Many of these associations were initially private and were recognized by the state later (Bricault 2014; Fraser 1972: 265).

The royal patronage of the cult of Isis and Sarapis continued under Ptolemy III Euergetes who reigned from 246 to 222/1 BCE. Foundation plaques from the major temple in the complex of Alexandrian Serapeum identify Ptolemy III and his wife Queen Berenice II as the ones responsible for the construction (Stambaugh 1972: 7; Pfeiffer 2008: 400). Following the examples of Ptolemy II and Arsinoe II, Ptolemy III and Berenice II were incorporated in the state cult of Alexander the Great as *Theoi Euergetai* (Benefactor gods) (Hölbl 2001: 49, 95). In the reign of Ptolemy III, Isis and Sarapis also played a role in the official oaths to king (*P.Eleph.* 23, 8–12; *P.Tebt.* III 1, 815, col. IV 21-3, translated by Stefan Pfeiffer in Pfeiffer 2008: 395):

> I swear by King Ptolemy, son of King Ptolemy and Arsinoe, the sibling gods, and by Queen Berenike, the sister and consort of the king, and by the sibling gods and the saviour gods, by their ancestors and by Isis and Serapis.

Double dedications to Isis, Sarapis, and the Ptolemaic king and queen are attested from the time of Ptolemy III as well (see e.g., SB I 585, 586; OGIS I 62, 63). We can turn again to the evidence from the island of Thera that offers a relevant and long-term insight into the Ptolemaic soldiers' devotion to the Ptolemaic rulers and to Egyptian gods. A certain Artemidorus of Perge, who was a former Ptolemaic officer, restored the sanctuary of Egyptian deities on Thera on behalf of Ptolemy III and his ancestors (IG XII.3 464; RICIS 202/1204; Chaniotis 2005: 152).

Ptolemy IV Philopator (reigned 222/1–204 BCE) finished the development of the collective dynastic cult by incorporating the *Theoi Soteres* (established by Ptolemy II in honor of his parents) into the cult of Alexander. Thus, all royal couples including *Theoi Philopatores* were officially legitimized by the kingship of Alexander (Buraselis 2008: 301; Hölbl 2001: 95, 169–77).

The relationship between the worship of the royal Ptolemaic couple and the cult of Isis and Sarapis can be observed on coins issued during the reign of Ptolemy IV. On these coins, the jugate busts of Isis and Sarapis are depicted posing as royal couple. Sarapis wears a *chiton*; however, he does not have the *kalathos*, his typical later feature, on his head but, according to John. E. Stambaugh, lotus or rather the adaptation of *atef* crown related mainly to the iconography of Osiris (Stambaugh 1972: 22). In the complex of Alexandrian Serapeum, plaques were found with a dedication of a temple to Isis, Sarapis, and to Ptolemy IV and Arsinoe III; the dedication was made probably by Ptolemy IV himself or by someone during his reign (Fraser 1960: 12; Stambaugh 1972: 30). Ptolemy IV promoted the cult of Isis and Sarapis also by his building activities. For example, dedication plaques from Alexandrian Serapeum attest that Ptolemy IV constructed a small shrine of Harpocrates (mythical son of Isis) within the temple complex (Stambaugh 1972: 7; Hölbl 2001: 170; Rowe 1946: 55). The text on the plaques states that he had received the command to build the shrine from Isis and Sarapis themselves (Hölbl 2001: 170; Rowe 1946: 55). Again, the evidence from the island of Thera points to the continuous merging of the ruler cult with the cult of Isis and Sarapis. A member of the Ptolemaic garrison on Thera, a man from Myndos, made a dedication to Isis, Sarapis, and Anubis for the well-being of Ptolemy IV and Arsinoe III (IG XII.3 1389; RICIS 202/1205; Chaniotis 2005: 152–3).

The royal patronage of the cult of Isis and Sarapis, however, declined after the death of Ptolemy IV, and the Ptolemaic rulers who followed began to favor native Egyptian gods, perhaps in order to soothe the anxiety among native Egyptians during the political crisis of the Ptolemaic empire. After the reign of Ptolemy IV Philopator, there is a significant lack in royal dedications to Isis and Sarapis, and there is no evidence of further building activities within the complex of Alexandrian Serapeum (Hölbl 2001: 122–51, 170; Stambaugh 1972: 97; Fraser 1972: 270). The cult of Isis and Sarapis then became officially promoted again later by the Roman emperors after the annexation of Egypt (Stambaugh 1972: 97; Hölbl 2001: 170; Fraser 1960: 9–12).

Based on the evidence discussed in this chapter, it seems that the Ptolemaic dynasty could have played a positive role in the early spread of the Isiac cults outside Egypt. The above presented examples of the double dedications to the Ptolemaic rulers and Isis and Sarapis outside Egypt suggest that by making these dedications, the people residing or traveling outside Egypt voluntarily expressed loyalty toward the dynasty and the related deities and thus affirmed their identities tied to their country—Egypt. The common identity expressed in worship of Egyptian deities is also apparent from the already discussed evidence mentioning a temple of Isis founded by Egyptian merchants in Piraeus (RICIS 101/0101).

3

Spread of the Isiac Cults: An Overview

3.1 Historical Context and the Academic Debate

The first mentions of the deities from the Isiac family outside Egypt are attested at the end of the fourth century and the beginning of the third century BCE. It is particularly Isis herself who precedes the other Egyptian gods in the dissemination of the evidence outside Egypt. Probably the most famous and the earliest attestation for the worship of Isis in Greece is the Athenian decree from Piraeus dated to 333/2 BCE (RICIS 101/0101), which I will quote here in its entirety to present the social context for the early cult of Isis in foreign territories (translation in Kloppenborg and Ascough 2011: 28):

> Gods!
>
> In the year that Nikokrates was archon, in the first prytany of the (tribe of) Aigeis, Theophilos of Phegaea, (chair) of the presiders, put the following to a vote: resolved by the Council (*boulē*) (the motion that) Antidotos son of Apollodoros of Sypalettos made:
>
> In regard to what the Kitians propose concerning the establishment of the temple to Aphrodite, it is resolved by the Council that the presiders, who are chosen by lot to preside in the first assembly (*ekklēsia*), shall bring them forward and deal with the business and put to the People (*dēmos*) the proposal of the Council: that it seems good to the Council that the People, having listened to the Kitians regarding the foundation of the temple and to any other Athenian who wishes (to speak), should decide whatever seems best.
>
> In the year that Nikokrates was archon, during the second prytany, of (the tribe of) Pandionis, the question was put by Phanostratos of the deme of Philaidae, (chair) of the presiders; resolved by the Council (the motion that) Lykourgos son of Lykophron, of the deme of Boutadai, made:
>
> Since the Kitian merchants are making a legitimate request in asking the People's assembly for (the right to) lease of the land on which they propose to establish a

temple of Aphrodite–: be it resolved by the People (*dēmos*) to grant to the Kitian merchants the lease of the land to establish the temple of Aphrodite, in the same way that the Egyptians also established the temple of Isis.

This text suggests that Egyptians, most probably merchants, who operated outside Egypt carried the worship of the deities from their homeland with themselves and dedicated a temple for Isis in the place of their operation. Another inscription with similar phrasing (i.e., Αἰγύπτιοι Ἴσιδι, Egyptians to Isis, RICIS 104/0101; Bruneau 1975: 17, 105, 115) from Eretria in Euboea dated between the end of the fourth century and the beginning of the third century BCE supports the suggestion that this was a trend. However, because this worship predates the establishment of the Ptolemaic dynasty and the introduction of the Hellenistic couple of Isis and Sarapis and its development in Alexandria, it is not entirely possible to categorize it as the spread of the Isiac cults. The spread of the Isiac cults is conceptualized here, and in the academic debate as well, as a cultural process that can be traced to the formation (or rather reformulation) of the theology for Isis and Sarapis as a couple and their divine family under the first Ptolemaic rulers; see discussions (Bricault 2004, 2013: 27; Heyob 1975: 6–7; Takács 1995: 29–30; Dunand 1973a: 4–5; Pfeiffer 2008: 392–8; Gasparini and Gordon 2018). The conceptual separation is thus built upon the rationale that the Hellenistic Isiac cults are a unique cultural product resulting from specific political and demographic developments in Ptolemaic Egypt and that the spread of these cults could have been potentially affected by different dynamics than the worship of individual Egyptian deities outside Egypt in the time before the death of Alexander the Great. It is the third century BCE, where we need to turn our attention to the majority of the evidence for the first phase of the spread of the Isiac cults in the Mediterranean. As Bricault lists (Bricault 2004), between 230 BCE and the early second century BCE, the Isiac cults had established temples on the shores of the Mediterranean Sea in cities such as Athens (RICIS 101/0201), Orchomenus (RICIS 105/0701), Rhamnous (RICIS 101/0502), Chaironeia (RICIS 105/0801), Thessalonica in continental Greece (RICIS 113/0501), Keramos (RICIS 305/1801), Halicarnassus (RICIS 305/1702) or Stratonikeia (RICIS 305/0501) in Asia Minor, or Rhodos (RICIS 204/0301, 204/0201).

The academic debate on the topic of factors of the spread of the Isiac cults is lengthy and offers ambitious and sometimes mutually opposing scenarios of how these cults successfully disseminated to the different areas and corners of the ancient Mediterranean. Before presenting an overview of the spatial dissemination of the Isiac cults in the ancient Mediterranean, it is relevant to describe the key arguments and milestones from the academic discussion first.

One of the earliest and most significant scholarly contributions to the topic of the factors behind the successful spread of the Isiac cults belongs to the Belgian historian, archaeologist, and philologist Franz Cumont. Cumont's well-known monograph *Les religions orientales dans le paganisme romain* was first published in 1906 following the centuries-long debates among Protestant and Roman Catholic theologians about the influence of the ancient Mysteries on emerging Christianity (Bremmer 2014: IX–XI). In his book, Cumont introduced the category of "Oriental religions," which incorporated original eastern cults practiced across the Graeco-Roman world such as the cult of the Phrygian goddess Cybele, the cult of the Egyptian goddess Isis and her divine husband Sarapis, the cult of the Persian god Mithra, and the cult of Jupiter Dolichenus and Jupiter Helipolitanus from Syria (Cumont 1911). Although Cumont perceived western culture as superior to eastern culture, as was common among many scholars at the beginning of the twentieth century, in his view there was one exception: religion (Stroumsa 2009). Cumont saw "Oriental religions" as more theologically and ritually sophisticated than Graeco-Roman paganism. According to Cumont, the spread of these "Oriental religions" gradually overshadowed the fading Graeco-Roman paganism and by putting the doctrinal emphasis on the soteriological issues the "Oriental religions" prepared ground for the emerging Christianity. In other words, Cumont attributed a very significant role to "Oriental religions" in the conversion of the Roman empire to Christianity (Cumont 1911: 1–45, 134). With the help of Cumont's students, especially of Maarten J. Vermaseren, his views on "Oriental religions" dominated the academic debate for decades (Pailler 1989). However, after 1970 his position began to weaken significantly under the academic critique of Richard Gordon, Ramsay MacMullen, and Walter Burkert who dismantled the individual arguments from Cumont's claims. Richard Gordon pointed out that the Roman cult of Mithras was significantly different when compared to its Persian predecessor, and therefore, it is not possible to label the Roman cult of Mithras as a purely Persian creation (Gordon 1975, 2003). Ramsay MacMullen analyzed the epigraphic evidence from the time of the Roman empire and concluded that the proclaimed triumph of "Oriental religions" over the Graeco-Roman paganism is speculative and without support in the epigraphic and literary evidence (MacMullen 1983). Walter Burkert argued that "Oriental religions" were not autonomous religious systems but, rather, they were cults not always focused on otherworldly salvation (Burkert 1987: 1–11). The typological feature of "Oriental" is, according to Burkert and

Corinne Bonnet, seriously outdated and unable to characterize or unify the cults with diverse cultural backgrounds (Burkert 1987: 2–3; Bonnet 2006).

The Hellenistic cult of Isis and Sarapis was, in Cumont's perspective, a successful attempt of Ptolemy I Soter to unite the Greeks and the native Egyptians inhabiting his new kingdom in one common worship. In accordance with his outline of "Oriental religions," Cumont described the Hellenistic cult of Isis and Osiris/Sarapis as very appealing to the Greeks, because "they found their own divinities and their own myths again with something more poignant and magnificent added" (Cumont 1911: 77). By "something more poignant and magnificent," Cumont meant advanced literary and artistic features together with the theological emphasis on afterlife embodied by the gods from the Isiac family (Cumont 1911: 77–8). Cumont attributed the success of the cult of Isis and Sarapis both in and outside Egypt to the political genius of the early Ptolemies. Cumont explained the mechanics of the early spread of this cult across the ancient Mediterranean as follows: "It was adopted wherever the authority or the prestige of the Lagides [i.e., the Ptolemies] was felt, and wherever the relations of Alexandria, the great commercial metropolis, extended. The Lagides induced the rulers and the nations with whom they concluded alliances to accept it." (Cumont 1911: 79). These Cumont's words had a very significant impact in the academic discussion on the spread of the Isiac cults in the ancient Mediterranean and are still referred to by modern researchers. This hypothesis, which claims that the Ptolemaic political propaganda was the key factor behind the successful spread of the Isiac cults, became known in the Isiac studies (represented mainly by French researchers) as "la théorie impérialiste" (Bricault 2004: 548; Malaise 1972: 256). What is, however, sometimes omitted in the discussion is Cumont's brief mention that the worship of Isis, the goddess of navigators, was also propagated by merchants and sailors under the protection of Egyptian squadrons, which shows that Cumont was, in fact, aware of other factors involved in the process of the spread (Cumont 1911: 79–80).

While the conceptual validity of "Oriental religions" started to be questioned in the 1970s, Cumont's imperialistic theory had become the subject of serious criticism already a decade earlier. In 1960, Peter M. Fraser argued extensively in *Two Studies on the Cult of Sarapis in the Hellenistic World* that Cumont's claims concerning the influence of the Ptolemaic propaganda on the spread of Isiac cults should be dismissed completely. Fraser shares with Cumont the idea that Alexandrian worship of Sarapis was established by Ptolemy I and that Sarapis adopted the attributes of Osiris (Fraser 1960: 1–5). However, the first significant difference between the two scholars comes with the assessment of

Ptolemy's ambitions with the royal cult of Isis and Sarapis. Fraser disagrees with Cumont's claim that Ptolemy I established the worship of Sarapis to unify the Greeks and the native Egyptians. According to Fraser, during the creation of the cult, Ptolemy I did not have the native Egyptian population in mind. Rather, in Fraser's view, he aimed to give the Greeks in Egypt, and particularly the denizens of Alexandria, a patron deity (Fraser 1960: 1-19). Whatever the case, Fraser argued that the ambitions of Ptolemy I with the cult were not successful, which is again in contradiction to Cumont's claims (Fraser 1960: 19). Fraser came to these conclusions based on a simple statistical evaluation of archaeological evidence from Hellenistic Egypt. He pointed out that the majority of the dedications to Sarapis are Greek, geographically confined to Alexandria, and dated mainly to the third century BCE (Fraser 1960: 1-19). The third century BCE is also connected to the construction of temples consecrated to Sarapis by the Ptolemaic royalty (Stambaugh 1972). However, the decline in official dedications after the reign of Ptolemy IV (i.e., from the second century BCE) suggests a decline in royal interest in the figure of Sarapis in Egypt (Fraser 1960: 17-19; Stambaugh 1972: 96-7). Fraser interpreted the evidence as follows: "The cult of Sarapis owed its main, if limited, popularity to the example and initiative of the royal house. The disappearance of the cult in Alexandria can then be satisfactorily explained as arising from the deflection of royal interest from this quasi-Greek cult to the native Egyptian cults" (Fraser 1960: 17). The American classical scholar John E. Stambaugh agrees that there was indeed a decline in royal patronage of the cult after Ptolemy IV. However, Stambaugh tries to offer an alternative explanation of the situation. He points out that, even after Ptolemy IV, the cult of Sarapis was practiced in the great temples of Rhacotis in Alexandria and in Memphis and that in the Memphian Serapeum, special devotees (*katochos* Ptolemaeus) continued to offer prayers on behalf of the Ptolemaic rulers. Stambaugh's interpretation is that the cult was at that time established to the extent that "it did not need the special encouragement of royal promotion" (Stambaugh 1972: 96-7).

Fraser went further on the conjectural level and speculated that the Greeks who newly arrived in Alexandria brought with them the traditional worship of the Olympian gods, however, without the particular gods of their home cities and that this was the gap Ptolemy I tried to fill in by establishing the Alexandrian cult of Sarapis. However, as Fraser admitted, there is no formal evidence attesting the god Sarapis *Polietus* until the Imperial period (Fraser 1960: 19). As was already mentioned earlier in the book, there is a general agreement in the modern academic discussion that if Ptolemy I intended to join the Greeks and Egyptians in one religious bond, he more or less failed because the evidence related to the cult of Sarapis in the Ptolemaic period is restricted to Greek social milieu with only little impact on the Egyptian one. The hypothesis that Ptolemy I established the cult of Sarapis specifically in order to tie Greek immigrants to the Ptolemaic dynasty and Egypt is also considered plausible in the discussion (see e.g., Moyer 2011: 148; Fraser 1960: 5–20; Stambaugh 1972: 94–6; Borgeaud and Volokhine 2000: 60).

Fraser agrees that Cumont's imperialistic theory seems reasonable, at least at first glance, because during the third century BCE, the cult of Sarapis could be, indeed, found in some Ptolemaic possessions in the Aegean Sea and Asia Minor. However, he claims that if the Ptolemies had propagated the worship of Sarapis, then the evidence in their possessions outside Egypt would have pointed to a public, and not private, cult. Fraser then demonstrates on selected pieces of evidence that this was not the case and therefore the imperialistic theory is untenable (Fraser 1960: 20–49). To sketch typical contours of Fraser's argument, his approach to the material evidence in Athens and on the island of Delos is discussed below.

The introduction of the Isiac cult to the island of Delos in Cyclades is attested in the inscription by the priest Apollonius (IG XI.4.1299; RICIS 202/0101; Constantakopoulou 2017; Moyer 2011: 153–75). The inscription tells a story of Apollonius's grandfather's arrival and introduction of the private cult on Delos. Later, during the time of Apollonius, who recorded the story, the cult became public. The dating of this inscription is complicated and still not completely resolved, but most researchers agree on a date between the end of the third century BCE and early second century BCE, and the first introduction of the cult by Apollonius's grandfather is dated around the first half of the third century BCE (Moyer 2008, 2011: 157; Fraser 1960: 22–3). As was already discussed above, the presence of the cult of Isis in Athens is dated to the fourth century BCE. In a decree from 333/2 BCE, *emporoi* from Kition were granted the right to own a plot of land on which they planned to build a sanctuary of Aphrodite, "as the Egyptians have founded a sanctuary of Isis" (IG II.² 337; RICIS 101/0101; Fraser 1960: 23; Reed 2003: 30–1; Harland n.d.a). The private cult of Sarapis in Athens is attested in 215/14 BCE (IG II.² 1292; RICIS 101/0201) by a decree of *Sarapiastai*, who were not Athenian citizens, honoring their magistrates. This decree is from the time of good diplomatic relations between Athens and Ptolemy III Euergetes after the retreat of Macedonian occupation troops from Attica in 229 BCE. In 224/3 BCE, Ptolemy III even received his own cult in Athens, and from the same year, the festival of *Ptolemaia* was held in Athens every four years (Fraser

1960: 23; Hölbl 2001: 51–2). However, the first evidence of the public cult of Isis and Sarapis in Athens is a dedication to Isis, Sarapis, and possibly Anubis written during the priesthood of an Athenian citizen in the early second century BCE (IG II.² 4692; RICIS 101/0202). Fraser thus concludes that in Delos and Athens, the private cult preceded the public cult and that in both cases the official Ptolemaic propaganda does not seem to have been the cause for the first instalment of the cult (Fraser 1960: 22–4).

The validity of the "imperialistic" theory was convincingly shaken by Fraser's argumentation. Fraser successfully proved that there was no general pattern in the archaeological and literary evidence with respect to the Isiac cults, which would point out to a single factor behind it—for a general overview of the discussion on the imperial theory, see also Malaise (1972: 255–7). Nevertheless, he implied that merchants and trade in general had a significant impact on the process of the spread of these cults. The problem is that Cumont and Fraser seem to fail in the recognition of the complexity of the spreading process. They both perceive spontaneous actions of people and Ptolemaic political/economic activity as separate, unrelated processes. While Cumont claims that the Isiac cults were directly induced by the Ptolemies in their possessions outside Egypt (Cumont 1911: 79), Fraser explicitly says that the Isiac cults spread "spontaneously, unaffected by political factors" (Fraser 1960: 47). The situation on the island of Thera in the Aegean Sea can perhaps clarify why their assumptions are problematic. There are dedications from Thera from the third century BCE that are connected both to the Ptolemaic rulers and Egyptian deities Sarapis, Isis, and Anubis (RICIS 202/1202-05). One of these inscriptions dated to the first half of the third century BCE (RICIS 202/1202) was dedicated by Diokles, a member of the group of *basilistai*, which was devoted to the dynastic cult and consisted of soldiers stationed in the Ptolemaic garrison on Thera. A table bearing the name of the Ptolemaic queen Arsinoe II Philadelphus from Thera, dated to ca. 270 BCE (RICIS 202/1201), creates the impression that the dynastic cult was deeply interwoven with the Isiac cults on Thera. The Isiac cults on the island were established spontaneously by individuals with their own intentions. But these individuals were also Ptolemaic soldiers sent there by the ruling dynasty in order to maintain the Ptolemaic garrison. This situation could have been similar for merchants traveling from Egypt. They built Egyptian temples in foreign lands in order to worship their own gods, but still the directions of their travels were also influenced by political and economic decisions on the higher level of Ptolemaic state hierarchy (this applies, e.g., to Athens and Rhodos). In other words, it seems highly probable that the spontaneous actions of people from Ptolemaic Egypt were at least partially related to the Ptolemaic state activities. Such an assumption (if accepted as valid) has the potential to further question some of Fraser's arguments. Fraser generally dismisses the evidence of the Isiac cults from the second century BCE as a proof of early Ptolemaic involvement in the spread of these cults because of the late date. Again, the metaphoric wall he built between the spontaneous action and political activity prevents him from seeing the process of the spread in the long term—when the Ptolemaic dynasty created a political or commercial channel somewhere and maintained it for decades or even a century, it could have taken time for a cult to be established in that place by traveling Egyptians and appear in material evidence. A suitable example could be the island of Keos. The island was used as a naval base for Ptolemaic troops from approximately half of the third century BCE, and the cult of Isis and Sarapis appeared there decades later, but the main person in the inscription attesting the cult is a son of a Ptolemaic official (RICIS 202/0801), which could demonstrate once again the role of the state in a spontaneous action. This direction was gradually pursued in the next stages of the academic discussion.

In comparison with the previous debate, the French historian and specialist of Graeco-Roman Egypt, Françoise Dunand, is more aware of the complexity of spreading processes in the long term (Dunand 1973a, 1980). From this perspective, Dunand describes the development of the Isiac cults in Athens and on Delos using the same evidence from the fourth to second centuries BCE as Fraser. In the earliest references from both Delos and Athens, the primary worshipers of Egyptian cults were not the local Greeks and Athenian citizens but Egyptians (for Athens see IG II.² 337; RICIS 101/0101; for Delos IG XI.4.1299). Evidence from Athens dated to the end of the third century and beginning of the second century BCE attests that at that time there was a priest of Isis and Sarapis, who was also an Athenian citizen. From then on, the trend continued, and the worshipers of the Isiac cults were gradually recruited more among the Greeks (Dunand 1980: 74). Dunand draws a similar conclusion for the island of Delos. Priests assigned to Sarapieion A on Delos at the beginning of the third century BCE were Egyptian. However, a few decades later, those who served in Sarapieion C were Delians (Dunand 1980: 74, 1973a: 83–115). Although Dunand's arguments are in agreement with Fraser's claim that the Isiac cults first spread mainly by private action, they render the situation more complicated. More specifically, Dunand's observations show that the first introduction of the Isiac cults in a place in the ancient Mediterranean cannot be considered as a delimited event. Rather, it is a first phase of a long-term process of cultural transmission during which a channel between two culturally specific social milieus is established.

Considering the "imperialistic" theory, Dunand comments on its general notion as logical at first look, in a similar way as Fraser did. She mentions that the cult of Isis and Sarapis was indeed closely tied to Ptolemaic rulers. She points out that during the third century BCE, Ptolemies consecrated big temples in Egypt both to Isis (Behbet el Bagar, Aswan, Philae) and Sarapis (Alexandria, Canopus, Memphis) and that Ptolemy IV even had the epithet "loved by Isis" (Dunand 1980: 107). The idea that the cult of Isis and Sarapis could have been propagated directly by a Ptolemaic kings is not, according to Dunand, unthinkable, especially in the context of their intense political activities across the Mediterranean (Dunand 1980: 107). However, Dunand claims that the archaeological evidence contradicts the "imperialistic" theory. She argues that there is no evidence exposing a direct and systematic organization of the Isiac cults in the lands belonging to Ptolemaic possessions. She uses the island of Crete as an example. As discussed above, although there are many traces of Ptolemaic military and diplomatic involvement on Crete during the whole third century BCE, the cult of Isis and Sarapis is only reliably attested to the second century BCE. To further question the "imperialistic" theory, Dunand also mentions the situation on Delos, where the cult was introduced by private action even though it belonged to the Nesiotic League administered by the Ptolemies at that time. Dunand dismisses the claim that the Isiac cults were directly propagated outside Egypt by the Ptolemies, which is also Fraser's conclusion. She believes, however, that the Ptolemaic political activity must have played a positive, although indirect, role in the spread of these cults. According to Dunand, it is no coincidence that there was a temple consecrated to Isis, Sarapis, and Anubis in Ephesus in the first half of the third century BCE, because Ephesus was under Ptolemaic control and had a Ptolemaic military base for decades (Dunand 1980: 108–9). Another example is Thera, where the already-mentioned member of the Ptolemaic garrison Diokles and the group of *basilistai* made a dedication to Egyptian deities. On the same island, a former Ptolemaic official, Artemidorus of Perge, restored a sanctuary of the Egyptian gods on behalf of Ptolemy III (IG XII.3 464; Dunand 1980: 109; Chaniotis 2005: 152). Dunand claims that in these cases, spontaneous religious actions are clearly connected to loyalty toward the Ptolemaic dynasty and Egypt (Dunand 1980: 109, 1973a: 123–9). This is a significant shift in argumentation when compared to Fraser's style as it admits interactions between a spontaneous action and political activity.

Dunand also focuses on the question of why the Isiac cults were successfully accepted in the Greek social milieu outside Egypt. She attempts to go beyond Cumont's statements that the Hellenistic Greeks were fascinated by the soteriological aspects of eastern cults and finds answers in the political development of the early Hellenistic Mediterranean. The conquests of Alexander the Great broadened the borders of the known world to many Greeks. This could have significantly weakened their identity, which was intrinsically tied to the traditional structures of the Greek *polis* and piety toward the Olympian deities (Dunand 1980: 97–101). Subsequent military conflicts between the *diadochoi* of Alexander at the end of the fourth century BCE and the Macedonian occupation of the Peloponnese during the third century BCE led to further economic and political instability in the region and diminished the significance of individual *poleis* and gods tied to them because they could no longer guarantee the safety and prosperity for their citizens (Dunand 1980: 94–101). Dunand points out that the decreased number of dedications to the goddess Athena at the end of fourth century BCE reflects this issue (Dunand 1980: 97). The topic of the weakening piety toward traditional gods of *poleis* also resonates in Onesimos's response to Smikrines in Menander's *The Arbitration* (i.e., *Epitrepontes*; verses 1085–1100, translation by W. Geoffrey Arnott in Menander and Arnott 1979), which was written in the same period:

Onesimos

I'll make it clear to you.

The world contains about a thousand towns,

Each one with thirty thousand residents.

Can every single man of them be damned

Or guarded by the gods? Absurd—you'd make

Their [lives] a drudgery. Then don't [the gods]

Look after us, you'll ask? They['ve introduced],

As each man's guardian, his character.

Inside us, it's [on duty (?)]—damns us if

[We treat] it badly, guards the others. That's

Our god, responsible for failure and

Success in each of us. To get on well,

You must placate it by avoiding error and

Stupidity!

Finally, Dunand mentions the "ithyphallic hymn" from 291 BCE sang by the Athenians to honor the Macedonian ruler Demetrius I Poliorcetes (Dunand 1980: 97–8; Austin 2006: 93–4). The following excerpt from the hymn illustrates clearly the transition of the attributed power from Olympian deities to human rulers (Athenaeus, *Deipnosophistae* VI.253b–f., translated by Michel Austin in Austin 2006, No. 43):

> Hail son [i.e., Demetrius] of the most powerful god Poseidon and of Aphrodite! For the other gods are either far away, or they do not have ears, or they do not exist, or do not take any notice of us, but you we can see present here; you are not made of wood or stone, you are real. And so we pray to you: first bring us peace, dearest one; for you have the power.

Dunand concludes that the general enlargement of the known world after the conquests of Alexander the Great combined with the existence of ethnically heterogeneous population constituted favorable conditions for the success of the Isiac cults. The disintegration of the traditional Greek religious and political structures further contributed to these conditions (Dunand 1980: 100–1). Dunand argues that identities of the Hellenistic Greeks tied to local *poleis* could not have been upheld in this dramatically changing world and that these identities had to anchor themselves more universally. This need, Dunand claims, could have been filled by worshiping universal deities from distant and prosperous countries. The Isiac cults closely tied to wealthy Ptolemaic Egypt fit naturally such a category (Dunand 1980: 98–101).

Dunand's arguments characterize the early spread of the Isiac cults across the ancient Mediterranean as a process involving multiple factors, which either directly or indirectly influenced the spread. Differentiating between the direct and indirect impact of these factors and explaining the process of the spread of these cults in the long term were significant and relevant changes in the style of argumentation in the academic discussion on the topic.

This "trend" continues in the work of the currently leading researcher in the *les études isiaques* (Isiac studies), Laurent Bricault. Bricault too offers a constructive criticism of previous scholarly debate. He completely dismisses the "imperialistic" theory for the lack of convincing arguments and points to Fraser's contribution in disproving Cumont's claims. Bricault particularly appreciates Fraser's differentiation between the private and public cult, which helped to seriously question Cumont's thesis (Bricault 2004: 548–9). Bricault admits that so far, the discussion has been revolving around these two opposing hypotheses, and modern researchers still tackle these arguments and have been trying to validate one or the other (e.g., Lefebvre 2008). However, similarly to Dunand, Bricault perceives the issue as more complicated. He argues that scholars involved in the debate on the topic of the spread of the Isiac cults often erroneously presumed homogenous and coherent patterns in the process of this spread and attempted to explain the process by all-encompassing theories. Bricault tries to dissociate his position from these views and frames the spread of the Isiac cults in terms of Dan Sperber (1996) as an ongoing epidemy of representations (Bricault 2013: 144–5). He claims that the spread (or in his words, *contagion culturelle*, Bricault 2013: 145) of the Isiac cults was influenced mainly by four factors, which were not mutually exclusive—commercial, economic, political, and social (Bricault 2004: 548–51). The research presented in this book follows this development in the academic debate and explores the role of the factors proposed by Bricault. He also contributed significantly to the Isiac studies by publishing a catalog of archaeological evidence related to the Isiac cults *Recueil des inscriptions concernant les cultes isiaques: RICIS* (Bricault 2005b). This corpus allows researchers to approach issues related to these cults more systematically. For the purposes of this book, Bricault's categorization of the material by type, date, and location is particularly relevant and suitable for various kinds of quantitative analysis. More specific arguments and problems of the debate related to the spread of the Isiac cults in the Aegean Sea and Asia Minor, that is, the two regions with the most significant density of the early Isiac material evidence outside Egypt, are discussed in the chapters focusing on the two case studies.

3.2 Spatial Overview of the Early Spread of the Isiac Cults

In *Atlas de la diffusion des cultes isiaques (IVe s. av. J.-C.—IVe s. apr. J.-C.)*, Bricault divides the spread of the Isiac cults outside Egypt into three periods or waves (Bricault 2001). Bricault identifies the year 333/2 BCE as a *terminus post quem* for the first wave of the spread of the Isiac cults outside Egypt (Bricault 2001: XIII). The year 333/2 BCE is related to the first evidence of a temple of Isis in the Greek world. As was discussed earlier, in the decree regarding a Kitian temple for the Syrian Aphrodite in Piraeus, an already-existing temple of Isis established by Egyptians (RICIS 101/0101) is mentioned (Harland n.d.a). Bricault puts the ending of the first wave of the spread to the year 88 BCE (Bricault 2001: XIII). In that year, Mithridates VI Eupator, king of Pontus, ransacked the island of Delos at the beginning of his war with the Roman republic (Pausanias,

Descriptio Graeciae III.23; Appian, *Mithridatic wars* 28; Plutarch, *Sulla* 11; Strabo, *Geographica* X.5.4). The island of Delos in Cyclades was culturally significant for the Mediterranean region because it hosted popular religious festivals and many temples were built there (Bruneau 1970; Reger 1994b: 270–1). The Isiac cults had been particularly well established on the island since the third century BCE (Bruneau 1970). The so-called Mithridatic wars changed the political balance in the Mediterranean dramatically, which probably also affected the channels through which the Isiac cults had been spreading earlier (McGing 1986). Bricault places the second wave of the spread of the Isiac cults in the period between the Mithridatic wars and the year 70 CE when the Roman emperor Vespasian visited the temple of Sarapis in Egypt and promoted the cult (Bricault 2001: XIII). The third wave is, according to Bricault, related to the time when the cult was favored by the members of the Flavian dynasty. Bricault places the ultimate end of the spreading to the year 391 CE when Theodosian decrees put an official end to Roman paganism (Bricault 2001: XIII). The focus of this book is on the early spread of the Isiac cults outside Egypt cults corresponding to the first wave in Bricault's typology, but for the contextual purposes, this chapter will summarize the evidence and process of this cultural transmission both in the early stages and in Roman times (Figure 3.1).

In the first wave of the spread of the Isiac cults, there are several re-occurring contexts accompanying the material evidence. The context of maritime connections is related to the majority of the early evidence of the spread of the Isiac cults outside Egypt as it is predominantly located in cities on the maritime transportation network (Bricault 2001). Another common condition for the spatial occurrence of the evidence for these cults is the previous contact of a location with the Ptolemaic Egypt (e.g., the island of Rhodos with a close commercial relationship with Egypt at that time). Finally, the Isiac cults can be attested in cities of Ptolemaic political interest with the presence of Ptolemaic officials or Ptolemaic garrisons (Bricault 2004). It was only later, mainly in the period of the Roman empire, when the Isiac cults were penetrating the Mediterranean further inland (Bricault 2001).

3.2.1 Greece

With its many islands and maritime connectivity, Greece is one of the main territories in providing rich evidence for the early spread of the Isiac cults. Because of the large scale of this area of interest and varying geographical

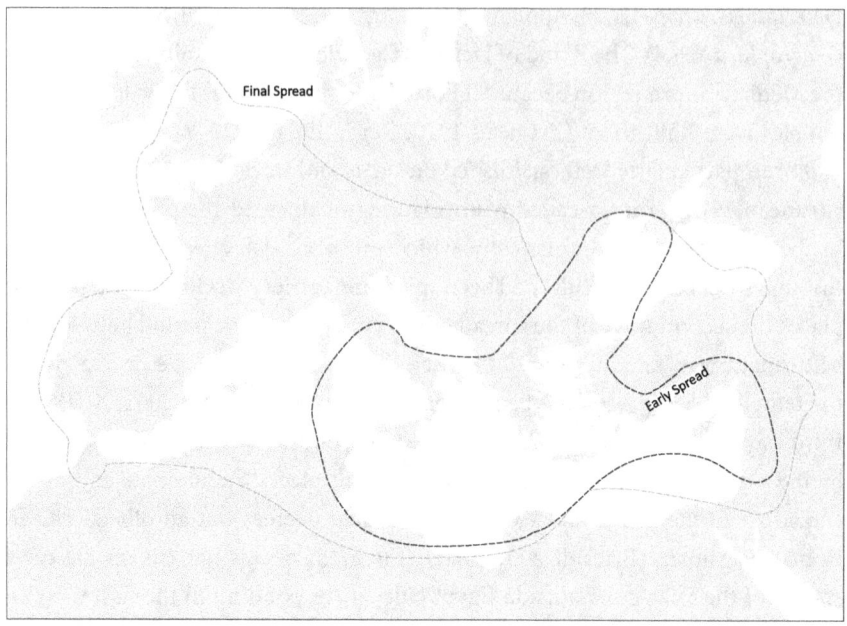

Figure 3.1 Spatial extent of the early and final spread of the Isiac cults outside Egypt. Base map source: "Natural Earth" n.d.

dynamics, it is appropriate to divide it into insular and continental Greece for the purposes of the overview.

The Cyclades at the heart of the Aegean Sea have particularly significant amount of material evidence for the early spread of these cults (Bricault 2001: 36–7). The islands provided anchoring points on the main maritime routes for ships traveling between Egypt and continental Greece. And because Egypt was one of the main exporters of grain in the Hellenistic period (Buraselis 2013; Casson 1954), busy maritime traffic with a lot of Egyptian merchants anchoring in Cyclades on their way elsewhere could have played a positive role in the early spread of the Isiac cults. Another potential favorable factor for this cultural transmission could have been Ptolemaic political presence on these islands. The Nesiotic League, that is, a league (*koinon*) associating the city-states in Cyclades, was under Ptolemaic control during the first half of the third century, and some of these islands were garrisoned by Ptolemaic troops, which only increased the presence of Egyptians in the region and potentially also increased the chances of successful spread of the Egyptian cults (Meadows 2013; Hölbl 2001: 23–4). These factors are further discussed in the case study in Chapters 4 and 5.

Despite being relatively small, only tens of kilometers wide, islands in the Cyclades yielded a substantial density of Isiac temples dated to the first phase of the spread of these cults. Namely, Delos, Amorgos, Astypalaia, Paros, and Thera had Isiac temples already in third and second centuries BCE with Tenos and Keos providing Isiac artifacts in the same time frame (Bricault 2001: 36–7). The most abundant evidence, however, comes from the island of Delos and points to the presence of these cults there already in the third century BCE (Heyob 1975: 7; Parker 2017: 154–72; Martzavou 2010; Bruneau 1970). The archaeological findings from this island and their diversity (spreading from inscriptions, through statues to temple itineraries) are crucial for understanding the Isiac cults in general. There were located temples of Sarapis, Isis, and Anubis, and hundreds of inscriptions related to these deities dated to the first phase of the spread of these cults outside Egypt (Bricault 2001: 36; RICIS 202/0101-0438). In addition to being located on major maritime routes in the center of Cyclades and in the sphere of the Ptolemaic influence, Delos was a major cult center for the worship of Greek deities and ritually purified for these purposes twice by Athens, long before the third century BCE (Parker 2017: 154–72; Rutishauser 2012: 55). The situation on Cyclades is discussed again in Chapter 4 (see Figure 3.2).

The island of Crete is also among those reached by the Isiac cults in the early phase; however, the earliest (and certain) evidence on the island for these cults can be dated to the second century BCE. The only city with an active temple in this period is Gortyn. The evidence for the worship of Isiac deities in Gortyn is most probably related to the frequent presence of Ptolemaic soldiers (Bricault 2001: 42). Crete also served as one of the prominent recruitment territories for Ptolemaic empire (Hölbl 2001: 130, 186), this reality being reflected on a dedication from Gortyn dated to the half of the second century BCE to Isis and Sarapis made by a Cretan archer, Pyroos, who was a mercenary soldier serving the Ptolemies (RICIS 203/0601). Denser dissemination of the Isiac cults along the southern coast of Crete is then attested in times of the Roman empire (Bricault 2001: 42–7).

In continental Greece, the earliest evidence of Isiac cults is again the mention of a sanctuary of Isis in the decree from Piraeus considering *emporoi* from Kition dated to 333/2 BCE (RICIS 101/0101). The traces of the early presence of the Isiac cults in Athens were already discussed here via arguments of Fraser and Dunand, but there is also another city in Attica that revealed evidence for the worship of the Isiac family in the third century BCE. It is the coastal city of Rhamnous in the northern Attica. There the Isiac cults were connected to a military context; however, this time, these deities were not worshiped by Ptolemaic army (Bricault

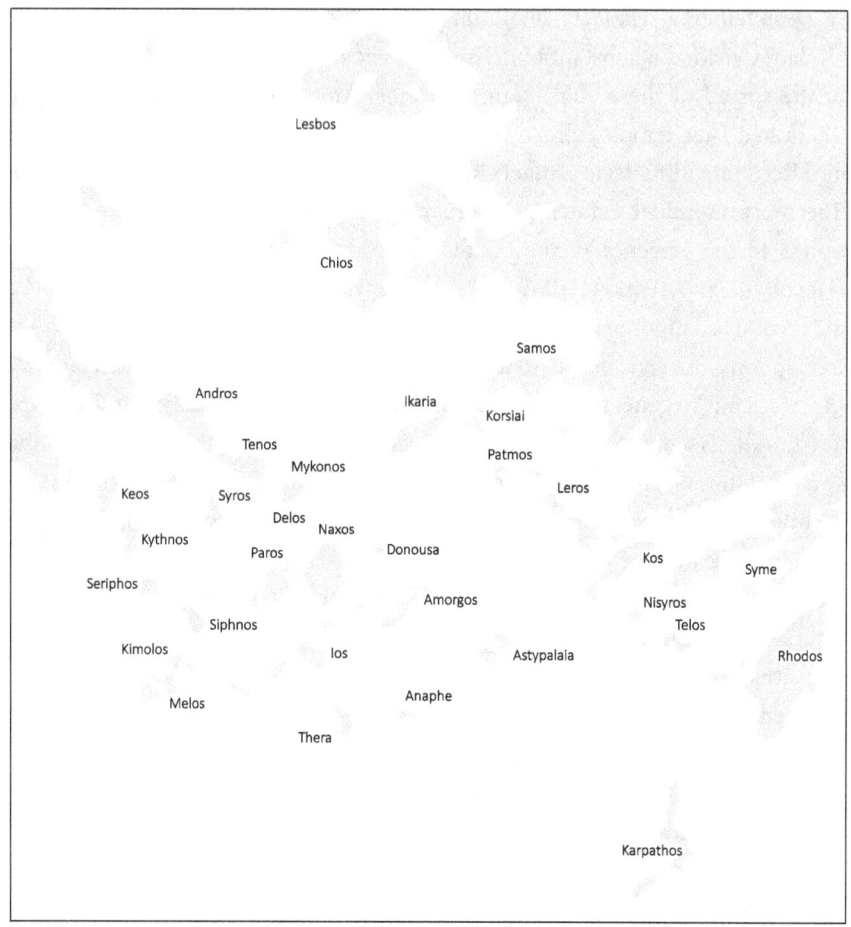

Figure 3.2 Islands in the Aegean Sea. Base map source: "Natural Earth" n.d.

2004). Specifically, there is a decree from Rhamnous dated to around 216/5 BCE written by an association of devotees of Sarapis (i.e., *Sarapiastai*, RICIS 101/0502, translation in Kloppenborg and Ascough 2011: 144–7; online in Harland n.d.d):

> Aphthonetos son of Aphthonetos of the deme Rhamnous made the following motion: Whereas Apollodoros, who was elected as commander (*stratēgos*), has at all times continued to be well-intentioned towards the People (*dēmos*)—both individually and collectively—and whereas the People crowned him when it accorded fitting recognition to all those who had been elected as commanders (*stratēgoi*), on account of which things the Council (*boulē*) has crowned him many times with gold crowns, and whereas he continues to be of service even individually in respect to whatever any of the citizens might ask him. Now, after

those citizens who perform military service in Rhamnous wrote in respect to a place that belonged to him, wishing to purchase it so that they could build a temple to Sarapis and Isis, not only did he not wish to be paid for it, but he even gave it to them without any charge, expressing to the highest degree piety towards the gods and good will and zeal with regard to his fellow citizens. So that the devotees of Sarapis (*Sarapiastai*) might be seen as rendering appropriate thanks to those who are zealous in respect to them, for good fortune the association of the devotees of Sarapis have resolved to commend Apollodoros son of Sogenes of the deme Otryne and to crown him with a crown of gold, for the piety that he has shown toward the gods and the zeal that he has displayed towards his fellows. They have resolved that the sacrifice makers (*hieropoioi*) who are responsible for the service (*leitourgia*) should also invite him to the sacrifices. They have resolved that they should inscribe this decree on a monument (stele) and erect it in front of the entrance to the sanctuary. And they have resolved that they shall choose men from among them who will take responsibility for inscribing the decree and for erecting the monument (stele). Let them make an accounting to the association of the expenses that are incurred. They were chosen as follows: Demokles of the deme Eupyridai, Antiphanes of Oioe, Kleodorides of Rhamnous, Bion of Phrearrhioi, Aphthonetos of Rhamnous, and Philokles of Erchia.

The association of the Sarapiasts honors Apollodoros son of Sogenes, of Otryne.

This text provides a very relevant social context for the early worship of the Isiac deities in continental Greece. We can read from it that toward the end of the third century BCE, the Isiac cults are practiced by an association consisting of Athenians serving in a garrison. This evidence is thus one of the indicators that at this time these cults were no longer worshiped solely by Egyptians outside their country and were part of local social networks (Arnaoutoglou 2013, 2018: 249–51; Bricault and Versluys 2014: 19). In the same temporal context (215/4 BCE), there is an honorary decree attesting a second group of *Sarapiastai*, this time noncitizens in Athens (RICIS 101/0201).

The diffusion of these cults to the regions in proximity to Attica such as Euboea and Boeotia was also successful. As was already mentioned earlier, there is the inscription Αἰγύπτιοι Ἴσιδι ("Egyptians to Isis," RICIS 104/010) from Eretria dated between the end of the fourth century and the beginning of the third century BCE. However, as in the case of the inscription from Piraeus dated to 333/2 BCE, the phrasing points to the probability that this is evidence for the worship of Isis before the introduction of the Isis-Sarapis couple under the Ptolemies. Not so far along the Euboean coast from Eretria was the city of Chalcis where a temple for the Isiac deities stood from the second century BCE (RICIS 104/0201). In Boeotia, the public cult of Isis and Sarapis was established around 220 BCE with temples standing in cities of Orchomenus (RICIS 105/0701-0703) and Chaironeia (RICIS 105/0801-0808). The region of Boeotia had good diplomatic relationships with the Ptolemaic dynasty in the reign of Ptolemy IV Philopator (ruled 222/1–204 BCE). The Ptolemaic diplomats intervened in these areas with donations and favorable policies on behalf of Ptolemy IV to help maintain peace in Greece and thus maintain good relations with this political power. That Boeotians recognized these efforts can be attested by statues erected in honor of Ptolemy IV and Arsinoe III in Oropos; the city of Tanagra and Orchomenus awarded the chief minister of Ptolemy IV, Sosibios, an honorary proxenos decree (Hölbl 2001: 132). This political context could thus have constituted a favorable condition for the spread of the Isiac cults in the Boeotian territory. In the neighboring region of Phocis, a public temple of Sarapis was located in the city of Daulis and is dated to the second century BCE (RICIS 106/0201). Similarly, Hyampolis had a public temple of Sarapis, Isis, and Anubis between the second and first centuries BCE (RICIS 106/0301-0302) (see Figure 3.3).

If we move further north to inland Greek territories toward Macedonia and Thessaly, the evidence becomes scarcer until it finally disappears north of Macedonia where it reappears only later under the Roman influence (Bricault 1997: 117–19). The cities in proximity to Boeotia and Phocis such as Boion (RICIS 107/0101), Naupactus (RICIS 108/0101), or Hypata (RICIS 112/0101) had the Isiac cults established there in the second century BCE. The last northern inland cities with the evidence of these cults in this area dated to the early spread (second century BCE) are Lete (RICIS 113/0801) and Beroia (RICIS 113/0301) in Macedonia. The situation, however, was different in ports and cities near the coast washed by the Aegean Sea. In Thessaly, the Isiac cults were present since the third century BCE (around 250 BCE) in the port of Demetrias (RICIS 112/0701), and in the same time frame, the city of Gonnos recognized the cult of Isis and Sarapis as official (RICIS 112/0801). In Macedonia, there is evidence for the Isiac cults established from the third century BCE in Dion (RICIS 113/0214-0215, 0219), and major ports of Amphipolis (RICIS 113/901-902) and Thessalonica (e.g., RICIS 113/0502-0507), where the amount of evidence is particularly high, with the first traces dated to the period between the end of the fourth century BCE and the beginning of the third century. A noteworthy political context appears in an inscription from Amphipolis dedicated to Isis, Sarapis, and King Philip (most probably V) from ca. 200 BCE (RICIS 113/0902), which is reminiscent of

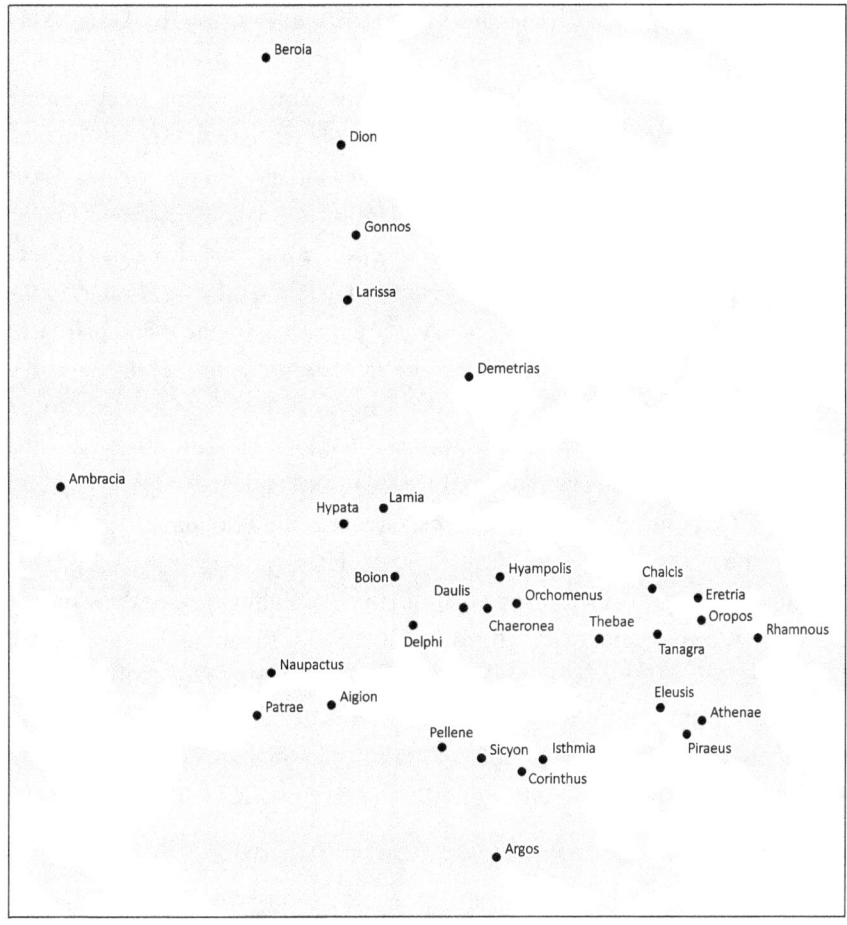

Figure 3.3 Greece with relevant ancient cities. Base map source: "Natural Earth" n.d.

the joint dedications to the Isiac deities and the Ptolemaic rulers who, in this case, are substituted by a king from the Antigonid dynasty (Veymiers 2009; Witt 1997: 260). The western coast of continental Greece, namely Epirus, connected to the Ionian Sea has only sporadic evidence for the early spread of the Isiac cults in this territory (Bricault 2001: 18–21), the traces being attested in Ambracia (a dedication dated to the third century BCE, RICIS 111/0101).

People in the border regions situated between continental Greece and Black Sea such as Thracia and the western corners of the Black Sea (later Roman province of Moesia Inferior) knew and worshiped the Isiac deities since the third century BCE (Braund 2018: 134–86; Bricault 2001: 48–53). The cities with the evidence of the Isiac cults from the third century in this area were exclusively ports connected to the maritime routes that were frequently used by Alexandrian and Rhodian sailors; it is Perinthus in Thracia (RICIS 114/0601) and Istrus in later Moesia Inferior (RICIS 618/1101). Additionally, according to epigraphic evidence, Ptolemy III managed to spread his influence in southern Thracian cities, and in 243 BCE, cities in Hellespont and southern Thracia such as Ainos and Maroneia were Ptolemaic (Hölbl 2001: 50). However, the evidence for the Isiac cults in Maroneia comes from the second century BCE (RICIS 114/0201-0202). Similarly, as in the case of Maroneia, there are temples dedicated to the Isiac deities dated to the second century BCE appearing on the island of Thasos in southern Thracia (RICIS 201/0101) and in Mesembria on the western shore of the Black Sea (RICIS 114/1401-1404). Temples and artifacts located further inland in provinces of Dacia and Moesia Superior are again attested to the Roman imperial period (Bricault 2001: 28–35) (see Figure 3.4).

The last area of interest in Hellenistic Greece is the Peloponnese peninsula. This region was not as much involved in the intensive maritime connectivity and mobility as its northern neighbors, and the Isiac cults appeared there mostly from the second century BCE (Bricault 2001: 6–9). There are, however, some exceptions sharing the common trait of proximity to the sea with evidence potentially from the third century BCE. Such artifacts were found in Aigion (RICIS 102/1301), Pellene (RICIS 102/1101), Sicyon (RICIS 102/1001), and Corinth (RICIS 102/0101) on the north and Argos (RICIS 102/0801) on the eastern side.

3.2.2 Asia Minor, Near East and Cyprus

The coast of Asia Minor, particularly the west coast, was one of the areas reached by the first phase of the spread of the Isiac cults outside Egypt (Dunand 1980: 107–9; Magie 1953; Bricault 2001: 54–63). The Anatolian coast is also a good example of the typical contexts accompanying this cultural transition combined. In addition to the proximity of the material evidence for the Isiac cults to port cities, the coast was subjected to Ptolemaic political interest and presence throughout the third century BCE (Bagnall 1976; Hölbl 2001; LaBuff 2016: 35–6; Fischer-Bovet 2014: 55–67).

The port cities of the west coast in Ionia and Caria such as Ephesus (RICIS 304/0601-0602), Priene (RICIS 304/0801), Bargylia (RICIS 305/1501), or Halicarnassus (RICIS 305/1701-1702) had Isiac sanctuaries already in the middle of the third century BCE (Bricault 2004: 550; 2001: 54–63). The geographically proximate island of Rhodos, a significant economic partner of Egypt at that time

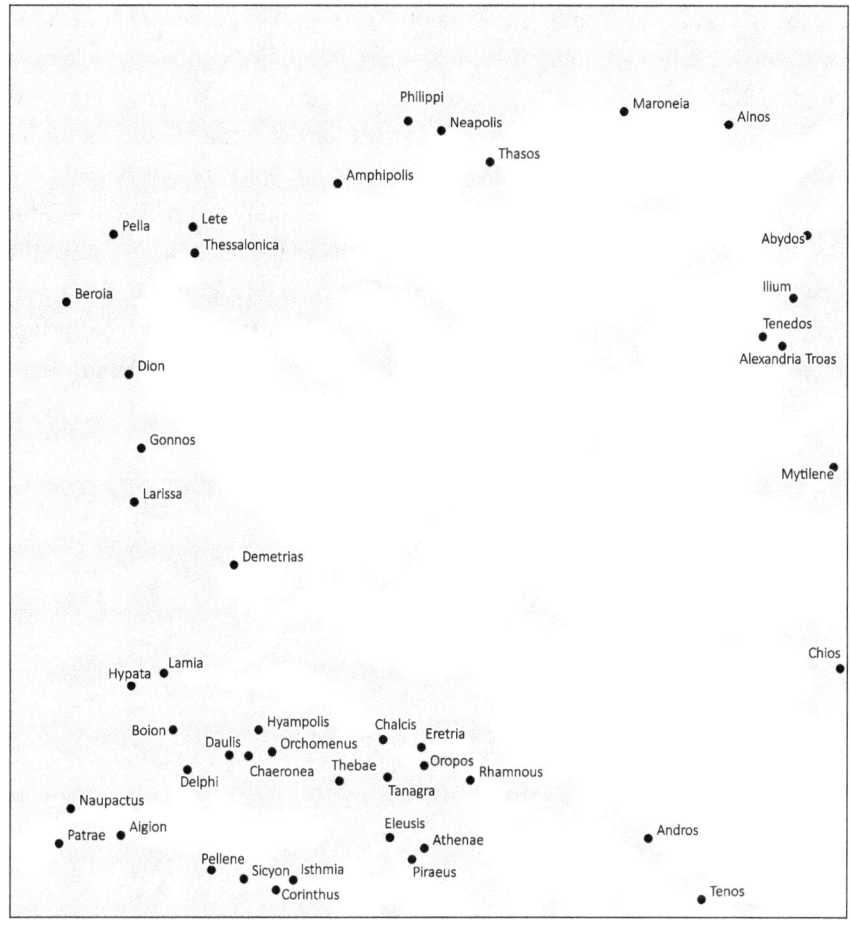

Figure 3.4 Northern Aegean with relevant ancient cities. Base map source: "Natural Earth" n.d.

frame (Gabrielsen 2013), hosted priests of Sarapis in two ports, Kamiros (RICIS 204/0201) and Lindos (RICIS 204/0301), in the middle of the third century BCE as well. Penetration of these cults further inland was, however, partially successful only in the time of the Roman empire (Bricault 2001: 54–63). The term partially is used because the evidence attested from locations in Roman times more distant from the shore is in majority consisting of artifacts, not temples (exceptions being mentions of Isiac priests in Tralles, RICIS 303/1301, and Apollonia Salbace, RICIS 305/0401).

The south coast of Asia Minor does not fall into the same pattern as the west coast. For the coastal regions of Pamphylia and Cilicia, there is almost no evidence for the Isiac cults that can be attested to the first wave of the spread of the Isiac cults, and the artifacts in those areas have their origins in the times of the Roman empire (Bricault 2001: 54–69). The situation in Lycia on the southwestern coast is slightly different with artifacts dated to the Ptolemaic times found in Limyra (RICIS 306/0601), Myra (RICIS 306/0401), and Xanthos (Bricault 2001: 64–6). When compared with Cilicia and Pisidia, Lycia had more favorable context for the potential spread of the Isiac cults as the ports in the region were one of the first possible anchoring points for ships traveling from Alexandria to the Aegean Sea, and cities such as Xanthos and Limyra were under the influence of the first Ptolemaic kings (Meadows 2006; Hölbl 2001: 23; Gygax 2005) (see Figure 3.5).

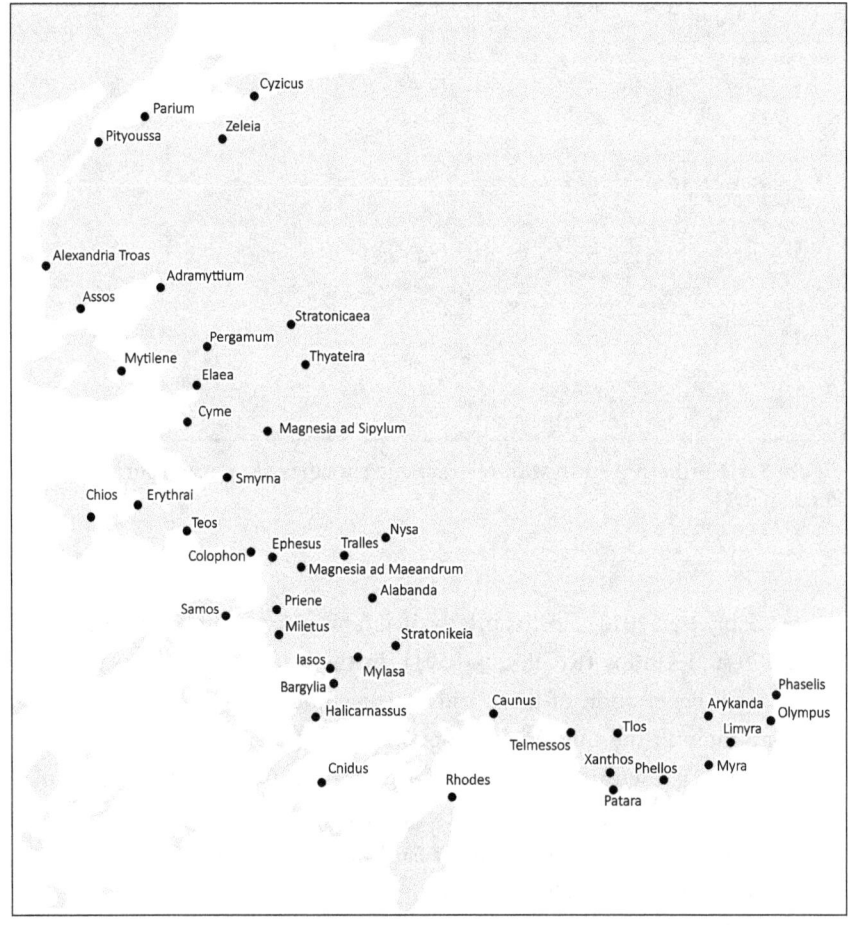

Figure 3.5 Western Asia Minor with relevant ancient cities. Base map source: "Natural Earth" n.d.

If we follow the coast further to the east, we reach Syria and Iran, more precisely, the territories belonging to the Seleucid empire, a great political rival of the Ptolemaic empire. The cult of Sarapis is attested in the Seleucid empire already in the reign of Antiochus I (281–261 BCE) in the region of Hyrcania located to the southeast of the Caspian Sea (RICIS 405/0101) (Bricault 2015: 83–4). There are also some traces of the Isiac cults belonging to the first phase of the spread on the Syrian coast, for example, a dedication to Isis and Sarapis in Libo dated to 217 BCE (RICIS 402/0601) or dedication to Sarapis in Tyrus from the third century BCE (RICIS 402/0801). There is an interesting dynamic present in the dissemination of the Isiac evidence in the Seleucid territory: while the Isiac cults were adopted in more eastern regions of the Seleucid empire, the amount of evidence for these cults in western parts of the Seleucid Asia Minor (with the exception of the western coast occupied by the Ptolemies) is minimal. John Ma addresses this issue and speculates that while the evidence for the Isiac cults in western Asia Minor belongs to the manifestation of Egyptian identities in the Ptolemaic context, in Seleucid east, the cults were rather associated with Greek (or Greek-Macedonian) identities within broader Hellenistic context without particular dynastic connotations (Ma 2014). The presence of Seleucid forces in the western parts of Asia Minor is considered as a potential immunological factor limiting the spread of the Isiac cults in the Case Study 2 in Chapter 5.

Cyprus, with its advantageous strategic position on the maritime network, abundance of metals, and strong agriculture, was the subject of Ptolemaic political and economic interest since Ptolemy I who began to actively shape the island's internal affairs in 312 BCE. The Ptolemaic influence in Cyprus was briefly interrupted by the Antigonid dynasty who seized control over the island after Ptolemy I had lost the battle of Salamis in 306 BCE to Demetrius I (later known as *Poliorcetes*, i.e., the besieger). In 294 BCE, the Ptolemies regained Cyprus, and it remained under their rule until 58 BCE when it became a Roman province. Politically, the island was a Ptolemaic possession and, as is documented from 217 BCE on, governed over by a Ptolemaic *strategos*. The island was also garrisoned by Ptolemaic troops as early as 294–290 BCE (on the Ptolemaic influence in Cyprus see e.g., Hölbl 2001: 17–23, 59–60, 226; Bagnall 1976: 38–79; Hauben 1987a). The economic importance of Cyprus to the Ptolemaic empire is attested in the so-called Canopus decree from 238 BCE, informing us that Ptolemy III imported grain from Cyprus to compensate for the lack of crop produced in Egypt caused by failure of the Nile floods, thus preventing further famine (Austin 2006, No. 271).

It is not, therefore, surprising that the earliest evidence for the presence of the Isiac cults in Cyprus is explicitly connected to the Ptolemaic dynasty, that is, a dedication to Sarapis, Isis, the king Ptolemy III, and his consort Berenice II (dated to 246–222 BCE; city of Salamis, RICIS 401/0101). The cult of Sarapis is also attested in the third century BCE on the western side of the island in the city of Soloi (RICIS 401/0604). Evidence for the cult of Isis and Sarapis from the second century BCE was found in the eastern tip of Cyprus on the peninsula of Carpasia (RICIS 401/0201) and in Amathous on the southern coast (RICIS 401/0401). First temples for the Isiac deities on Cyprus are documented in first centuries BCE and CE, which is outside the time frame of the first wave of the spread and overlaps with the beginnings of the Roman rule over the island (Bricault 2001: 42–7) (see Figure 3.6).

3.2.3 Africa

In Africa, the early spread of the Isiac cults can be located around the city of Cyrene (RICIS 701/0101), and in Carthage (RICIS 703/0101), in the area that later became the Roman province Africa Proconsularis. However, the spatial proximity between Cyrene and Egypt makes it difficult to differentiate between the "Isiac" and earlier presence of Egyptian deities. With this issue in mind, the temple of Isis in the precinct of the sanctuary of Apollo in Cyrene is dated to the fourth century BCE (Bricault, Bohec, and Podvin 2004: 222). Isis is appearing on coinage in Cyrene in similar time frame, and from the third century, there is a statue dedicated to Horus (RICIS 701/0101). Sarapis can be attested in the material evidence from this area only several centuries later in the time of the Roman presence (RICIS 701/0102). The port city of Carthage is the key location for the oldest traces of the cult of Isis in Africa Proconsularis. Here, the Phoenician-Punic social milieu holds the answer to the process of this cultural transmission. The Egyptian theophoric names (including Isis) appearing in the Phoenician-Punic onomastics can be traced to the eighth century BCE (Bricault, Bohec, and Podvin 2004; Nagel 2012: 71; Lipinski 1995). Moreover, Isis, adapted from her original ancient Egyptian setting, is also present in the Phoenician iconography and Punic epigraphic evidence. A Neo-Punic inscription then attests the presence of the temple of Isis in Carthage in the third century BCE (RICIS 703/0101) (Bricault, Bohec, and Podvin 2004: 222), that is, well before the time of Roman conquest in 146 BCE. Denser spatial dissemination of the Isiac cults outside of these big cities in Africa Proconsularis, Mauretania, and Numidia can be observed later, particularly in the times of the Roman empire

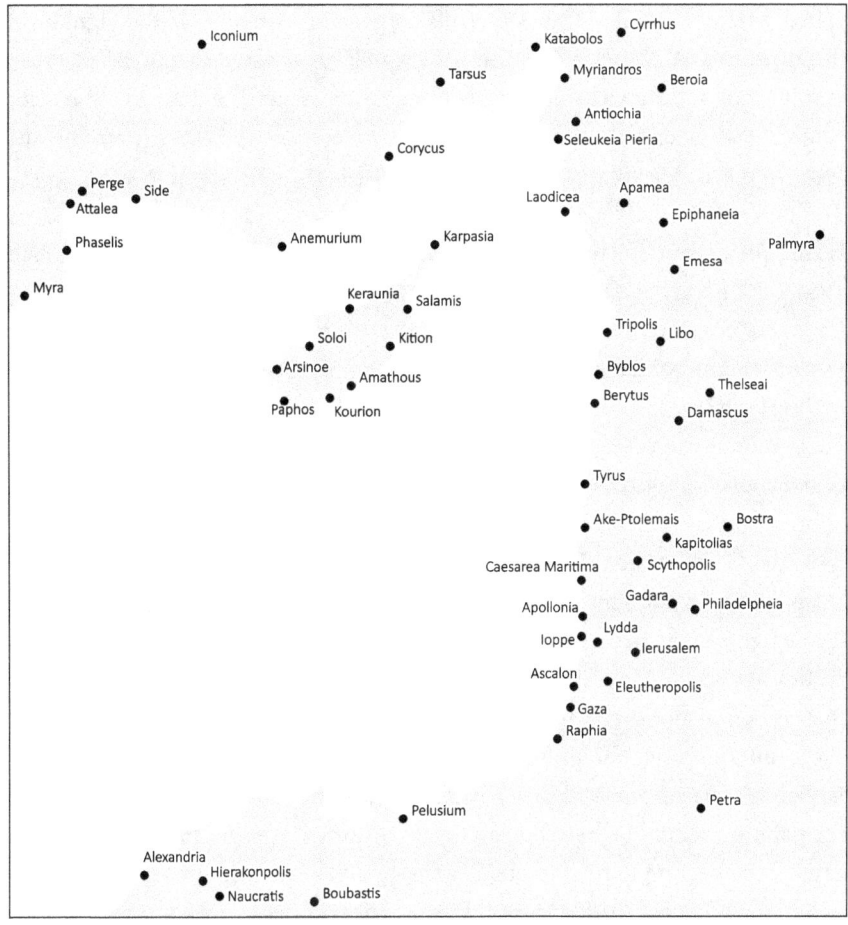

Figure 3.6 Eastern Mediterranean with relevant ancient cities. Base map source: "Natural Earth" n.d.

(Bricault 2001: 78–89). On the Isiac cults in Africa, see (Bricault, Bohec, and Podvin 2004; Nagel 2012; Bricault 2005a, 2001: 78–89).

3.2.4 Black Sea

The spatial density of material evidence related to the Isiac cults in the area of the Black Sea is low, and the bulk of the material found around its shores is dated to Roman times. However, the Isiac cults did reach as far as the Bosporan kingdom in the third century BCE (Bricault 2001: 48–53). The trace in question is the so-called Isis trireme, that is, a wall painting in the city of Nymphaeum with the name of Isis engraved on the body of an ancient vessel called trireme (RICIS 115/0401). This important evidence of the significant distance from Alexandria that the worship of Isis covered in the early spread is subject of some controversy in the academic debate. The dating to the third century BCE is agreed upon by the scholars; however, the context around the Isis trireme is heavily discussed (Braund 2018: 160–77; Bricault 2020: 23–7). The narrative around the Isis trireme set up by the excavator Nonna Grach is that the artist depicted a ship that arrived in Bosporus from Egypt (Grach 1984). The names Satyrus and Paerisades referencing the rulers of the Bosporan kingdom inscribed on the wall led scholars to further speculate that the Isis trireme might be depicting a royal envoy sent by Ptolemy II to Paerisades II (ruling between 284 and 245 BCE) (Braund 2018: 160–77; Bricault 2020: 23–7). Lucien Basch supported this argument by recognizing the Isis trireme as one of the enormous vessels of Ptolemy II (Basch 1985: 148–9). This idea was then opposed by John S. Morrison in his study *Greek and Roman Oared Warships 399-30 B.C.* who stated that the names of the boats were hinted at by figures on the prow rather than by names on the ship's body (Morrison 1996: 209). There is one figure scratched at the front part of the ship, one of the Dioscuri, patron deities of sailors. More recently, David Braund pointed out several problems that are often not taken into account in the debate and stand in the way of successful interpretation of this material: (1) the relationship between the name Isis and the vessel is not clear; (2) there is no evidence directly suggesting that the painting should be based on an actual historical voyage; and (3) there is no explicit connection to the Ptolemaic dynasty on the Isis trireme (apart from the name Isis) (Braund 2018: 134–86). Despite these concerns, the fact that the Isis trireme is an indicator of the spread of the Isiac cults in the city of Nymphaeum in the third century BCE is undisputed.

Although the Isis trireme raises some questions, it is too found in typical context of the first phase of the spread of the Isiac cults outside Egypt. In addition to being situated on the maritime network, there is evidence for diplomatic connections between the Bosporan kingdom and the Ptolemaic Egypt in the third century BCE (Archibald 2007; Hölbl 2001: 40–1, 63). One type of material attesting these relations are signet rings bearing the profile portraits of early Ptolemaic rulers and their spouses found in the cities of Bosporan kingdom, mainly in its capital Panticapaeum (Braund 2018: 163–4). Another trace of the diplomatic connection between these two political powers is a letter from a Ptolemaic official Apollonius sent to his secretary Zenon in Fayum in 254 BCE during the rule of Ptolemy II. The text is as follows (translation in Skeat 1974: 62–6; Archibald 2007: 253):

Apollonios to Zenon, greetings.

As soon as you have read this letter, send to Ptolemais the chariots, the other conveyances for the journey, and the luggage-mules for the ambassadors from Pairisades and the delegates from Argos whom the King has sent to see the sights in the Arsinoe district. Take care they are not late for when they are needed, for when I wrote this letter to you, they had already sailed up-river. Farewell. Year 32. The 26th of Panemos—the 1st of Mesore.

The Pairisades in the letter refers to the Paerisades II ruling at that time in the Bosporan kingdom, and the letter attests the official visit of envoys from the Bosporan kingdom and Argos in Ptolemaic Egypt (Archibald 2007: 253).

Later evidence, but still within the early spread of the Isiac cults, in this geographical area comes from Tyras (sanctuary dated between the second and first centuries BCE, RICIS 115/0101). In more southern areas near the Black Sea, such as Abydos (RICIS 301/0900) or Parium (RICIS 301/0700) in the Troad in the northwestern part of Asia Minor, the Isiac cults are documented mainly on coinage bearing the headdress of Isis (*basileion*) since ca. 175 BCE (see Figure 3.7).

3.3 Spread of the Isiac Cults in Roman Times

It is certain that from the second century BCE on, the Romans knew the Isiac cults (Bricault 2001, 2018, 2019; Christodoulou 2015; Bøgh 2013; Heyob 1975: 10). We do not have the evidence to pinpoint when and where exactly the first introduction of these cults to the Roman environment happened. However, since the spread of the Isiac cults is a cultural transmission from one socio-spatial milieu to another and the key prerequisite in this process is social contact, we can at least explore the first possible social encounters that could have facilitated the cultural transmission.

One of the areas of interest here is Sicily in the third and second centuries BCE. It was especially during the reign of Hieron II of Syracuse (270–215 BCE) when Sicily maintained close political and economic relationships with the Ptolemaic Egypt. Together with the geographical proximity of Sicily to Italy, this island provided favorable conditions for the spread of the Isiac cults in the Roman environment (Heyob 1975: 11–12; Martzavou 2010; Bricault 2019: 198–9, 2018: 227; Hölbl 2001: 133; cf. Malaise 1972: 261–3). The kingdom of Syracuse was located in the southeastern part of Sicily, and Hieron II aimed to keep the

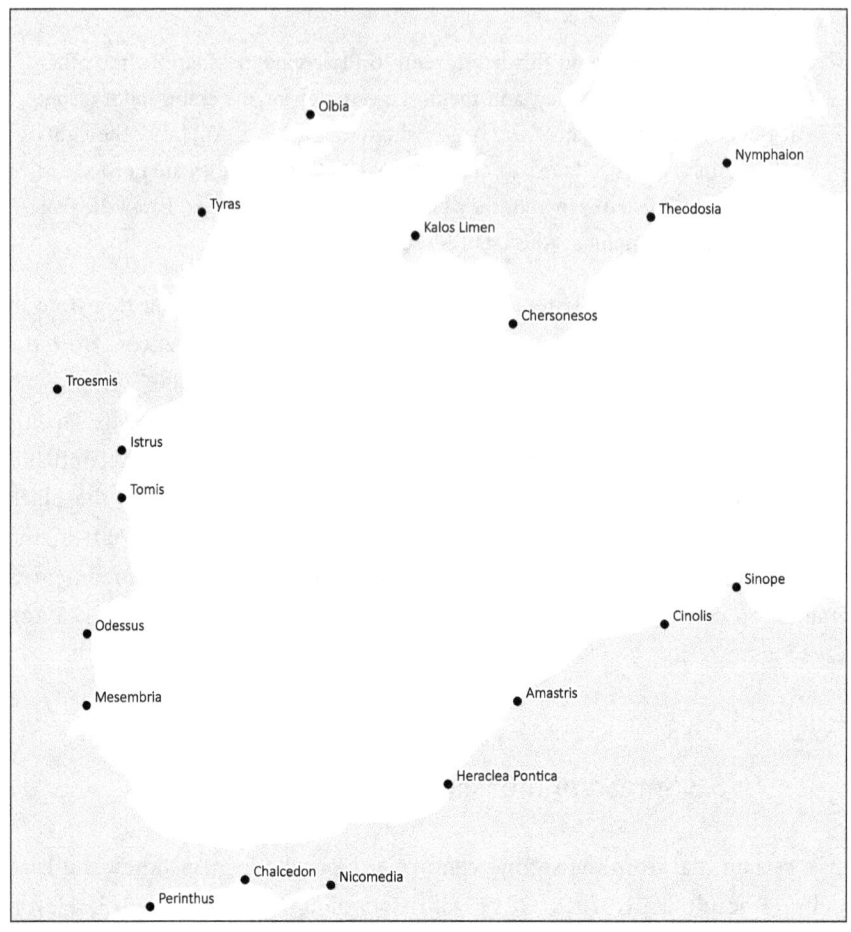

Figure 3.7 Black Sea region with relevant ancient cities. Base map source: "Natural Earth" n.d.

kingdom independent despite being caught between two opposing powers, Carthage and Rome. It is thus logical that Hieron II sought support and kept diplomatic relations with the Ptolemaic Egypt, as can be, for example, attested by his gift of a luxury ship loaded with grain delivered to the Ptolemies (Hölbl 2001: 133; Bricault 2019: 198). However, after Hireon's II death in 215 BCE, his successor, Hieronymus, entered into a coalition with Carthage, and despite diplomatic efforts, the provoked Rome laid siege to Syracuse (213/2 BCE), which eventually led to extending the Roman influence over the whole Sicily. It is in this environment where the first archaeological evidence of the Isiac cults appears at the end of the third century or beginning of the second century BCE

(Hölbl 2001: 133; Eckstein 2008: 201–2, 371; Grainger 2017: 145–60, 166–8). There is, however, no evidence suggesting that these cults were introduced to this territory by official action of the Ptolemies.

The second area of interest with respect to initial social contacts between Romans and the carriers of the Isiac cults is constituted by the island of Delos in Cyclades. The island of Delos was significantly influenced by Ptolemaic politics in the third century BCE. Already in 287/6 Ptolemy I received divine honors on Delos for taking action against Demetrius I Poliorcetes, a member of the Antigonid dynasty, who conquered Athens several years before and threatened the political balance at that time. Firm Ptolemaic grip in Cyclades is then attested by the festival of *Ptolemaia*, honoring the Ptolemaic royal family, taking place on Delos in 270s BCE and followed by *Ptolemaia* II and III honoring the Delian gods in 249 and 246 BCE (Hölbl 2001: 93, 98). The introduction of the Isiac cults to the island is attested to the third century BCE (RICIS 202/0101), however, by a private and not state initiative. These cults only flourished and were officially recognized on Delos in the second century BCE. Also from the second century BCE, there are attested Italian merchants (*negotiatores*) worshiping the Isiac deities in the *Sarapieia* on the island, which points to another possible route of the spread of the Isiac cults to Italy (Heyob 1975: 10–11; Malaise 1972: 318, 331–2; Veymiers 2018: 32–3). In 166 BCE, Rome made Delos a free port, and the island prospered as a strategically well-placed key trade center for the political powers in the Mediterranean, which could have only contributed to the spread of the Isiac cults as merchants were one of the most mobile groups (Bricault 2019: 199). Directly on the Italian peninsula, there is a Serapeum attested in the inscription from 105 BCE (RICIS 504/0401) from the port of Puteoli, which served as a Roman center for trans-Mediterranean trade since the second century BCE (Bricault 2004; Heyob 1975: 12). As there is evidence of many Campanians worshiping Isiac deities on Delos (Takács 1995: 34; Malaise 1972: 469–70) and Lucilius used a nickname for Puteoli, calling it *Delus minor* (fragment no. 123; Fontana and Murgia 2010: 27), the probable routes of transmission become even clearer.

A similar approach of tracing scattered social contacts and introductions of the Isiac cults in the political context can be applied in the case of the city of Rome. The presence of the cult of Isis in the city can be with high certainty dated to the first half of the first century BCE. The first clue in this respect can be found in Apuleius's *Metamorphoses*, specifically in the section where he describes how the main character, Lucius, assumes the Isiac priesthood (XI, 30; translation in Apuleius and Ruden 2012): "Soon, shaved to the skin again, I went joyfully about the duties of this venerable priesthood, founded in the time of Sulla." The reference to a time of a Roman statesman, general, and eventually dictator Sulla puts the foundation of the priesthood somewhere in the context of the so-called Mithridatic wars (88–63 BCE), probably to the 80s BCE because Sulla retired in 79 BCE (Takács 1995: 30, 67; Bricault 2011). *Metamorphoses* is an ancient Roman novel from the second century CE and thus not the best source for historical accuracy. There is, however, supporting evidence that the cult of Isis existed in Rome around the half of the first century BCE, that is, an inscription mentioning "sac(erdotis) Isid(is) Capitolin(ae)" (RICIS 501/0109; Lipka 2009: 54; Heyob 1975: 16). Moreover, in 88 BCE, one of Mithridates's generals sacked the island of Delos, which could have intensified the spread of the Isiac cults in Italy because many Italian merchants needed to return from the island where the cults were flourishing for a long time by then (Bricault 2011, 2019: 201, 2018: 227; Takács 1995: 56). Another presence of the cult of Isis in the form of a temple in this temporal frame in Rome is documented by *Historia Augusta* (*Tyranni Triginta 25*, translation in Magie 2014): "The house of the Tetrici is still standing to-day, situated on the Caelian Hill between the two groves and facing the Temple of Isis built by Metellus," and with probability also archaeologically identified by Mariette de Vos (1996). The *Iseum Metellinum* was probably built by Quintus Caecilius Metellus Pius between 71 and 63 BCE (Bricault 2011, 2019: 202; Versluys 2004).

So far, we have been speaking more about the private form of the worship of the Isiac family in the city of Rome, and the path toward the officialization of the Isiac cults in this city is not a straightforward one. It was in 58 BCE when the Isiac cults in Rome faced the first repressive action from the Roman authorities. The incident is described by Varro through the words of Tertullian (*Ad Nationes* I, 10, translation by Peter Holmes in Roberts, Donaldson, and Coxe 1993):

> Varro informs us that Serapis also, and Isis, and Arpocrates, and Anubis, were excluded from the Capitol and that their altars which the senate had thrown down were only restored by the popular violence. The Consul Gabinius, however, on the first day of the ensuing January, although he gave a tardy consent to some sacrifices, in deference to the crowd which assembled because he had failed to decide about Serapis and Isis, yet held the judgment of the senate to be more potent than the clamour of the multitude, and forbade the altars to be built.

Although it is a report of a difficult situation for the worshipers of Isis in Rome, it also confirms the picture drawn above, that is, that the Isiac cults already thrived on the Capitol before 58 BCE. A couple of years later, in 53

BCE, according to Cassius Dio (40.47), the Senate issued a decree that ordered the destruction of private shrines (*naos*) of the Egyptian gods. This decree, however, as it seems, was not carried out until 50 BCE when the consul Lucius Aemilius Paulus himself took an ax to hack up the doors of the temple (*Valerius Maximus* 1.3.4, Heyob 1975: 18; Takács 1995: 56–70; Bricault 2011, 2019, 202–3; Hayne 1992: 145; Christodoulou 2015: 186; Scheid 2016: 131). Another destructive event aimed at the worshipers of the Isiac deities took place in 48 BCE as is reported by Cassius Dio (42.26, translation by Earnest Cary in Cassius Dio, Cary, and Foster 1987): "Among other things that happened toward the end of that year bees settled on the Capitol beside the statue of Hercules. Sacrifices to Isis chanced to be going on there at the time, and the soothsayers gave their opinion to the effect that all precincts of that goddess and of Serapis should be razed to the ground once more." The exact motives for issuing the senatorial decree to tear down the shrines of Egyptian gods are unknown, and consensus in the discussion is lacking since the period of the Late Republic offers several political tensions to choose from (Orlin 2008; Takács 1995: 65–6; Hayne 1992: 143–9; Bricault 2011). For example, Tarolta A. Takács speculates a scenario that the territory inside the sacred precinct of Rome (*pomerium*) was intended only for official cults and that the growing popularity and presence of unofficial Isiac cults inside the *pomerium* threatened both the balance in the perceived divine order and the senatorial authority (Takács 1995: 65–6). A final act in the era of the Late Republic, more specifically in the time of Gaius Julius Caesar, between the Roman authorities and the Isiac cults in Rome, is again reported by Cassius Dio (47.15–16) who tells us that in 43 BCE, the Second Triumvirate decided to build a temple for Sarapis and Isis. However, the decision was not acted upon, probably because the *triumviri* were occupied with political issues following the death of Caesar (Takács 1995: 69; Heyob 1975: 19; Bricault 2011, 2019: 203; Malaise 1972: 378; Christodoulou 2015: 186).

The Isiac cults in Rome were also affected in the context of the civil war resulting from the tensions between Octavian, Mark Antony, and Cleopatra. In 28 BCE, Octavian issued a decree that banned the Egyptian rites inside the *pomerium*. The act of moving the Egyptian cults outside the sacred border means that they were officially considered foreign (Orlin 2008; Heyob 1975: 22; Bricault 2018: 227–8). This should not, however, be interpreted as a sign of Octavian's hatred of anything Egyptian because (1) relocating Egyptian rites *extra pomerium* is very far from forbidding the worship of Egyptian deities entirely and (2) Octavian, at the same time, repaired and restored the Egyptian temples in the city (Orlin 2008). In other words, Octavian allowed and supported Egyptian cults in Rome as long as they were bound to specific areas.

After enduring further suppressions, mainly in the reign of Tiberius, no later than in the time of Vespasian, the Isiac cults finally gained an official public and prominent position among the Roman deities (Pachis 2010). The relationship between Vespasian and the Isiac family is reminiscent of the early Ptolemaic times and certainly relevant in the context of the further spread and popularity of these cults (Levick 2020: 78–9). After Nero had committed suicide in 68 CE, the following political turmoil in the empire became known as the Year of the Four Emperors, that is, a conflict leading to four men ruling in quick succession (i.e., Galba, Otho, Vitellius, and Vespasian) with Vespasian emerging victorious and becoming the new Roman emperor and founder of the Flavian dynasty (Morgan 2007). It was mainly Vespasian's need for his legitimization as a successor to the Roman throne that invited the Isiac family into play. Vespasian was a son of a tax collector, and although he had the necessary military strength of his legions stationed in the eastern provinces, he lacked the proper *maiestas* and *auctoritas* (majesty and prestige) to be considered a worthy successor (Bricault 2019: 206, 2018: 228–9; Takács 1995: 95–7; Levick 2020: 77). During the Year of the Four Emperors, Vespasian took control over Egypt, and he was there when in 69 CE his rival Vitellius was killed in Rome and Vespasian was proclaimed the emperor. While in Alexandria, Vespasian supposedly visited Serapeum to receive the oracle about his bright future, healed two cripples that were sent to him by Sarapis in their dreams, and assumed the role of pharaoh similarly as did Alexander the Great or Ptolemy I before him (Levick 2020: 79; Christodoulou 2015: 188–9; Bricault 2019: 206–7). With these acts and miracles ascribed to him, Vespasian acquired the necessary qualities to be considered a legitimate ruler. Later, in 71 CE, Vespasian and Titus spent a night in the temple of Isis in the *Campus Martius* in their triumphant return to Rome (Bricault 2018: 228; Scheid 2009, 2016: 132). The Isiac deities firmly tied with Vespasian's ascension to the Roman throne thus became the patron and protector deities of the Flavian dynasty (Scheid 2009, 2016: 132). Since the Isiac family became a member of the official Roman pantheon, the spread of the Isiac cults was not limited by Roman political barriers, and eventually, in the course of the following centuries, the cults disseminated across the whole Roman empire (see Figure 3.1).

Although Vespasian emphasized Sarapis from the divine couple of Isis and Sarapis, on the level of the general population, it was Isis who rose to significant popularity. From the available literary and epigraphic evidence for the worship of Isis from that time on, it is apparent that the traditional maternal role of Isis/

Eset in the ancient Egyptian pantheon gave way for more universal aspects of the goddess represented by attributes such as victorious (*victrix*), ruling (*domina, regina, or invicta*), or protector of the sea travel (*pelagia* or *pharia*) (Bricault 2018: 229; Bøgh 2013: 234). Isis also received a new iconographical rendering since the first century CE, which lasted until the fourth century CE; in this period she was frequently depicted on coins and sculptures holding a *sistrum* in one hand and *situla* (carrying the sacred water of the Nile) in the other (Bricault 2018: 229).

After the Flavian dynasty, there was a continuation in the royal interest for Egypt and its culture. Emperor Hadrian (ruled 117–138 CE) included buildings and statues in Egyptian style in his villa at Tibur, and he restored, among other important temples, the Alexandrian Serapeum (Takács 1995: 105–6; Heyob 1975: 29–30). We can observe a very close connection between Hadrian and the Isiac deities on coins issued during his reign bearing the text on the reverse side *ADVENTVI AVG ALEXANDRIAE* (entry to Alexandria) depicting Hadrian and Sabina facing Sarapis and Isis (Manders 2012: 75). This motif is a clear indication of another continuity—Ptolemaic tradition of identifying the royal couple with Isis and Sarapis. The emperor who followed, Antoninus Pius, did not show such interest in Egyptian culture as his predecessor. Still, the attachment of the Isiac family to the royal couple remained. In 141 CE, Antoninus's wife Faustina died, which grieved the emperor greatly. Antoninus asked the Senate to proclaim her goddess and dedicated a temple to her. In the year of her death, the emperor issued a coin type depicting veiled Faustina on the obverse side and the goddess Isis holding sistrum on the reverse (Heyob 1975: 30; Takács 1995: 107). Similarly, Faustina II, the wife of the emperor Marcus Aurelius (ruled 161–180), was associated with the goddess Isis, mainly with her aspect of the protector of seafaring (*pharia*) (Bricault 2018: 229; Takács 1995: 107–12). Despite co-occurring with Isis on coins issued by Marcus Aurelius, Faustina II is mentioned in this particular role in an Alexandrian inscription dated to 161–169 CE: "P. Aelius Panopaios, who was procurator (*epitropos*) of our lords the Augusti. For the sake of goodwill to their household, those from the banqueting hall (*syssition*) of the Augustan images and of Faustina Pharia ('of the Vessel') Sostitolos ('Protector of the Fleet'), new Augusta, set this up for their fellow-banqueter (*syssitos*)" (Harland n.d.c). The last member of the Antonine dynasty, Commodus, was very familiar with the Isiac cults. *Historia Augusta* (*Commodus* 9.4.) states that he participated in the festivities of the Isiac cults and carried the statue of Anubis. Cassius Dio (73.15.3) then mentions a golden statue of Commodus with a bull and a cow, which is usually interpreted as a representation of Commodus-Horus with Osiris-Apis (bull) and Isis-Hathor (cow). Even though Cassius Dio is not explicit in this Egyptianizing interpretation and, together with the *Historia Augusta*, is biased to paint Commodus as insane (Hekster 2002: 4–8), the Roman coinage attests this connection on coins issued under Commodus depicting Sarapis with the inscription *SERAPIDI CONSERV AVG* (*Serapidi Conservatori Augusti*) indicating the protective aspect of the god (Manolaraki 2013: 230–1; Heyob 1975: 30–1; Takács 1995: 112–14).

The Severan emperors favored the Isiac cults, and based on the numerous and diverse archaeological, epigraphic, and numismatic evidence, it may appear that the Isiac cults reached the peak in that period (193–235 CE) with respect to spatial dissemination. Bricault admits that the widespread popularity, however, also points out the term "peak" might also be misleading and the observation biased by the increased epigraphic habit in the Roman empire in those times (Bricault 2004, 2018: 229). Emperor Caracalla (ruled 211–217 CE) is an illustrative example of the Severan inclination to Egyptian gods. A number of coin types with the Isiac deities were issued under Caracalla, with two of these commemorating his visit in Egypt in 215 CE; they are depicting Caracalla and Isis on the reverse side where Isis presents two corn-ears to Caracalla who is in military attire trampling on a crocodile (Łukaszewicz 1998; Manders 2012: 243–44). Cassius Dio informs that Caracalla on this visit in Egypt resided in the precinct of the temple of Sarapis (77.23) and sacrificed to this god (77.15). Caracalla also built Serapeum in Rome (Regio VI, Quirinal; RICIS 501/0106), thus supporting the cult inside *pomerium* (Roullet 1972: 39–40; Versluys 2002: 24). Finally, in an inscription from Alexandria dated to 216 CE honoring Caracalla, his mother Julia Doma, and father Septimius Severus, the emperor is called φιλοσάραπιν (philosarapis), that is, a friend of Sarapis (SB I, 4275; Takács 1995: 117; Podvin 2014).

This trend continued after the end of the Severan dynasty. The perception of the emperor as *philosarapis* and Sarapis as *comes Augusti* (emperor's companion) is visible on coins issued during the reign of Gordian III (238–244 CE) where Sarapis is facing the emperor on the obverse side (Manders 2012: 235; Heyob 1975: 34; Christodoulou 2015: 189). However, the era of Tetrarchs is the last period of intensive and positive relations between the emperors and the Isiac cults. Tetrarchy was established in 293 CE and represented a model of rule where four authorities (two Augusti, Diocletian and Maximian, and two Caesars, Galerius and Constantius Chlorus) were overseeing different parts of the empire in order to maintain control over a vast territory. The ideal of the Tetrarchy is visually represented on the Arch of Galerius in Thessalonica where the two emperors and the two Caesars are accompanied by the main Roman gods such as

Virtus, Fortuna, Mars, Dioscuri, and Isis and Sarapis (Christodoulou 2015: 190–2). The Egyptian gods and their company on this relief are a clear statement of their prominent position in the Roman pantheon at that time. Moreover, in the period of Tetrarchy, temples for both Isis and Sarapis were built in Rome, and the Isiac deities appeared on the coinage issued in relation to the *Vota Publica*, that is, annual vows for the *salus* (health and welfare) of the emperor and the empire (Bricault 2018: 229–30).

Eventually giving place to rising Christianity, the last available inscription connected to Isiac cults is from Rome and dated to May 25, 390 CE, mentioning Cecin(i)a Lolliana, a priestess of the goddess Isis (RICIS 501/0212). Only two years later, the Serapeum in Alexandria was destroyed during skirmishes between Christians, pagans, and Roman soldiers, which represents a symbolic end to the worship of the Isiac family (Bricault 2018: 231; Heyob 1975: 35–6). In their long journey, the Isiac deities subsequently spread from Egypt to the most distant corners of the Roman empire such as western shores of Spain, province Britannia, Chersonesos on the Crimean Peninsula, or Dura-Europos in Syria.

3.4 Concluding Remarks on the Patterns of the Spread of the Isiac Cults

Based on the discussion and evidence of the Isiac cults presented in this chapter, it is apparent that there indeed are several re-occurring factors entangled with the spread of the Isiac cults—these are mainly trade, politics, and, for the period of the early spread, closeness to the maritime network. Despite the tendencies in the earlier stages of the academic discussion to favor only one of these factors as the exclusive force behind the spread, the material evidence and its contexts described here point to a more complicated picture of interrelated impact of several factors together.

The impact of Hellenistic trade is very tangible in the spread of the Isiac cults outside Egypt from the beginning. Commercial activities in connection to the presence of the Isiac cults are attested in Piraeus, Rhodos, Delos, and Puteoli in the context of the spread of these cults into Roman territory. The debate on the political aspects of this cultural transmission, however, suffered by focusing the majority of the arguments on the validity of Cumont's imperialistic theory. Instead of nuancing the different layers of potential political influences on the spread of the Isiac cults, the results of the debate were largely formed to answer the question whether the Ptolemies directly propagated these cults abroad or not. If we, however, step out of the shadow of this aspect of the debate, it is visible that the Ptolemaic political sphere is present in the context of the evidence of the spread of the Isiac cults. It can be attested, for example, by the joint dedications to Sarapis, Isis, and the Ptolemaic rulers in territories under the Ptolemaic influence or by the Ptolemaic soldiers worshiping these gods (e.g., Thera, Ephesus, Kaunos, Crete). The next logical step is to move beyond the logic of arguments revolving around the imperialistic theory and recognize different modes of political influences on cultural transmission that nuance the research problem using categories such as direct, indirect, spontaneous, or contextual influence. The factor of maritime connectivity present mainly in the early phase of the spread of the Isiac cults is tied to the geographical fact that Egypt communicated with the rest of the Mediterranean mainly using seaways. In other words, Egyptian trade, political, or cultural products reached inland territories almost exclusively by reaching port cities first. This geographical aspect that was strongly impacting many aspects of life in the ancient Mediterranean (including culture, trade, and politics), both on micro and macro scales, only shows how important it is to take into account the mutual interaction of these factors when assessing problems such as cultural transmission.

This book follows the rationale of more nuanced approach to the factors of influence on the early spread of the Isiac cults and their potential interactions. The next chapters present two case studies that explore quantitatively, using methods such as network analysis and mathematic modeling, the interplay of these factors and their comparative impact on the spatial dissemination of these cults in two regions—the Aegean Sea and the west coast of Asia Minor.

4

Case Study 1: Spread of the Isiac Cults across the Aegean Sea

4.1 Area and Period of Interest

As was summarized in the previous chapter, the Isiac cults spread from the end of the fourth century BCE first to the ports of the ancient Mediterranean and subsequently reached further into the mainland until they were disseminated across the whole Roman empire in the fourth century CE (Bricault 2014, 2004, 2001, 2005b). However, it is not possible to perceive the process of the spread of these cults as homogenous in time and space mainly because the channels of the spread were interconnected with the unstable political and economic sphere of the Mediterranean region.

The definition of the spatio-temporal focus of this book is significantly inspired by Bricault's differentiation of the spread of the Isiac cults into the three temporal phases. The book focuses mainly on the early spread of the Isiac cults corresponding to the first wave in Bricault's classification. However, there are some differences between Bricault and this book in framing the temporal extent of the spread of the Isiac cults that should be described in greater detail (see below). Geographically, this case study observes and analyzes the dissemination of the Isiac cults in the specific region of the Aegean Sea with the emphasis on the Aegean Islands (Figure 4.1). Generally, this case study analyzes quantitatively the impact of individual factors on the spread of the Isiac cults in the period between the end of the fourth century BCE and the end of the second century BCE, in the area of the Aegean Sea region and especially on the Aegean Islands. Following sections 4.1.1, Temporal Extent, and 4.1.2, Geographical Extent, explain the reasons behind this selection.

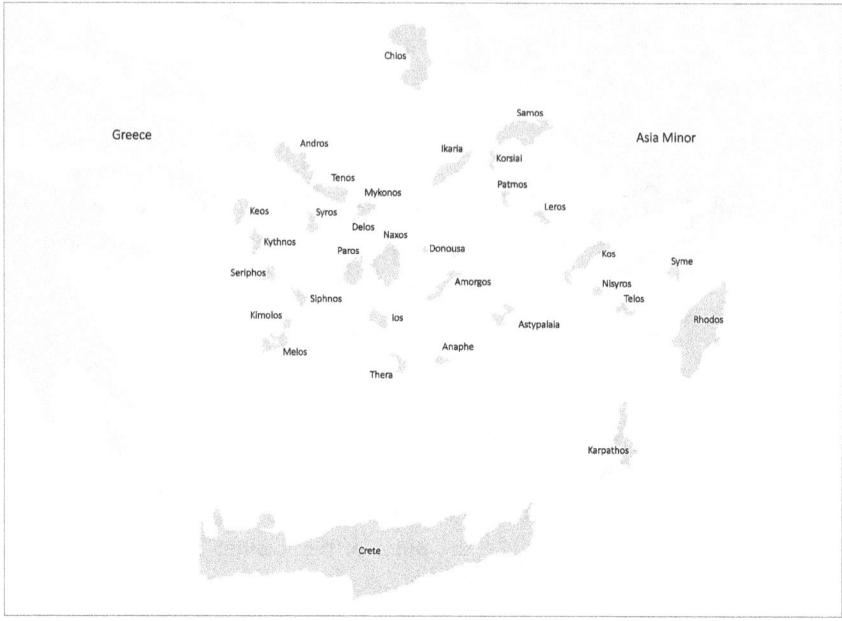

Figure 4.1 Area of interest—case study 1. Base map source: "Natural Earth" n.d.; Data source: Glomb et al. 2018.

4.1.1 Temporal Extent

1. The beginnings of the spread of the cult of Isis and Sarapis and other Egyptian deities outside Egypt are closely tied with the rule of Ptolemy I Soter in Egypt, who gave royal patronage to the cult of Isis and Sarapis and thus made it more accessible for the Greek audience. Ptolemy I Soter ascended to the Egyptian throne in 305/4 BCE (Stambaugh 1972; Pfeiffer 2008: 398). The earliest mention of the cult of Isis outside Egypt is dated to 333/2 BCE and placed to the Athenian port of Piraeus (RICIS 101/0101). However, this case study focuses mainly on the spread of the Isiac cults from Alexandria after they were promoted in Egypt by the Ptolemies in order to examine the possible role of the Ptolemies in the process of this spread. The starting point of the spread is therefore the year of Ptolemy I's ascension to the throne.

2. According to Bricault, the military acts of Mithridates on the island of Delos in 88 BCE mark the end of the first wave of the spread of the Isiac cults. However, the channels of the spread could have been restructured even earlier. In 167/6 BCE, Rome gifted the strategically important island of Delos to Athens on the condition that Delos would be a free port. With that act, the island of Rhodos lost its influence on the Island League,

and the commercial traffic shifted from Rhodos to Delos. Moreover, in the same time, the Roman Senate gave freedom to some of the Rhodian possessions (e.g., Caria and Lycia). In 164 BCE, Rome offered Rhodos a treaty, which restored their friendship but, on the other hand, put a definitive end to their equal partnership (Habicht 1989: 337–8). These steps disbalanced previous political and commercial flows on the transportation network of the Aegean Sea region. The crucial nodes for Egyptian export were impacted by Roman influence, and with that situation, the early spread of the Isiac cults could have been seriously affected. It is therefore difficult to decide the specific date of the end of the early spread of the Isiac cults across the Aegean Sea. Moreover, many pieces of archaeological evidence related to the Isiac cults cannot be dated precisely—they are often dated only to a certain century. For these reasons, the end of the early spread of the Isiac cults in this case study is set to the end of the second century BCE, and the evidence from the first century BCE was excluded from the analysis as it could have originated later than 88 BCE.

4.1.2 Geographical Extent

1. The main trading routes between Alexandria and continental Greece led through the Aegean Sea with the Aegean Islands as potential places of Egyptian interest (Casson 1954; Roebuck 1950; Buraselis 2013).
2. Ptolemies were also politically invested in the Aegean using the islands as strategic locations for military bases and administering the Island League (Hölbl 2001: 35–76).
3. In comparison with continents, islands are small and closed worlds with clear physical borders and therefore are more suitable for small-scale demographical and geographical analyses—in other words, the Aegean Islands are, in this case, seen as a specific kind of "laboratory specimen," which can be, in certain aspects, observed more transparently and systematically than cities and areas on the continent.

4.2 Academic Discussion on the Early Spread of the Isiac Cults across the Aegean Sea

Since the early introduction of the Isiac cults to the island of Delos in the third century BCE by a private initiative—grandfather of the Isiac priest Apollonius

(RICIS 202/0101)—was already discussed in detail in Chapter 3, section 3.1. This section provides the key turns and arguments in the debate focusing on the Isiac evidence from other islands in the Aegean Sea. The arguments in the lengthy debate on this region are again mostly defined based on positions toward Cumont's imperialistic theory that Ptolemies directly propagated the Isiac cults abroad. As Peter M. Fraser represents one of the loudest voices against Cumont's theory and chronologically belongs to the earlier stages of the discussion (1960s), his assessment of the spread of the Isiac cults across the Aegean Sea is presented first.

As is hinted in the previous paragraph, Fraser discusses the evidence from Cyclades in order to test the validity of the imperialistic theory (Fraser 1960: 24–32). Besides Delos, the island of Thera is a place of abundant evidence of the Isiac cults in Cyclades. As was already discussed earlier in the book, there are several dedications from Thera dated to the third century BCE jointly dedicated to the Ptolemaic rulers and the Isiac family (RICIS 202/1202-05). Again, the example of the inscription dedicated to the Isiac deities by Diokles, a member of the *basilistai* devoted to the Ptolemaic dynastic cult, is of relevance here since the group on Thera consisted of soldiers stationed in the Ptolemaic garrison (RICIS 202/1202, first half of the third century BCE). Thera, as Fraser claims, had an exceptional status in the region because of the presence of the aforementioned Ptolemaic garrison (Fraser 1960: 24–5). The only other island with the evidence from the third century BCE is, according to Fraser, Amorgos (Fraser 1960: 25). A marble table from the end of the third century BCE found on Amorgos attests the presence of the state cult of Sarapis and the annual festival of *Sarapieia* (RICIS 202/1501). No later than 280 BCE, the island of Amorgos was under the Ptolemaic control as a member of the Nesiotic League (also known as the Island League or League of Islanders) (Fraser 1960: 25; Hölbl 2001: 23–4; Meadows 2013; Austin 2006, No. 256). Based on this evidence, Fraser admits that the cult could have been introduced to Amorgos in the middle of the third century BCE (Fraser 1960: 25). Fraser then states that the evidence from the remaining islands (Ios, Andros, Tenos, Keos, and Anaphe) is in almost all cases confined to the second century BCE and could therefore be dismissed as late and irrelevant with respect to the validation of the imperialistic theory (Fraser 1960: 25). Fraser somehow omitted to describe in greater detail the evidence and the context on the island of Keos. He does describe a decree of *Sarapiastai* mentioning the celebration of *Isideia* (IG XII.5.14; RICIS 202/0801), which is dated to the third or second century BCE, but his note ends with the declaration that he favors the second century as the correct date for the decree (Fraser 1960: 25). What is missing in Fraser's text is the information that the island of Keos had in fact a Ptolemaic military and naval base stationed there during the Chremonidean War (ca. 267–261 BCE) (Bagnall 1976: 141–5; Fischer-Bovet 2014: 60; Chaniotis 2005: 90) and that Epameinon honored in the decree of *Sarapiastai* was a son of a Ptolemaic official Somenes (RICIS 202/0801 L.2; IG XII.3.320).

Fraser concludes that in the case of Cyclades, the imperialistic theory finds little support due to the lack of evidence (Fraser 1960: 25). This is a very interesting moment in Fraser's argumentation. At the beginning of the article, Fraser declares that his aim is to disprove the imperialistic theory, and the evidence from Delos and Athens indeed suggests that there is only a small chance that the cult was systematically propagated by the Ptolemies outside Egypt. However, in the case of Thera (and possibly Amorgos and Keos), the connection between the Ptolemaic dynasty and the Egyptian cults is indisputable. Yet instead of admitting a limited local plausibility of Cumont's notions or offering a more elaborated commentary, Fraser only provides the short conclusion that Cumont's theory "finds little support." Moreover, Fraser tries to isolate Thera—a weak part of his argument against Cumont—by stating that the island's status was an exception (Fraser 1960, 25). It should be, however, noted that the presence of Ptolemaic garrisons or short-term military camps in the ancient Mediterranean was not exceptional at that time because the Ptolemies took part in several wars, and garrisoning their possessions was a common procedure (Hölbl 2001; Chaniotis 2005).

After summarizing the situation in Cyclades, Fraser focuses on the evidence from the northern Aegean Islands—Chios, Lesbos, and Samos (Fraser 1960: 25–6). Lesbos and Samos were Ptolemaic possessions during the third century BCE; Samos also had a Ptolemaic naval base at the time (Bagnall 1976: 80–8, 159–65). Chios, Fraser claims, was not a Ptolemaic dependency but had close commercial relations with Egypt (Fraser 1960: 25). Indeed, a papyrus from the Zenon archive dated to 259 BCE reports a shipment of expensive Chian wine to Egypt and therefore proves mercantile connections between Chios and the Ptolemies (Fraser 1960: 25; Gabrielsen 2013: 72; Austin 2006, No. 298). There is, however, a decree from Chios that mentions king Ptolemy and his wife Arsinoe, which attests at least some diplomatic connection between Egypt and Chios during the third century BCE. Fraser dates the decree to the reign of Ptolemy IV and Arsinoe III (221–204 BCE) (Fraser 1960: 25), but Roger S. Bagnall dates it to the reign of Ptolemy II and Arsinoe II (283–246 BCE) (Bagnall 1976: 168–9). The evidence connected to the presence of the Isiac cults on Chios can be, according to Fraser, dismissed in validation of the imperialistic theory because both dedications to Isiac deities found there are of too late a date (RICIS 205/0201-03) (Fraser 1960: 26). The case is, according to Fraser, similar for Samos where the evidence of the Isiac cults appears to be from the second century BCE despite the fact that Samos was Ptolemaic throughout the third century BCE (Fraser 1960: 26). It is, however, possible, that this claim is not entirely correct. There is a Samian dedication by Horos, son of Phaon, who was originally from Canopus, to the god Apollo-Horus, which is dated by Laurent Bricault to the third century BCE (RICIS 205/0101). However, there is no mention of Isis or Sarapis in the dedication. Furthermore, a marble stela from Samos bearing the mention of a priest of Isis is dated by Bricault somewhere between the third and second century BCE (RICIS 205/0102). On Lesbos, more specifically in Mytilene, a dedication to Sarapis and Isis was found and dated by Bricault to the third century BCE (RICIS 205/0301). The evidence collected on Samos, Lesbos, and Chios is rather inconclusive with respect to either validation or falsification of the imperialistic theory.

In Fraser's perspective, the dense spatial dissemination of public Isiac cults on Dorian islands during the third century BCE is caused by the exceptional status of the island of Rhodos (Fraser 1960: 27–8). Indeed, Rhodos had been one of the main commercial and political partners of Ptolemaic Egypt from the time of Ptolemy I Soter and served as a main distribution point for Egyptian grain heading to Aegean cities (Gabrielsen 2013). The status of Rhodos and its possible role in the early spread of the Isiac cults will be discussed in more detail in the following sections. It should be noted here that Rhodos was a sovereign state and was never subjugated by the Ptolemies. Fraser sees the natural explanation of the spread of these cults on Rhodos and around this island in commercial ties between Rhodos and Egypt. However, he also agrees that the fact that the figure of Sarapis overshadows Isis in the evidence could be a sign of political gratitude toward the Ptolemaic dynasty (Fraser 1960: 27–30). It is noteworthy that Fraser mentions the island of Astypalaia as an exception in the pattern of the spread of the Isiac cults around Rhodos. Although Astypalaia was not under Rhodian influence, it has a dedication of a shrine to Sarapis and Isis (RICIS 202/1301) from the end of the third century or the beginning of the second century BCE (Fraser 1960: 28–9). There is, however, a piece of evidence suggesting the connection between Astypalaia and the Ptolemaic dynasty—a statue base of Ptolemy III Euergetes (reigned 246–222 BCE). According to Fraser, and also Bagnall, it is not possible to decide if the island was under Ptolemaic direct control solely on the basis of this evidence (Fraser 1960: 29; Bagnall 1976: 149; Dunand 1973a: 123).

To complete the picture of the Aegean Sea region, Fraser summarizes the situation on Crete. The island of Crete was a place of Ptolemaic interest throughout the Hellenistic period. First, Crete served as a rich source of mercenaries recruited to the Ptolemaic army (Launey 1987; Bagnall 1976: 117; Fraser 1960: 30). Second, dedications to various Ptolemaic kings were found across the island (IC II 19.2; 12.25; 16.11; Bagnall 1976: 117). This evidence, however, does not attest a direct Ptolemaic control of the island of Crete or its cities. Fraser moves further and argues that during the third and second centuries BCE, the Ptolemies controlled at least two cities, Gortyn and Itanos, by maintaining a garrison in both of them (Fraser 1960: 30–1). In case of Gortyn, Fraser mentions the testimony of Strabo (*Geographica* X.4) according to which Ptolemy IV, who ruled from 221 to 204 BCE, began to build a wall around this city (Fraser 1960: 30–1). Bagnall disagrees with Fraser and claims that although this demonstrates a military alliance between the Ptolemies and Gortyn, it does not prove that Ptolemy IV controlled the city directly (Bagnall 1976: 117–18). Fraser also mentions a situation when Ptolemy VI (ruled from 180 to 145 BCE) sent Egyptian soldiers to help Gortyn in a war with Cnossos (IC IV.195; Fraser 1960: 31; Fischer-Bovet 2014: 165; Bagnall 1976: 118). Bagnall is in opposition and claims that this military mission only proves that there were no Egyptian forces stationed regularly in Gortyn (Bagnall 1976: 118). The situation in Cretan Itanos is much clearer. Ptolemaic admiral Patroclus most probably garrisoned the city of Itanos in the beginning of the Chremonidean War (around 267/266 BCE) (Bagnall 1976: 120–3; Fraser 1960: 30; Fischer-Bovet 2014: 60). An Itanian inscription (IC III.4.2) recognizes him as "Πάτροκλ[ος] Πάτρωνος Μακεδὼν ἀποσταλεὶς ὑπὸ βασιλέος Πτολεμαίου στραταγός"; the title of στραταγός (*strategos*) represents Patroclus's military command (Bagnall 1976: 120–1). Fraser argues that if the imperialistic theory was valid, then rich evidence of the Isiac cults would have to be found in both Gortyn and Itanos, which, according to Fraser, is not the case: there is no evidence of the Isiac cults in Itanos and the Isiac cults in Gortyn are attested only from the second century BCE (Fraser 1960: 30–1). While Fraser is correct with respect to the evidence in Gortyn, there is a possibility that the cult of Isis was known in Itanos at the end of the third century or the beginning of the second century BCE. Stylianos Spyridakis (1969) follows an earlier claim of Adolphe J. Reinach (1911) according to which Tyche Protogeneia from an Itanian inscription (IC III.4.14) could be assimilated with the goddess Isis (this is also mentioned by Bricault in RICIS 203/0901). This hypothesis is based on an inscription from the second-century Delos (ID 2072) where Isis is indeed identified with Tyche Protogeneia: "Ἴσιδι Τύχηι

Πρωτογενείαι." Fraser is aware of this hypothesis but dismisses it as improbable (Fraser 1960: 30).

Finally, based on his previous arguments and findings concerning the validity of the imperialistic theory in the Aegean Sea region, Fraser draws the following conclusions: he claims that with the exception of Thera, the evidence of the Isiac cults is scanty in Ptolemaic possessions. To the contrary, Fraser argues, the public cult was established in places that were not under Ptolemaic control (e.g., Rhodos) or in places where the private cult preceded the public one (e.g., Delos, Athens). Therefore, he concludes, the theory that these cults spread across the Aegean Sea by Ptolemaic propaganda cannot stand. Fraser hypothesizes that "the normal movement of commerce and trade combined with a certain desire to stand well with Egypt, suffices to explain the diffusion of the cult in this region" (Fraser 1960: 32). Later in his text, Fraser is even more radical toward the imperialistic theory and claims that it must be completely abandoned, because the cult spread spontaneously, unaffected by political factors (Fraser 1960: 47).

Françoise Dunand scrutinizes the evidence for the presence of the Isiac cults in the Aegean in a similar fashion as Fraser, that is, with focus on the potential role of the Ptolemies and differentiating between private and public cult (Dunand 1973a: 72–130). This is another testament how significant position the question of Ptolemaic involvement in the spread of the Isiac cults outside Egypt had in the debate: the material evidence of these cults in the Aegean was presented by these scholars frequently as part of arguments against Cumont's imperialistic theory. As was already discussed earlier in this book, Dunand is an opponent of the imperialistic theory. However, on several occasions, Dunand points out that situation is not as black and white as Fraser often describes, and she argues that Ptolemaic influence must have played a role in this cultural transmission even when the Ptolemaic state did not propagate these cults abroad directly. This is indeed a crucial milestone in the debate as it brings more nuance into conceptualization of political influence: where Fraser was able to perceive Ptolemaic role in the cultural spread only as direct and intentional, Dunand thinks of the possibility of indirect and unintentional Ptolemaic involvement. This change in the debate represents one of the first steps in conceptualization the spread of the Isiac cults as a complex process impacted by different variables without the previous emphasis on intentionality behind it.

For the Aegean Islands, Dunand's treatment of the Isiac material branches from Fraser's interpretations on several occasions and brings forward more politically nuanced context. This is not the case for the situation on Delos, which was already discussed earlier, and Dunand here agrees with Fraser that nothing indicates a Ptolemaic involvement in the spread of the Isiac cults to this island where the cult first appeared by means of a private initiative (Dunand 1973a: 83–115). For the island of Keos, however, Dunand highlights the Ptolemaic context of the decree of *Sarapiastai* from the island (RICIS 202/0801). Dunand is inclined to date this decree to the second century BCE as Fraser does rather than third century, but Dunand mentions that Epameion, who was honored in the inscription, was a son of a Ptolemaic official. Dunand then states that it is possible that there might have been interest in Egyptian cults in this family, but still there is no evidence indicating that the cult was brought to the island by the initiative of Ptolemaic rulers (Dunand 1973a: 115–16). With respect to Amorgos, Dunand considers the island's position in the Nesiotic League in the third century BCE, which was controlled by the Ptolemies, as enough favorable context for the appearance of the Isiac temples in that time frame on the island (Dunand 1973a: 119–20). Dunand is offering similar interpretation for the island of Astypalaia. While Fraser was hesitant about the Ptolemaic presence on Astypalaia, Dunand argues that this island was well in the zone of Ptolemaic influence in the third century BCE, and it is thus unsurprising to find a temple of Isis and Sarapis there at the end of the third century BCE/beginning of the second century BCE (Dunand 1973a: 123). In case of Thera, which had a Ptolemaic garrison in the third century BCE, Dunand explicitly states the different possible modes of political influence on the spread of the Isiac cults. While Fraser treats the evidence from Thera as an exception from the pattern, Dunand approaches it as an example of a place where the durable Ptolemaic presence must have prepared the ground for the spread of the Isiac cults even without any direct initiative of the Ptolemaic rulers in exporting this cult outside Egypt (Dunand 1973a: 124–9). More closely to the shores of the western Asia Minor, Dunand also comments the contexts of the spread of the Isiac cults on the island of Samos that was a Ptolemaic naval base and strongly politically connected with Egypt in the third century BCE (Dunand 1973b: 60–5). Fraser dismisses the evidence from this island dated to the second century as too late for validation of the imperialistic theory (Fraser 1960: 26), but Dunand argues that the long-term commercial and political ties between Samos and Ptolemaic Egypt could have led to introduction and development of the Isiac cults there (Dunand 1973b: 60–1).

Dunand also approaches the situation on Crete differently from Fraser. While Fraser speculates that if the imperialistic theory is valid, then there should be plenty of evidence for the Isiac cults on Crete as the island was subject of Ptolemaic political interests throughout the third century BCE, Dunand does not dismiss the potential role of Ptolemies in the spread of the Isiac cults on Crete, even when the early evidence is scarce. Although the evidence from the city of Gortyn attests the presence of the Isiac cults only to the second century BCE, Dunand speculates that these cults might have been established there earlier due to long-term Ptolemaic presence. In this regard, Dunand mentions inscriptions from the second century BCE from Gortyn dedicated to Isis and Sarapis by a Cretan archer Pyroos (RICIS 203/0601-0602) who was a mercenary in the Ptolemaic service (Dunand 1973a: 73–82). This is also an important change in the use of the Isiac evidence when compared with Fraser. Fraser dismissed the evidence from the second century BCE as not relevant for his arguments, but Dunand incorporates this evidence and uses the case of the Cretan archer as an indicator of the entanglements between the Ptolemaic politics and the cultural transmission.

As was already pointed out earlier in this book, Laurent Bricault, who represents the current state of the debate, considers the spread of the Isiac cults as multifactorial epidemiological process. Such conceptualization helps overcome polarizing views demonstrated by Cumont and Fraser and opens doors toward more formal approaches to this topic. With respect to Bricault's view on the factors beneficial for the spread of the Isiac cults across the Aegean Sea, he argues that in Cyclades, the factors were Ptolemaic occupation together with the presence of Rhodians, who knew the Isiac cults and had commercial ties with Ptolemaic Egypt (Bricault 2001: 36). In case of Crete, Bricault has similar opinion as Dunand and states that Ptolemaic troops present on the island probably played a positive role in the introduction of the Isiac cults on the island. Bricault demonstrates this context also on the example of the Cretan archer Pyroos in Ptolemaic service worshiping Isiac deities (RICIS 203/0601-0602; Bricault 2001: 42).

4.3 Factors of the Spread

Several factors are mentioned in the academic discussion as significantly responsible for the successful spread of the Isiac cults across the ancient Aegean Sea. These factors are related especially to political, economic/commercial, and social spheres. However, this book is focused more on a large spatio-populational scale, and therefore, small-scale social factors related to individual associations devoted to worship of Isis and Sarapis are not incorporated into the quantitative analysis. This chapter identifies the specific trade and political factors that could have affected the process of the early spread of Isiac cults across the Aegean Sea in the long run and can be tested by means of quantitative methods.

4.3.1 Economic Level

Because of the geographical layout of the Mediterranean, maritime trade was an indispensable part of ancient economies. Hellenistic Egypt was one of the main exporters of grain, a staple food in antiquity (Foxhall and Forbes 1982). Egyptian grain was channeled to the Aegean Sea and finally to continental Greece mainly through the island of Rhodos, Egypt's main partner in maritime trade. The major Hellenistic trade route connecting Athens and Egypt, with the island of Rhodos as the major transit point, is mentioned frequently by Demosthenes who lived in the second half of the fourth century BCE (see e.g., Demosthenes 56; Casson 1954; Roebuck 1950; Buraselis 2013).

A proof of Athenian import of Egyptian grain during the third century BCE can also be found in texts from the *Inscriptiones Graecae* collections. One of them is the Phaidros of Sphettos's honorific decree (IG II.³ 1, 985; IG II.² 682), which describes the embassy to Ptolemy I Soter securing the grain for Athens. The embassy is dated between the years 294 and 287 BCE (Oliver 2007: 249–50). A similar action from about the year 282 BCE during the reign of Ptolemy II Philadelphus is described in the decree for Kallias of Sphettos (translated by Theodore L. Shear in Shear 1978: 5, lines 43–54):

> And whereas, upon the succession to the monarchy of the younger King Ptolemy, Kallias was staying in the City and when the generals called upon him, explained the situation in which the city found itself, and begged him for the sake of the city to hasten to King Ptolemy in order that aid in the form of grain and money might be forthcoming as quickly as possible for the City, Kallias himself sailing at his own expense to Cyprus and there conversing earnestly with the king in behalf of the city brought back fifty talents of silver for the Demos and a gift of twenty thousand medimnoi of wheat, which were measured out from Delos to the agents sent by the Demos.

Not only does this text illustrate the diplomatic and commercial relationship between Egypt and Athens but it also includes the island of Delos on the map of the Hellenistic grain trade. Moreover, from 287 BCE, the Ptolemies remotely controlled other islands surrounding Delos by administering the Island League for about thirty years (Hölbl 2001: 23–4, 44; Casson 1954).

The thesis of an important grain trade partnership between Egypt and the island of Rhodos is, besides Demosthenes's account, further strengthened by the fact that Alexander's governor in Egypt, Cleomenes, chose Rhodos as the center for his operations with grain (Gabrielsen 2013; Buraselis 2013). That was the situation on the island in the time of Alexander the Great. However, historical evidence shows that the status between these two commercial powers was upheld even during the rule of the first Ptolemies in Egypt. Diodorus describes the relationship from the end of the fourth century BCE as follows (*Bibliotheca Historica* XX.81, translated by Michel Austin in Austin 2006, No. 47):

> The Rhodians, then, by establishing friendship with all the dynasts, kept themselves immune of any justifiable complaint, but their sympathies inclined mostly towards Ptolemy. For it so happened that they derived the majority of their revenues from the merchants sailing to Egypt and that in general their city was sustained by that kingdom.

When a member of the Antigonid dynasty and the future king of Macedonia, Demetrius Poliorcetes, besieged Rhodos in 305–304 BCE, Ptolemy I provided the islanders with about 600,000 artabas of grain, which helped them to outlast the siege. A similar gesture was repeated in 227/6 BCE by Ptolemy III Euergetes, who donated about one million artabas of grain to the Rhodians who suffered from an earthquake. Finally, the strong tie between Egypt and Rhodos is attested by the large number of Rhodian amphorae found in Alexandria (Gabrielsen 2013: 67–8; Diodorus, *Bibliotheca Historica* XX.88.9, 96.1, 98.1, 99.2; Polybius V.88.1–90.4).

The evidence presented here also supports the assumption that the inhabitants of the Aegean Islands imported grain primarily from Ptolemaic Egypt and not as much from other exporting regions (e.g., the Black Sea coast). Moreover, Egypt had an advantage over the other exporters of grain due to the favorable weather conditions. While ships carrying grain from the Black Sea could have been trapped north of the Dardanelles due to early winter, Egypt was able to dispatch ships continuously throughout the year (Bissa 2009: 163).

Previous descriptions attempted to sketch a broader network of commercial relationships between ancient Egypt and the Aegean Sea region. However, any attempt to characterize this broad network of commercial relationships between ancient Egypt and the Aegean Sea region and to determine which islands in the Aegean Sea imported Egyptian grain is hampered by the lack of detail in ancient literary and archaeological evidence. This is a serious problem when considering merchants traveling from Egypt as potential carriers of the Isiac cults. This issue, however, could be partially resolved by analyzing pieces of data that are not primarily considered as archaeological or literary evidence but that indicate which islands in the Aegean Sea were, for example, fertile or barren. This approach can answer the question of which islands were potentially more dependent on Egyptian grain imports than others. This issue is elaborated in the section 4.4.2.

4.3.2 Political Level

The second major factor frequently discussed among scholars focusing on the early spread of the Isiac cults concerns Ptolemaic political actions. As mentioned previously, the Ptolemies were very active politically during the Hellenistic period in the area of the ancient Mediterranean. To keep the issue relatively simple, transparent, and connected to the research question, Ptolemaic political actions were categorized by their time span and geographical traceability. During the period of interest, there were several wars where Ptolemaic Egypt played an important role. The ports in the Aegean Sea were affected especially by the so-called Fifth War of the Successors (288–286 BCE) (Worthington 2016: 180; Hölbl 2001: 23–4) and the Chremonidean War (267–261 BCE) (Hölbl 2001: 40–3; Oneil 2008).

The actions of the son of Antigonus the One-Eyed, Demetrius Poliorcetes, were among the main causes of the Ptolemaic military activities during the years 288–285 BCE. This particular conflict, later known as the Fifth War of the Successors, began to escalate in 294 BCE when the diplomatic partnership between Athens and the Ptolemies was disrupted by Demetrius conquering the Greek city. Six years after that, in 288 BCE, Ptolemy I formed a coalition with two *diadochoi* of Alexander the Great, Lysimachus and Seleucus, and with Demetrius's former ally Pyrrhus of Epirus to drive Demetrius from Macedonia. In 287 BCE, a thousand Ptolemaic soldiers under the command of Kallias of Sphettos left a temporary base on the Aegean island of Andros and reached the shores of Attica. Ptolemaic forces then joined the Athenian revolt against Demetrius who, at the time, was besieging Athens. Demetrius lost and had to leave the country. Although the Athenians were freed by treaty, the situation was not yet completely stable because the Athenian port of Piraeus remained under Antigonid control. However, Ptolemy I managed to leave his mark in the Aegean when around 287 BCE he took the Island League from the hands of the Antigonid dynasty. The Ptolemies then controlled the Cyclades for the next three decades. Demetrius Poliorcetes was finally captured by Seleucus in

285 BCE, and at the same time Lysimachus, who ruled jointly with Pyrrhus in Macedonia, expelled the latter from the country. Demetrius Poliorcetes died in captivity in 283 BCE (Hölbl 2001: 23–4; Fischer-Bovet 2014: 54–5; Anson 2014: 179–83; Shear 1978).

Another major conflict that shook the region of the Aegean Sea was the Chremonidean War (ca. 267–261 BCE). In the 270s, the son of Demetrius Poliorcetes, Antigonus Gonatas, defeated Pyrrhus of Epirus and strengthened again the Macedonian position in Greece. This political development was inconvenient particularly for the Ptolemaic thalassocracy over the Aegean Islands. At the request of the Athenian statesman Chremonides in 268 BCE, Sparta, Athens, and Ptolemy II Philadelphus formed an alliance with the purpose of defeating Antigonus Gonatas. Patroclus, the strategos of the Ptolemaic forces, led the Ptolemaic fleet to Attica, and on his way, he garrisoned strategic ports and thus secured the route for reinforcements and supplies. Neither the Ptolemaic army nor any of the allies were able to cause significant damage to the superior Macedonian army, and the war was lost in 261 BCE. However, by stationing military bases in Cretan Itanos, the island of Thera, the island of Keos, and the Arsinoe-Methana peninsula in Attica, the Ptolemies yet again tightened their grip on the Aegean for upcoming decades (Hölbl 2001: 40–3; Fischer-Bovet 2014: 60; Marquaille 2008: 47–8; Oneil 2008). Other Ptolemaic garrisons that could have influenced the mobility in the eastern part of the Aegean Sea region during the third and second centuries BCE were placed in Ephesus and Samos (Bagnall 1976: 80–8; Chaniotis 2002).

The Ptolemaic garrisons dispersed in the Aegean Sea (see section 4.4.2, Appendix, and Figure A.1) are of great importance for the subsequent quantitative analysis because they are (a) easily traceable both in time and space and (b) many of them were stationed there for a long period of time, thus increasing the chance of spreading the Isiac cults by Ptolemaic soldiers. The list of Ptolemaic garrisons used in the analysis and description of their time spans is described in the Appendix.

Another potential political factor in the question of influencing the spread of the Isiac cults, besides Ptolemaic garrisons, are political leagues that helped to unify islands or regions under a common administration. In the context of the Aegean Sea, the Ptolemies led the Island League from ca. 287 to the 250s BCE (Hölbl 2001: 23–4; Constantakopoulou 2012; Meadows 2013). Again, this political factor could be of importance because it is geographically delimited and lasted for a longer period of time. However, the question of the membership in the league is not completely clear, and the topic is still up for debate in the academic discussion (Meadows 2013; Constantakopoulou 2012). For this reason, it has been decided to exclude this factor from the quantitative analysis.

Finally, there are diplomatic missions and specific battles. However, such events lasted only for a brief period of time. Because the book is focusing mainly on long-lasting factors, adding short-term events could potentially disrupt the outcome. These events were thus excluded from the quantitative analysis.

4.4 Quantitative Analysis

In order to successfully compare the potential individual impact of different factors on the early spread of the Isiac cults taking place on the ancient transportation network in the Aegean Sea region, three crucial steps had to be followed through:

1. construction of a model of the ancient maritime transportation network as a platform for quantitative analysis;
2. transformation of selected factors of possible influence on the spread of the Isiac cults into geocoded parameters of the network;
3. definition of a mathematical model that allows to determine which parameters of the network explain the spatial dissemination of archaeological evidence connected to the Isiac cults with higher statistical significance than the others.

Each of these steps is elaborated in the following technical sections.

4.4.1 Transportation Network

A significant step forward in research focusing on the ancient transportation network has been made by the Stanford geospatial network model of the Roman world (ORBIS), which "reconstructs the time, cost and financial expense associated with a wide range of different types of travel in antiquity. The model is based on a simplified version of the giant networks of cities, roads, rivers and sea lanes that framed movement across the Roman Empire" (Scheidel and Meeks n.d.). The maritime transportation network in ORBIS is based on many ancient and modern sources; however, the scale of the network is large, and it focuses primarily on rendering routes that cover long distances.

This sometimes leads to inaccuracies and erroneous traveling scenarios within more restricted regions such as the Cyclades in the Aegean Sea, where the designed network is on too large a scale. This is a significant drawback with respect to the research task of this case study, which focuses mainly on the maritime transportation network between Egypt and Greece, where the short routes between the Aegean Islands possibly played a role in the spread of the Isiac cults. Thus, it has been decided that for the purposes of the case study, it would be more suitable to construct a new maritime transportation network of the Aegean Sea region based on ancient navigational guides, with particular attention to detail and scale.

First, the geometries of all relevant islands in the selected region were extracted. These were then generalized with a simplifying function (based on Douglas-Peucker algorithm) in order to obtain the identical level of detail for the islands, and afterward, they were validated by satellite images. Then, the relevant major ancient ports from *A Catalogue of Ancient Ports and Harbours* (Graauw 2016) were filtered, and their positions were validated with the Ancient World Mapping Center (Ancient World Mapping Center n.d.) and satellite images. In the subsequent steps, these ports were used as nodes in the new transportation network.

The maps and directions described in Pascal Arnaud's collection of ancient maritime routes (Arnaud 2005) were interpreted, scanned, and geocoded in a geographic information system (GIS) software, and all routes within the area of interest were re-drawn as polylines (i.e., continuous lines composed of one or more line segments). The vertices (i.e., corners) of these polylines were snapped to the port geometries obtained in the previous step. Then, each island had two buffers created around them. One buffer at a "hypothetical critical" distance of 100 meters was meant to represent the minimum safe sailing distance from the shore. The value of the second "ideal" buffer was set at 2,000 meters, which was considered as the safe distance from which sailors could see the coast, this distant visual cue allowing them to navigate more accurately but without risk of entering water that was too shallow. These buffers were then used to correct the geometries of the routes. Layers with edges and nodes were exported into a comma-separated values (CSV) format and loaded into Python script to calculate the shortest paths for every combination of port nodes using the maritime routes on the constructed network and to store these calculated geographical distances (in km) for the purposes of the final quantitative analysis. The exact script packages and libraries can be found in the original study (Glomb et al. 2018). This model of the ancient maritime transportation network met the conditions

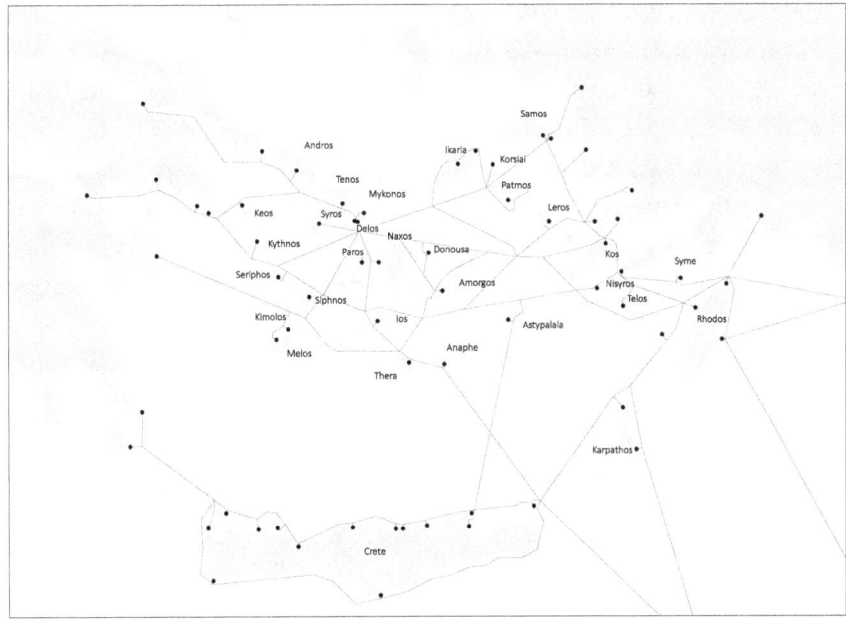

Figure 4.2 Transportation network of the case study 1. Base map source: "Natural Earth" n.d.; Data source: Glomb et al. 2018.

for using an adequate scale in the area of interest and was used as a platform for the final quantitative analysis (Figure 4.2).

The next step was to measure the centrality values using network analysis of individual ports in order to derive a proxy for the potential strategic importance of particular ports within the network. To be able to calculate centrality values for each port, the structure of the network had to be simplified by the elimination of nodes representing maritime "crossroads" outside ports; the ports were then reconnected directly. Besides the usual centrality values that allow for identifying important nodes within a network, parameters reflecting specifically the amount of "Egyptian" traffic for each port in the network were needed to be derived. One possibility was to measure the eigenvector centrality value that was described by Ray Rivers, Carl Knappett, and Tim Evans in maritime context as the "busyness of harbours as a measure of the flow of goods, people and ideas between them" (Rivers, Knappett, and Evans 2013: 146). However, this option was not suitable in this case as it does not respect historical directions. The research of this case study focuses mainly on ships from the main Egyptian port, Alexandria, carrying sailors potentially practicing the Isiac cults. Therefore, a Python script was created, whose task was to send one ship from Alexandria to each node in the network using the calculated shortest geographical path on the network. These paths still respected the directions and maritime routes from the ancient navigational guides collected by Arnaud. By removing maritime crossroads outside ports and by calculating the most advantageous maritime routes on the network, a simple and "idealized" scenario for the script was created where ships travel from port to port until they reach their destination. The output values represented how many times each node was visited by an Egyptian ship traveling elsewhere on the network. The islands of Rhodos and Delos obtained high values calculated by the script, which is in accord with the previously mentioned historical evidence pointing to high political and economic significance of these Aegean Islands. This is a simplistic and idealized way of revealing important ports in a network, but from all the network measurements and types of centralities, this approach seems to be the most relevant and transparent for the intended goal.

4.4.2 The Operationalization of Factors Involved in the Spread

The archaeological evidence related to the Isiac cults from the time and area of interest was geocoded based on Bricault's corpus *Recueil des inscriptions concernant les cultes isiaques, RICIS* (2005b). The data from RICIS were categorized into two groups for the purposes of the analysis: (a) artifacts (altars, statues, inscriptions, etc.); (b) evidence related to temples of Isis and Sarapis (see Figure 4.3). The evidence from both groups indicates the presence of these cults; however, the Egyptian temples are considered as more significant proxies, which is also reflected in the final quantitative analysis. The parameters of the transportation network derived from the connectivity and traffic measurements reflect the general strategic importance of each port on the network. The next set of node parameters was obtained by geocoding Ptolemaic military garrisons (see Figures 4.3 and A.1), these reflecting long-term Ptolemaic political interests in the area of the Aegean Sea. Data on Ptolemaic garrisons were collected mainly from Roger S. Bagnall's monograph *The Administration of the Ptolemaic Possessions Outside Egypt* (Bagnall 1976) and checked with more recent studies for consensus on the evidence (Chaniotis 2011, 2002; Fischer-Bovet 2014; Hölbl 2001). The third set of parameters was derived by identifying potential markets for imported Egyptian grain. However, the procedure in the case of economic parameters was rather complicated. The lack of archaeological and literary evidence did

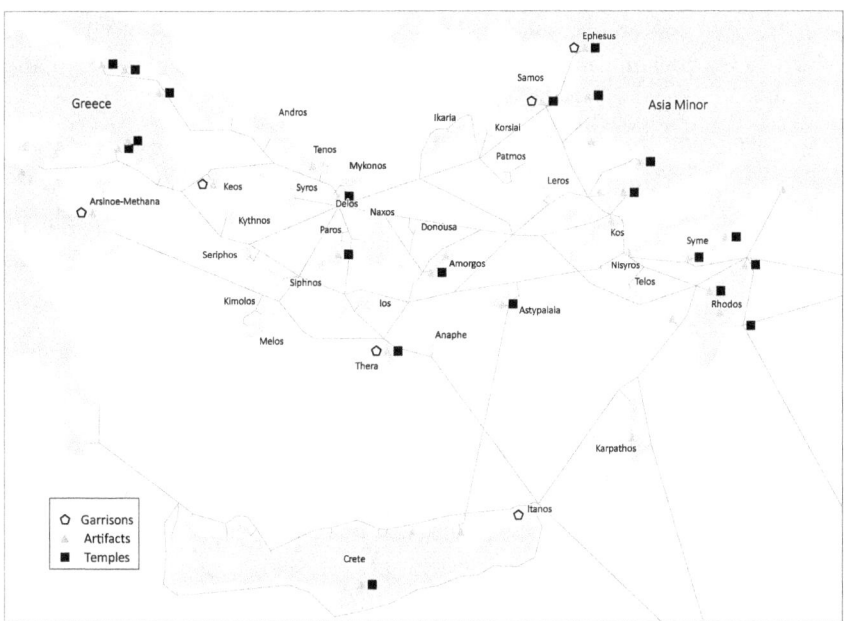

Figure 4.3 Dissemination of relevant Ptolemaic military garrisons together with temples and artifacts related to the Isiac cults in the area of interest on the transportation network. Base map source: "Natural Earth" n.d.; Data source: Glomb et al. 2018.

not allow to identify exactly which islands or ports between Alexandria and continental Greece imported Egyptian grain, and therefore, it was not possible to conclude which nodes could have been in more direct contact with Egyptian sailors possibly carrying practices and artifacts connected to the Isiac cults. To help overcome this deficiency, a model was developed that, based on environmental and demographical datasets, determined whether an island in the Aegean Sea suffered from possible food shortages and could therefore have been in need of grain imports. The specifics of this model are elaborated in the next section 4.4.2.1, Environmental Model.

4.4.2.1 Environmental Model

The main task of this model was to identify potential markets for imported Egyptian grain. To fully understand the mechanics of the model, it is necessary to describe the geographical and climatological profile of the Aegean Islands and its impact on the islands' agricultural fertility.

Orography, that is, the properties of elevated terrain, is one of the key geographical features, which influences the climate in the area of the Aegean

Islands. More specifically, mountain ranges affect the flow of liquids and gases, which has further impact on rainfall. The interrelation between elevation and rainfall is particularly significant in the case of the Aegean Islands. The Pindos range stretching from the northern Epiros to Peloponnese creates a natural barrier catching large amounts of rainfall. The higher islands in the northern Aegean Sea, Andros and Tenos, capture the orographic rainfall brought by northern weather, and even the highest southern islands have only small amounts of precipitation because only few clouds reach them. These factors combined leave the Cyclades in a fairly arid zone (Isager and Skydsgaard 1995: 11–13; Broodbank 2000: 76–80; Figure 4.4).

Another relevant climatological feature of the Aegean Islands and especially Cyclades is unpredictability of weather conditions with respect to time. Collected data suggest that there are significant inter-annual fluctuations in rainfall (Broodbank 2000: 78). This means that inhabitants of the Hellenistic Cyclades could not have relied on consistent yields of crops in the long term. The lower quality of soil and relatively small size of majority of islands in Cyclades further contribute to their agricultural vulnerability (Bissa 2009: 197). The assumption

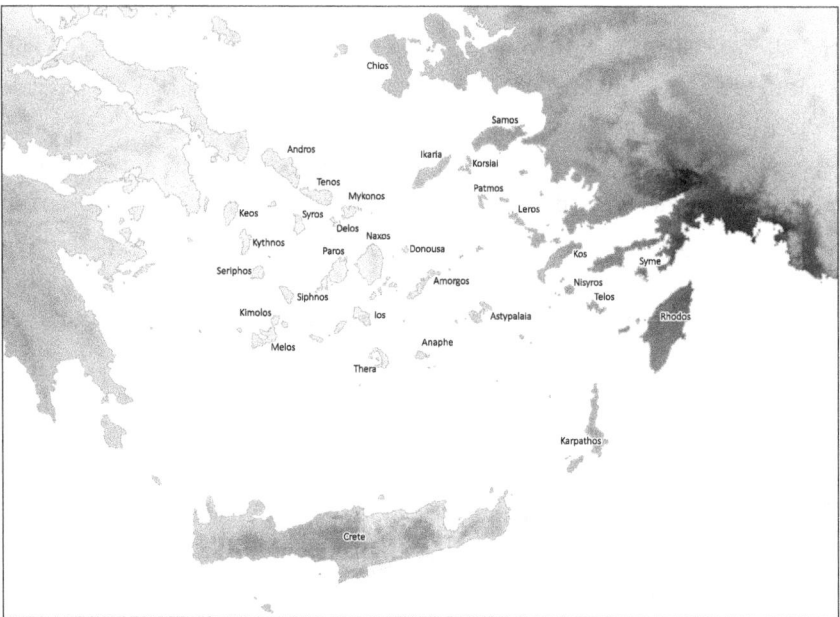

Figure 4.4 Average monthly precipitation (mm) in the Aegean Sea between 1960 and 1990. Darker shades in the raster indicate higher precipitation; lighter shades indicate lower precipitation. Data source: "WorldClim 1.4: Current Conditions" n.d.

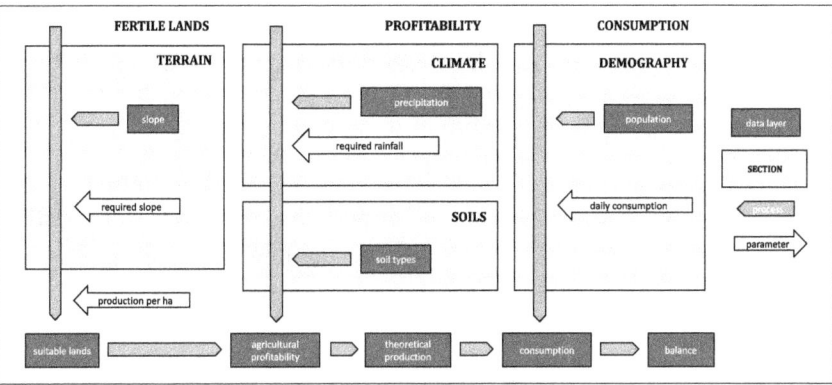

Figure 4.5 Overall scheme of the famine vulnerability model.

that at least some of the Aegean Islands imported grain seems, under these conditions, plausible. This hypothesis can be also supported by selected pieces of historical evidence from the late fourth century BCE such as inscriptions from islands of Andros and Amorgos honoring traders importing grain (IG XII.5.714; IG XII.7.11).

In order to determine the potential vulnerability to food shortages of the Aegean Islands, the model measures the ratio between the theoretical production and consumption for each island (Figure 4.5). The model reduces the complexity of the problem by adopting three assumptions:

- over the course of time, key factors such as terrain and climate have not changed *dramatically* in the region in question (Broodbank 2000: 77–9; Isager and Skydsgaard 1995: 11). Although recent research shows that some climatic conditions may have changed during antiquity in the Mediterranean region—(see e.g., Harper and McCormick 2018)—the model is focused mainly on establishing an order between the Aegean Islands with regard to their comparative vulnerability to food shortages. This order would most probably have remained unaffected by admitting those possible climatic changes because of the stable physical and spatial predispositions of individual islands in the region of the Aegean Sea;
- the predisposition of the terrain and the climate determined the quantity of food produced;
- food production could have been limited to barley, which (in comparison to wheat) can be produced in harsher environments (Arnon 1972: 74; Reger 1994b: 90–103).

The first part of the model rates the production potential of each spatial unit (pixel) on the basis of the local climate, soil quality, and terrain slope. Climate data ("WorldClim 1.4: Current Conditions" n.d.) were normalized on the basis of the minimal requirements for barley production (Arnon 1972: 74). The bulk density of soil ("European Soil Database" n.d.) was used as a proxy for soil quality due to its relationships with other properties (porosity, soil moisture, hydraulic conductivity, etc.). The maximum limiting value for terrain slope for agriculture was selected and validated via the analysis of CORINE Land Cover data ("Corine Land Cover 2006 Seamless Vector Data V17" n.d.)—land cover categories related to agriculture were extracted; then correlations for particular islands between model outputs and the real situation were identified in order to select the most suitable value. Areas above this threshold were then filtered out as inappropriate for agricultural production, and areas below it were rated by measuring the difference from this limit. The theoretical average yield for barley was set to 680 kg/ha based on the pre-fertilizer average yields of barley from the early twentieth-century Greece (Ruschenbusch 1988; Reger 1994b: 98–9). In the case of the environmental model, this value was assigned to areas (pixels) with a score of 1 representing "normal" agricultural conditions; other values were assigned proportionally to their score. Finally, to estimate the yield for each island, these areas were spatially aggregated, and their values summed.

The second part of the model estimates the hypothetical food consumption on the Aegean Islands. In order to obtain the consumption numbers, the model needs demographical data—specifically, the population sizes on the Aegean Islands in antiquity. Indeed, modern literature provides some population estimates or methods for estimating the populations of the ancient Aegean Islands; however, the data are unreliable, and consensus among researchers has not been achieved.

Chronologically, the first major work on this topic is Karl J. Beloch's *Die Bevölkerung der griechisch-römischen Welt* published in 1886 (Beloch 1886). Although Beloch's work deserves recognition for promoting the topic of ancient demography in the academic discussion, the archaeological evidence grew significantly since then, making the book and the results based mainly on literary and epigraphical evidence seriously outdated. Generally, Beloch worked with the assumption that the majority of the Greek *poleis* were defended by one-quarter of the free population. The first major problem with that assumption is that the number of soldiers in literary sources is often exaggerated and unreliable. Second, Beloch also assumed that every male citizen between twenty and fifty years of age served in the army. According to modern scholars, at least 20–25 percent of male citizens within the abovementioned age category were unfit for military service (Beloch 1886; Hansen 2006: 4–6).

In 1939, the *Athenian Tribute Lists* were published (Meritt, Wade-Gery, and McGregor 1939), which subsequently led to other attempts in estimating the population sizes of ancient Greece. Eberhard Ruschenbusch, for example, hypothesizes that the height of the *phoros* paid by *poleis* to Athens can be correlated with their population sizes. Ruschenbusch founded his argument on a mention from Diodorus describing the incident from 405 BCE in the polis of Iasos (*Bibliotheca Historica* XIII.104.7, translated by Charles H. Oldfather in Diodorus Siculus and Oldfather 1989):

> Lysander, sailing with the larger part of his ships to Iasus in Caria, took the city, which was an ally of the Athenians, by storm, put to the sword the males of military age to the number of eight hundred, sold the children and women as booty, and razed the city to the ground.

The tribute list then states that Iasos paid *phoros* of one talent. From these two pieces of information, Ruschenbusch derived that *phoros* of one talent equals 800 male citizens. From that, Ruschenbusch, using Beloch's rule of thumb that the number of male citizens is one-quarter of the total population in the polis, reached the conclusion that the *phoros* of one talent corresponds to 3,200 inhabitants (Ruschenbusch 1984b, 1984a, 1983). However, once more, the method is not flawless. The incident happened in 405 BCE, but earlier in 412 BCE, the polis of Iasos was already destroyed once (Thucydides VIII.28.2–4), and the data from the tribute list are from the years between 449 and 431 BCE. Therefore, it is doubtful that the polis of Iasos, which was several times endangered and conquered, had the same size of the population in 440s or 430s BCE and in 405 BCE. Also, such an unstable polis could hardly be a "role model" for estimating population sizes for all Greece (Hansen 2006: 8–10). Ruschenbusch's method was applied in this research; however, the results in the case of the Aegean Islands showed significant and unrealistic population spikes. Therefore, the results obtained by Ruschenbusch's method were not taken into consideration.

One of the more recent methods elaborated especially by Herman M. Hansen tries to derive population estimates from the archaeological remains of walled *poleis*. More concretely, it uses the degree of urbanization as a proxy for the population size. Based on archaeological surveys, Hansen claims that half of the area enclosed by the defense walls in a polis was used for public buildings and roads, whereas the other half was inhabited. By observing the spatial patterns of buildings outside the walls, Hansen derived the ratio between the size of the population living in hinterlands and on the inner side of the walls (Hansen 2006). This approach could be helpful in estimating the population numbers in large *poleis* and especially in those on the continent, but the relation between the urban area and its surroundings is far less consistent on the islands. Therefore, it was decided not to use this method as the area of interest contains tens of islands.

As population growth factors such as the environment, technology, agriculture, and health care remained substantially unchanged in this region up to the beginning of the twentieth century CE, it can be assumed that the population distribution in the time of interest should correlate closely to numbers from the first modern population census (end of the nineteenth century CE). Also, Ruschenbusch and Hansen compared their estimates with population sizes on the Aegean Islands from the end of the nineteenth century CE. They did so, because during the nineteenth century, the population sizes reached the islands' carrying capacity, which was probably also the case for the fourth century BCE (Hansen 2006: 9–12). That said, it is necessary to admit the very hypothetical character of this approach. However, for research purposes and also for the purposes of the model's goal, which was to compare the food production/consumption ratio between the selected islands, the focus was mainly oriented on the relative population sizes of particular islands than on exact historical numbers, the latter probably being unreachable.

After the extraction of these population estimates (Karpat 1985; Booth and Booth 1928; "Ministry of Interior: Résultats statistiques du recensement de la population de 5-6 October 1896" n.d.), it was possible to implement food consumption in the model. The average intake of a person in ancient Greece was estimated by Foxhall and Forbes to be 212 kilograms of grain per year (Foxhall and Forbes 1982; Bissa 2009: 173). The difference between the food production and consumption was then relativized by the number of inhabitants to get a nondimensional coefficient—islands with values under 1 were marked as potentially vulnerable to food shortages; islands with a higher number were considered as self-sufficient (Figure 4.6). It should be noted that this model has no ambition to serve as the only tool for assessing the question of which islands in the Aegean Sea region imported grain from Egypt. Rather, its purpose is to offer a basic comparative perspective on the islands' agricultural potential.

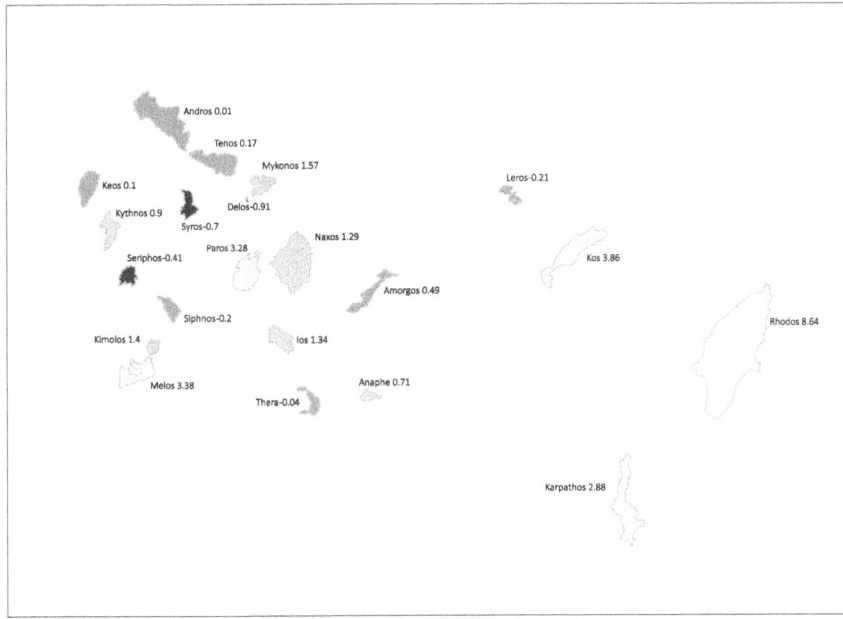

Figure 4.6 Food shortage vulnerability—output from the environmental model. Islands with a darker shade (and lower number than 1) are more vulnerable to food shortages. Islands with insufficient and incomplete datasets were not analyzed by the model. Base map source: "Natural Earth" n.d.; Data source: Glomb et al. 2018.

4.4.3 Statistical Analysis

Statistical analysis was used to evaluate and compare the possible impact of the factors quantified and transformed into parameters in previous steps on the early spread of the Isiac cults in the Aegean Sea region. The data were organized in a table (Glomb et al. 2018), listing each island and its maritime network centrality value, the geographical distance on the network (in km) to the closest Egyptian temple and artifact, the distance to the closest Ptolemaic garrison, and the value that approximates the need for grain import. The task was to find a suitable and interpretable mathematical model that would be able to explain the relations between these values, mainly the dependency of a place on the distance to the closest Egyptian (Isiac) temple or artifact.

First, standard descriptive statistics were used to evaluate pairwise correlations between the factors described in this case study. Since the histograms showed that the variables do not possess a normal (Gaussian) distribution, the correlations were quantified by the Spearman rank correlation coefficient. The Spearman rank correlation coefficient (R_s; always between 1.0, i.e., a perfect negative

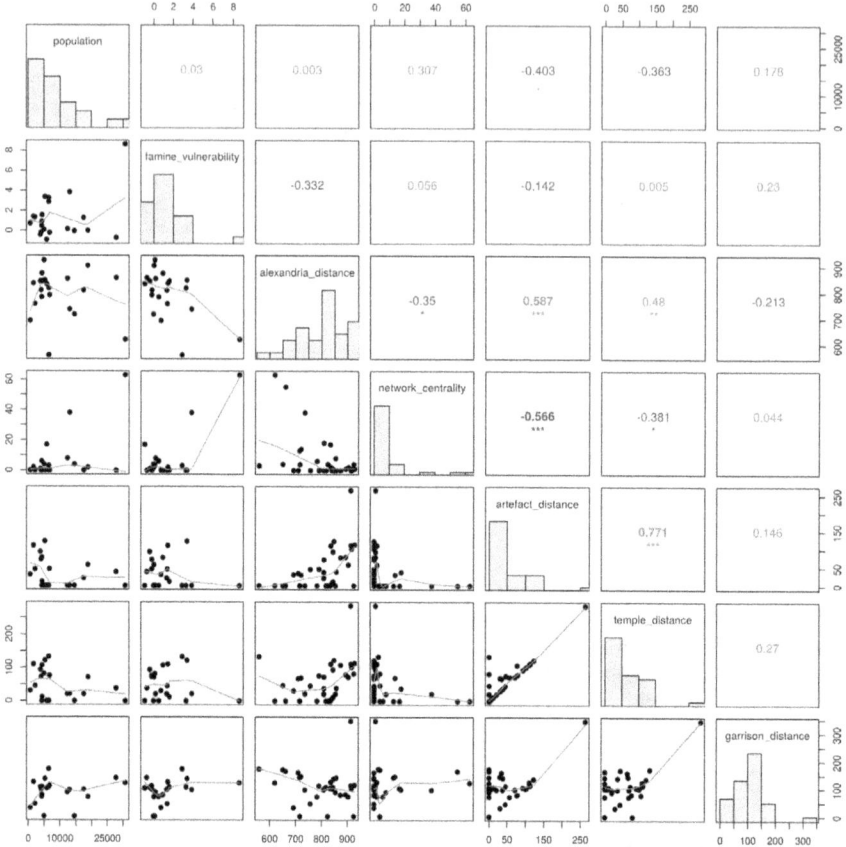

Figure 4.7 Visualization of the parameters. The diagonal includes the frequency histograms of the analyzed variables; above the diagonal are their pairwise correlations (Spearman rank correlation coefficients; stars indicate statistical significancy, and darker shades indicate greater distance from 0), and below the diagonal are dot-plots of the variable pairs complemented by nonparametric estimates of their "dependence." Data source: Glomb et al. 2018.

correlation, and 1.0, i.e., a perfect positive correlation) ranks the parameters based on their value and measures the strength, or "tightness," and direction of the association between two ranked variables (Figure 4.7).

The outcome of the analysis, which correlated each variable to one another, rendered some significant correlations. For example, the positive correlations between the distances of ports to Alexandria and the distances of ports to religious proxies (i.e., distance on the network to the closest Egyptian temple and artifact) are in accord with the fact that the Isiac cults are assumed to have spread from Alexandria. These findings were expected, but more importantly, they show that the data yielded by the abovementioned methods (transportation network construction, environmental/population condition processing, political/military records evaluation) do not contradict the historical reality. Hence, it was possible to deal with them using more sophisticated data description methods or analyses.

The consensus in current academic discussion is that the early spread of the Isiac cults cannot be explained by a single factor. Therefore, to be able to evaluate statistically the joint impact of several factors, it was desirable to use a multivariate statistical method. The standard tool for such evaluation is analysis of variance. The principle of this analysis is that it determines which factors/predictors better explain the spatial occurrences of evidence for the Isiac cults by correlating distances among variables on the transportation network (Figure 4.3). The response variable (the explained quantity) represents the spatial intensity of the Isiac cults and should be inversely proportional to the distance from the temple, the distance from the artifact, or a combination of both distances (with temples as more important proxies than artifacts). The predictors, that is, the variables influencing the response variable (spatial intensity of the Isiac cults), are proxies quantifying local political (military), geographical (environmental, strategic), and trade factors.

Since an assumption of simple linear dependence of explained variable on factors under consideration is not very realistic, this case study utilized generalized linear models with interactions of factors up to the third order. Computations and testing of various regression models found two appropriate models fitting the data. The first model (M1) with three predictors reads:

$$y_1 = -0.524 \cdot g - 7.09 \cdot \ln(1 + f) + 1.29 \cdot c$$

where y_1 denotes the proxy of cult intensity computed by the formula: $-(2 \cdot \text{temple\_distance} + \text{artifact\_distance}) / 3$; it expresses that both distances determine the cult intensity, and it defines the distance from a temple as more important than the distance from an artifact. The variables g, f, and c denote the distance to the Ptolemaic garrison (in km), the famine vulnerability coefficient, and network centrality, respectively. The coefficient of determination $R^2 = 0.68$. F-value 12.76 with 3 and 18 degrees of freedom (DF) is highly significant ($p < 0.001$); the Akaike information criterion (AIC) is 506. The outcome of the model is that 68 percent of the variability in the response variable (intensity of the Isiac cults) can be explained by the simultaneous impact of the three predictors; that is, military influence, famine vulnerability, and centrality explain 48 percent, 11 percent, and 9 percent, respectively, of the variance.

The second appropriate model (M2), which puts aside centrality values and focuses more on the relationship between the Ptolemaic garrisons and famine vulnerability, is

$$y_2 = -0.497 \cdot g + 17.8 \cdot \ln(1 + f) - 0.77 \cdot g \cdot \ln(1 + f)$$

where y_2 denotes the proxy of cult intensity expressed by: – temple_distance, and g and f again denote the distance of a place to the Ptolemaic garrison (in km) and famine vulnerability coefficient, respectively. Now, $R^2 = 0.60$, $F = 8.81$ with $DF = 3, 18$, $p < 0.001$, and $AIC = 515$. By this model, 60 percent of the variability in the distance of a place to a temple can be explained by the two predictors; that is, military influence and famine vulnerability themselves explain 47 percent and 12 percent of variance, respectively; the interaction of the two factors adds 1 percent of explanation.

This model also reveals a certain ambiguity with respect to the political (military) and environmental impact on the spread of these cults since it is not linear. For example, if the Ptolemaic garrison is sufficiently far from an island, then higher resistance to food shortages on that island reduces the local intensity of the Isiac cults. If a garrison is near to an island, then the effect is reversed, that is, the impact of the food factor on the spatial intensity of the Isiac cults diminishes.

The construction of mathematical regression models was crucial here for the quantification of the results, as descriptive statistics do not provide deep insights in this particular case. The numerical outcomes (percentage of explained variability) of both created models do not differ significantly. On the other hand, the models have different levels of complexity, which provide a greater variety of possible outcomes and data patterns to be interpreted. Only selected variables were used as model inputs; others were auxiliary and were used to validate the dataset and the models against the historical reality. Both models are summarized in Table 4.1.

4.4.4 Results

The mathematical models presented in this case study revealed statistically significant patterns and correlations with respect to the different factors involved in the process of the early spread of the Isiac cults across the Hellenistic Aegean Sea.

Table 4.1 Variance in Spatial Intensity of the Isiac Cults Explained by Selected Factors

Predictor		β	E β	t		SumSq	F		SumSq / Σ SumSq	R^2	AIC
Model 1: response variable $-\frac{1}{3}(2d_T + d_A)$										0.68	505.7
Army	g	−0.524	0.09	5.6	***	36 410	27.1	***	0.4822		
Trade	$\log(1+f)$	−7.09	0.42	0.84		7 878	5.9	*	0.1043		
Centrality	c	1.29	0.56	2.3	*	7 076	5.3	*	0.0934		
residual						24 146					
Model 2: response variable $-d_T$										0.60	515.2
Army	g	−0.497	0.11	4.5	***	44 275	21.0	***	0.4727		
Trade	$\log(1+f)$	17.8	41.1	0.43		10 924	5.2	*	0.1166		
Interaction	$g \log(1+f)$	−0.77	0.36	0.50		53	0.3		0.0057		
residual						37 937					

The statistical significance of t and F values is marked by asterisks: "***" $p < 0.001$; "*" $p < 0.05$. Data source: (Glomb et al. 2018).

Probably the most relevant outcome of the analysis is the statistically significant connection between the placement of Ptolemaic garrisons and the spatial dissemination of archaeological evidence related to the Isiac cults. In more precise and technical language, the presence of Ptolemaic garrisons in the Aegean Sea region explains 48 percent of the variance of the spatial dissemination of the Isiac cults. This generally means that (a) people residing on an island garrisoned by the Ptolemies often had an Egyptian temple (or artifact) on the same island or in their proximity (i.e., in a near port on the maritime network); or (b) there is a high probability that people situated on an island with a Ptolemaic garrison would have an Egyptian temple (or artifact) in their proximity in the (relatively near) future. Ptolemaic garrisons remained, in many cases, for decades, and one interpretation could be that Ptolemaic soldiers residing on islands contributed significantly to the successful spread of the Isiac cults. To analyze how concretely the cultural transmission between Ptolemaic soldiers and native inhabitants happened, it would be necessary to focus more on the micro-social perspective and to use social simulation methods or possibly the tools of the social network analysis, which is beyond the scope of this book.

Another statistically relevant result, this from the first mathematical model (M1), is that agriculturally self-sufficient islands were spatially related to the weak presence of the Isiac cults (explaining 11 percent of the variance). This outcome suggests the possibility that islands that were agriculturally self-sufficient and therefore not completely dependent on import were not, in some cases, as attractive to merchants exporting grain from Egypt as those suffering from food shortages. However, the outcome of the second mathematical model (M2) suggests that the situation is more complicated. More specifically, it indicates that the agricultural factor gained significance in areas further away from Ptolemaic garrisons. This highlights the possibility that Ptolemaic garrisons had more weight with regard to the early spread of the Isiac cults in the Aegean Sea region than the agricultural factor.

A further relevant result from the first mathematical model (M1), explaining 9 percent of the variance in the dissemination of the Isiac cults, is that higher levels of centrality intensified the presence of these cults. Here, the interpretation is that the strategic position of a port could attract the attention of the Ptolemaic dynasty and people traveling from Egypt in general.

The results show that factors from different levels such as trade, politics, network position, and distance probably all worked together in a complex manner that allowed the successful spread of the Isiac cults in the Aegean Sea region. This finding supports and elaborates Bricault's hypothesis, claiming that the cults connected to Isis and Sarapis spread successfully in the first phase because of a combination of commercial, economic, political, and social factors. The main aim of this case study was to compare the possible impacts of individual factors on the process of the spread. Statistical results from the mathematical models suggest that the spatial distribution of Ptolemaic garrisons from the third and second centuries BCE probably had a more significant impact on the dissemination of the Isiac cults in the Aegean Sea region than other factors considered in the analysis. However, it should be noted that the analysis is tied to a specific region and that the factors discussed could have had different weights in other parts of the ancient Mediterranean. With respect to temporal dynamics, a relatively broad and uncertain dating (often connected only to a certain century or to its part) of the archaeological evidence related to the Isiac cults limits the possibility to statistically uncover different stages of the spread of these cults during the third and second centuries BCE.

4.5 Conclusion of the Case Study 1

This case study attempted to integrate the methods of mathematical and geospatial modeling and network science into the historical study of the factors involved in the early spread of the Isiac cults outside Egypt in order to overcome the limits of established historiographical methods and contribute to the discussion with new arguments. Another goal of this case study was to demonstrate that approaching history as a result of complex processes can lead to a better understanding of the past when compared to approaching history solely as a set of events tied to intentions of important historical figures.

This innovative approach led to relevant results, which can be subjected to academic scrutiny. In summary, the results of selected quantitative analyses suggest that the strong and long-term Ptolemaic military presence could have contributed significantly to the process of the successful spread of the Isiac cults in the Aegean Sea region mainly in the third and second centuries BCE. Available historical evidence from the island of Thera in the region of interest attests that this scenario is not in contradiction with the historical reality. An example is the already-discussed situation of Diokles, a member of the Ptolemaic garrison on the island of Thera, who made a dedication to

Sarapis, Isis, and Anubis—the deities closely tied to the Ptolemaic dynasty (IG XII.3 443). Later, during the third century BCE, a former Ptolemaic official, Artemidorus of Perge, restored the sanctuary of the Egyptian gods on the same island on behalf of Ptolemy III (IG XII.3 464). In addition, the garrisons used to secure the maritime routes in their proximity by defending ships and ports from pirate attacks (IG XII.3 1291; IG II.² 650, lines 15–16). This also means that the Ptolemaic troops could have further contributed to the spread of the Isiac cults by keeping the key routes between Alexandria and the Aegean Sea safe for soldiers, merchants, and the population in general. Although the role of this factor seems to be dominant, the mathematical models employed here show that the commercial demand for Egyptian grain and the strategic position of an island on the maritime transportation network also probably played specific roles, even if their impact on the spread of the Isiac cults in the region was lower.

However, it should be noted here that it is not currently possible to perceive the results presented in this case study as "hard" and "bulletproof" findings because of the degree of uncertainty in the incomplete or otherwise problematic input datasets. The uncertain dating of some of the archaeological evidence, not completely reliable estimates of the ancient population numbers, reconstruction of the ancient maritime routes, and other specific analytical steps involving incomplete historical evidence could have created "gray areas" in the quantitative analysis and to a certain degree limit the reliability of the results. Nevertheless, the statistically significant patterns revealed in this case study support parts of existing hypotheses and could possibly signpost more specific directions in future historical studies, which is demonstrated in the Case Study 2.

This case study provides strong support to the argument interwoven throughout the book that the spatial dissemination of the Isiac cults emerged as a result of multivariate and interconnected processes. It also demonstrates that it is possible, to certain extent, to disentangle these processes and identify, with the help of quantitative methods, which of them had more weight than others in connection to this cultural transmission. While Cumont's imperialistic theory that claimed the Ptolemies intentionally and directly propagated the Isiac cults outside Egypt was disproven in the academic debate, the results presented here reveal that Ptolemaic politics still probably played an important role. Contrary to the imperialistic theory that emphasizes direct and intentional political impact, the findings of the Case Study 1 indicate that military and diplomatic decisions of the Ptolemaic empire contributed indirectly to the spread of the Isiac cults by opening new communication zones in the Aegean Sea and increasing the presence of the Egyptian element in these zones by, for example, stationing Ptolemaic troops. Since the Ptolemaic presence was evaluated as the most influential in the interplay of the selected factors in the Aegean Sea, Case Study 2 builds on this result and explores whether the Ptolemaic political factor was similarly impactful in the region of western Asia Minor.

5

Case Study 2: Spread of the Isiac Cults on the West Coast of Asia Minor

The results of the Case Study 1, which focused on quantitative evaluation of the impact of individual factors on the spread of the Isiac cults across the ancient Aegean Sea (Glomb et al. 2018), demonstrated that Bricault's view is a promising premise. Informed by multivariate statistical analysis, the conclusion from the Case Study 1 is that the early spread of the Isiac cults across the islands in the Aegean Sea benefited from military and commercial activities of the Ptolemaic dynasty, although the model presented there identified the Ptolemaic military operations as the most influential factor in the process of the spread. Following the results from the Case Study 1, this research contributes to the question of whether the positive role of the Ptolemaic political activities in the process of the spread of the Isiac cults was a trend that can be revealed in other regions of the ancient Mediterranean. More specifically, this case study focuses on the quantitative evaluation of the early spread of the Isiac cults on the west coast of Hellenistic Asia Minor, that is, a region with a very specific political situation related to the actions of the first Ptolemaic kings (Hölbl 2001; Austin 2006; Kosmin 2018; Bagnall 1976).

5.1 Area and Period of Interest

The Anatolian coast had already become a place of Ptolemaic interest during the reign of Ptolemy I Soter. In his struggles with Antigonus I Monophthalmus (the One-Eyed) and Antigonus's son, Demetrius I of Macedon, over the eastern Mediterranean, Ptolemy managed to gain and lose again territories such as Syria, Phoenicia, or Cyprus. In this context, Ptolemy launched a campaign in 309 BCE to the western Asia Minor and seized parts of Lycia and Caria probably in order to protect the outer borders of the Ptolemaic area of influence in the Aegean and to maintain safe passage to Greece (Hölbl 2001: 19, 28; Meadows 2006: 460). Ptolemy's efforts to gain a stronger territorial foothold were, however, stopped again by Demetrius near Halicarnassus (Hölbl 2001: 19). Nevertheless, Ptolemy I was successful in introducing Ptolemaic presence in the regions of Aegean Sea and Asia Minor and laid foundations to territorial policies further developed and enforced by Ptolemaic kings that followed until Ptolemy VI. Temporary bases placed by Ptolemy I in the Aegean such as on Samos, Arsinoe-Methana, or Cretan Itanos were then transformed into long-term Ptolemaic garrisons by Ptolemy II, who further expanded the Ptolemaic influence in the Mediterranean also by using Ptolemaic generals and admirals such as Patroclus of Macedon, Callicrates of Samos, or Philocles of Sidon as well as alliances with individual cities in Asia Minor (see Appendix, Figure A.1; for Ptolemaic officials see Hauben 2013, 1987b, 2004; Bagnall 1976).

Since the late 280s, Ptolemy II Philadelphus subsequently solidified the Ptolemaic presence not only in ports on the west and south-west coast of Anatolia but also in cities further inland (e.g., Amyzon, Mylasa, or Stratonikeia) (Hölbl 2001: 35–76). However, the authority over this region was also claimed by the Seleucid empire, a rival Hellenistic state to the Ptolemies, established by one of the *diaodochi*, Seleucus I Nicator (Habicht 1989; Ma 2002; Kosmin 2018). The Ptolemaic control in Asia Minor was thus under a constant pressure from the Seleucid empire campaigning from the east. During several military clashes between the Ptolemaic and Seleucid dynasty known as the Syrian Wars, the Ptolemaic grip on regions of the Asia Minor was repeatedly loosened and tightened again (Grainger 2010). One of the early opportunities for Ptolemy II Philadelphus to extend the Ptolemaic influence in the western Asia Minor was the so-called Syrian War of Succession (280–279 BCE) (Hölbl 2001: 37–8). After the death of Seleucus I Nicator in 281 BCE, Antiochus I Soter succeeded his father on the Seleucid throne, but before any attempt at solidifying his rule in the western Asia Minor, he was occupied by settling down a rebellion in northern Syria. Ptolemy II exploited this window of chaos in the Seleucid empire and gained several cities on the Anatolian coast such as Halicarnassus, Kaunos, or Iasos. In 279 BCE, the Ptolemaic and Seleucid empire made peace; however, this peace was only a momentary respite, and the Ptolemaic dominance in western Anatolia was later repeatedly challenged by Seleucid forces again. The First Syrian War (274–271 BCE) initiated by Ptolemy II who aimed to conquer Seleucid Syria ended with the continuation of status quo in Asia Minor (Grainger 2010: 73–87; Hölbl 2001: 38–40). Ptolemy was initially unsuccessful and had to retreat and prepare for the invasion of Seleucid forces, but Antiochus I was forced to abandon the attack because of economic and health crisis in Babylonia. Thus, a poet Theocritus listed in his poem, composed probably around 270 BCE, the territories of Lycia, Caria, Pamphylia, and Cilicia as Ptolemaic (Theocritus and Hunter 2003: 75–91).

The Second Syrian War (260–253 BCE) significantly complicated the Ptolemaic grip in the Asia Minor. Initially, the so-called Ptolemy "the son," who was, as is assumed by historians, a successor to Ptolemy II at that time, strengthened Ptolemaic power in Ionia as a military commander. However, eventually, this Ptolemy rebelled against Ptolemy II, and Timarchos, an Aetolian mercenary commander, joined Ptolemy's rebellion and became a self-appointed tyrant of Miletus. Their efforts, however, were soon stopped, and since 259 BCE, Ptolemy "the son" was no longer appearing as co-regent in Ptolemaic dating formulas, and Antiochus II took Miletus in 259/8 BCE (Grainger 2017: 79–81; Hölbl 2001: 43–5; LaBuff 2016: 36–7). In this temporal context, the Seleucid king Antiochus II was in an agreement with the Antigonid ruler, Antigonus II Gonatas, which only helped the Seleucids to make a move against Ptolemaic positions in Asia Minor even if the actual Antigonid involvement is rather speculative (Grainger 2010: 132–3; Hölbl 2001: 44). Antiochus II thus was able to seize territories from the Ptolemies in Ionia (Miletus, Ephesus, Samos), Cilicia, and Pamphylia. A peace was struck in 253 BCE, and Ptolemy, showing his strong diplomatic skills, solidified it by marriage of his daughter Berenice and Antiochus II (Hölbl 2001: 43–5).

The aforementioned marriage, however, eventually contributed to dynastic tensions leading to the Third Syrian War (246–241 BCE). In 246 BCE, both Ptolemy II and Antiochus II died, and while Ptolemy III assumed the throne in Egypt shortly after the death of his father, situation in the Seleucid empire was more complicated. The succession to the Seleucid throne was claimed by two branches of Antiochus's family—his first wife, Laodice, with her son Seleucus II as the heir, and his second wife, Berenice, sister of Ptolemy III who proclaimed her son, whose name is unknown, as the rightful ruler. This eventually resulted in the murder of Berenice and her son instigated by Laodice and Seleucus II and a Ptolemaic campaign deep into the Seleucid territory. At the end of the war in 241 BCE, the Ptolemaic kingdom was in its greatest territorial extent. As a result, in Asia Minor, Ptolemies controlled positions around Seleucia in Pieria (northern Syria), in Cilicia, Pamphylia (lost again under Ptolemy III), Lycia, Ionia, Caria, and Hellespont (Grainger 2017: 81–2, 2010: 137–70; Hölbl 2001: 48–51; Fischer-Bovet 2014: 64–6).

The chapter that subsequently led to the end of Ptolemaic influence in Asia Minor started with the ascension of several young kings to the thrones of powerful Mediterranean empires. In 221 BCE, Ptolemy IV Philopator became the king, but his political decisions were influenced by Sosibios of Alexandria who was skilled in intrigues at the Ptolemaic court (Hölbl 2001: 127–8). Antiochus III, who began to rule the Seleucid empire in 222 BCE, and Philip V, who became the leader of the Antigonids in 221 BCE, were, however, more ambitious than the Ptolemaic ruler (Chaniotis 2005: 45). Antiochus III aimed to bring the Seleucids back to their former power in Asia, and his capturing of Seleucia in Pieria from the Ptolemaic hands marks the beginning of the Fourth Syrian War (219–217 BCE) (Ma 2002). During Antiochus's prolonged stay in Phoenicia and Palestine, Ptolemy IV eventually amassed enough troops to defeat Antiochus in the battle at Raphia (217 BCE) (Fischer-Bovet 2014: 86–92; Ma 2002: 59–60; Hölbl 2001: 128–31). Although Ptolemy IV celebrated the victory in one of the biggest battles of ancient history and preserved his control over Coele-Syria, the war was costly, and together with social-economic unrests in Egypt, it contributed to the gradual fading of Ptolemaic control outside Egypt (Hölbl 2001: 134; Fischer-Bovet 2014: 92–6).

After the death of Ptolemy IV in 204 BCE, Ptolemy V ascended to the throne when he was five years old. The unpopular Ptolemaic regent of Ptolemy V, Agathocles, was overthrown by a revolution in 202 BCE, and the beginning of Ptolemy V's rule was thus very unstable. Antiochus III and Philip V of Macedon exploited the situation in Alexandria, and following their secret agreement, they invaded Ptolemaic foreign territories both from the east and west, and they successfully stripped the Ptolemaic empire of its power abroad (Ma 2002: 53–105; Will 1982; Hölbl 2001: 134–41). (For the regions of interest, see Figure 5.1.)

5.2 Academic Discussion on the Early Spread of the Isiac Cults on the West Coast of Asia Minor

The academic discussion on the favorable factors facilitating the early spread of the Isiac cults in the Asia Minor revolves around specific variations of the known arguments from the more general debate, that is, the validity of Franz Cumont's imperialistic theory and the role of economic contacts are the key issues.

As is the case in the debate described in sections 3.1 and 4.2, Peter M. Fraser aims to disprove Cumont's imperialistic theory and argues, based on specific pieces of material evidence, that the Isiac cults in ancient Asia Minor appeared

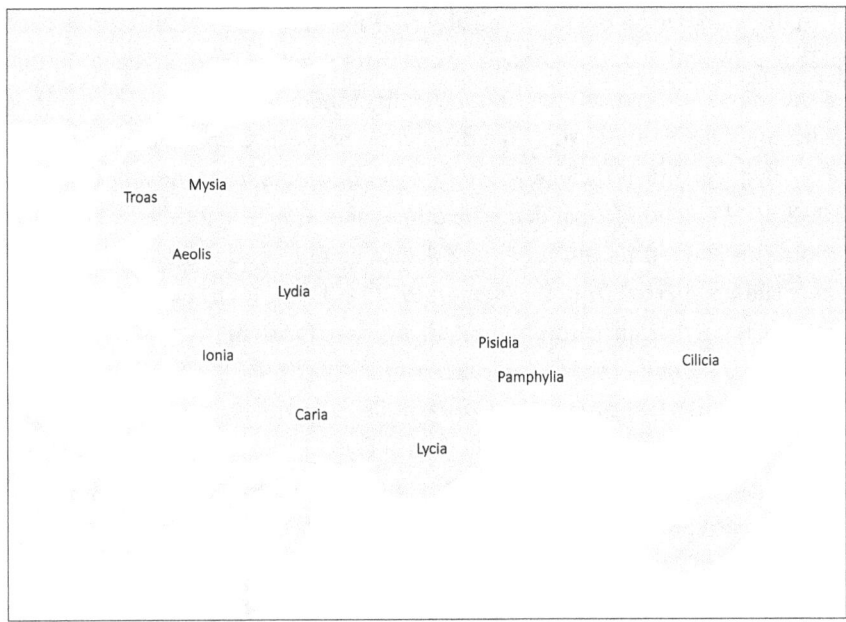

Figure 5.1 Area of interest with regions—case study 2. Base map source: "Natural Earth" n.d.

in ports and cities with commercial contacts and not in cities under Ptolemaic sovereignty (Fraser 1960: 32–7). Since the bulk of the archaeological finds of the Isiac cults in Asia Minor is located on the western coast, mainly in Ionia and Caria, Fraser builds his argumentation around the situation in this region. First, Fraser issues a warning that the proximity between cities under the Ptolemaic sovereignty in Ionia and Caria and the evidence for the Isiac cults must not be considered relevant for the argument that these cults appeared there because of Ptolemaic influence or propaganda and that this proximity was already proven misleading, according to Fraser, in the case of the Aegean Sea (Fraser 1960: 33). The validity of Fraser's arguments with respect to the area of the Aegean Sea was already discussed in the previous case study, and in this chapter, the focus is on Fraser's approach toward the material from Asia Minor.

First evidence brought forward by Fraser is the mention of Osiris in a letter to people of Miletus concerning dedications made by the Seleucid kings, Seleucus I and Antiochus I, to the temple of Didymean Apollo dated to 288/7 BCE (Fraser 1960: 33). Fraser presents this evidence to create a contrast against nonexisting evidence of similar dedications to Egyptian deities made by Ptolemaic rulers at the same time at Delos and thus to point out that while the Seleucid kings directly promoted an Egyptian cult abroad, Ptolemies were not engaged in such practices around that time. Fraser is aware that the cult of Osiris at the beginning of the third century BCE could not be straightforwardly connected to the Isiac cults; however, he states that "the distinction between Osiris and Sarapis is so slight that worship of the one would easily lead to worship of the other" (Fraser 1960: 33). Françoise Dunand, on the other hand, argues that this material only informs us about the attitude of first Seleucid kings toward Osiris and not much more can be inferred from it (Dunand 1973b: 49–50). John Ma points out that this case is not that surprising as the dedications to Osiris in Greek were common long before the end of the fourth century BCE (Ma 2014: 117–22).

After discussing the mention of Osiris by Seleucid rulers, Fraser focuses on the earliest evidence of the Isiac cults in Carian coastal cities such as Halicarnassus and Bargylia dated to the first half of the third century BCE (Fraser 1960: 33–5). In this regard, there is a dedication from Halicarnassus to Isis and Sarapis from the early third century BCE (RICIS 305/1701) and a dedication to Sarapis, Isis, and Arsinoe II, the queen and spouse of Ptolemy II, dated to ca. 270–246 BCE (RICIS 305/1702). Fraser admits that because Halicarnassus was a Ptolemaic possession throughout the third century BCE, the evidence mentioning a Ptolemaic queen might be used as an argument for a Ptolemaic influence. Fraser, however, dismisses this option as there is no indication that the shrine where the dedication was made was a public one (Fraser 1960: 34). Here again, the conceptual limits of Fraser's perspective are apparent. Repeatedly, in his text, Fraser argues that the spread of the Isiac cults was not due to Ptolemaic influence or propaganda. Although Fraser considers influence and propaganda as one category, there is a significant difference between the two. While Fraser can convincingly argue that there are no traces of a direct propagation of the Isiac cults abroad by the ruling Ptolemaic dynasty, this argumentation does not cover the potential impact of Ptolemaic "influence"—if there is a joint dedication to the Isiac cults and the Ptolemaic queen Arsinoe II in a city that was Ptolemaic, then it is difficult to argue that the inscription is not resulting from the Ptolemaic political influence. The conceptual difference that Fraser omits is, as was already discussed in the previous case study, that the Ptolemaic state, by its political actions, could have impacted the spread indirectly by increasing the presence of people carrying the Isiac cults with themselves in cities abroad, and it is important to repeat and highlight this to overcome this conceptually flawed heritage from the lengthy discussion.

Fraser aims to put the situation in Halicarnassus in contrast with Bargylia where he argues that the Isiac cults were public already in the third century, although the city has never been Ptolemaic (Fraser 1960: 34–5). Indeed, there is a dedication from an Isiac temple in Bargylia to Isis, Sarapis, and Anubis from the third century (RICIS 305/1501). The problem is, however, the second part of Fraser's argument. Despite his emphasis on the statement that Bargylia has never been Ptolemaic, the consensus in current debate on the political clashes between the Ptolemaic and Seleucid dynasty in Caria is that Bargylia was under Ptolemaic control most of the third century BCE until Philip V of Macedon seized it in 201 BCE (Eckstein 2008: 156; Bremen 2003; Bresson 2012; Grainger 2010: 253, 2017: 180; Ma 2002: 68, 77). Similarly, Fraser assesses the case of Knidos, which was not, according to him, a Ptolemaic city and speculates that there might have been a temple of Sarapis in the third century BCE based on the Zenon papyrus mentioning a Kinidian attempting to build a Serapeum in an unknown city (Fraser 1960: 35–6). This indirect evidence is not listed by Bricault in RICIS in connection to Knidos, and the earliest local trace of the Isiac cults in RICIS is dated to the second century BCE (RICIS 305/1901). With respect to the question of Ptolemaic influence in Knidos, the matter is more complicated. A direct Ptolemaic rule over the city is difficult to assess. However, it can be concluded that Ptolemaic influence was present in the third century BCE in Knidos based on the statue erected there in honor of the chief minister of Ptolemy IV Philopator, Sosibios (LaBuff 2016: 35–54; Bagnall 1976: 98; Hölbl 2001: 127; Shear 1978: 24; Eckstein 2008: 162).

Fraser then accurately points out that in Miletus, a Ptolemaic city in the third century BCE (LaBuff 2016: 35–54; Bagnall 1976: 98; Hölbl 2001: 127), there is no evidence of the Isiac cults until the Roman period (Fraser 1960: 35; RICIS 304/0901). Fraser than closes his argumentation on Caria by stating that with respect to inland Caria, there are very few traces of the Isiac cults before the Roman period despite certain parts of it were under Ptolemaic control (Fraser 1960: 36). To clarify, inland Carian cities Mylasa and the future Stratonikeia (name given to the city by Seleucids) are attested as under Ptolemaic control in the reign of Ptolemy II Philadelphus (Bremen 2017, 2003; Ma 2002: 40–85), and there is evidence for the Isiac cults in both cities. In Stratonikeia, RICIS lists a Sarapieion dated to the third century BCE (RICIS 305/0501), and for Mylasa, there are the cults attested later to the period between the second and first centuries BCE (RICIS 305/1302-1303).

In connection to Ionia, Fraser discusses the cases of Priene and Magnesia ad Meandrum (Fraser 1960: 36–7). In Priene, there was a temple of the Isiac deities in the third century BCE (RICIS 304/0801-0802), and in Magnesia, there was a temple in the second century BCE (RICIS 304/0701). Fraser states that neither of these cities was under Ptolemaic control. However, there is evidence for Magnesia ad Meandrum being in the zone of influence of Ptolemy III in the Third Syrian War (246–241 BCE) (Ma 2002: 44–5; Grainger 2010: 179; Chrubasik 2016: 250–2), and in the same time frame in Priene, there is a Ptolemaic official being mentioned (Hiller von Gaertringen 1906; Fischer-Bovet 2014: 65). In this context, Ma lists Priene as potentially under direct Ptolemaic rule (Ma 2002: 44–5), and Hölbl lists it in Ptolemaic possessions without further detail (Hölbl 2001, sec. Appendix). It is becoming apparent that with more and more evidence of diversity in the intensity and modes of Ptolemaic influence abroad, it is no longer viable for the academic debate to speak about Ptolemaic control using only the limits of the spectrum such as "direct" and "absent," as Fraser does. For Ephesus, which was a Ptolemaic military base for decades in the third century BCE (Hölbl 2001: 50; Bagnall 1976: 170–1), Fraser admits the Ptolemaic presence there but reminds that the cult there, richly attested to the third century BCE, was private and not public (Fraser 1960: 36–7). However, the connection between the Ptolemaic dynasty and the Isiac cults in Ephesus is explicit in a dedication from probably 282–270 BCE to Ptolemy (II), Arsinoe (I), Sarapis, and Isis (RICIS 304/0601).

Fraser concludes the situation in Ionia and Caria as follows:

> Thus the only places in Caria and Ionia where state cults of Sarapis are at present known were not Ptolemaic, and even if evidence of state cults in the Ptolemaic cities should come to light, it could not be argued that it was due to Ptolemaic influence. Thus the coast of Asia Minor supports the conclusion drawn from the islands of the Aegean. The cult appears in harbours and cities with considerable commercial and international contacts—Rhodes, Eretria, Priene, Ephesus (closely connected in the third century with Rhodes, it may be noted) and Magnesia, and not in cities under Ptolemaic suzerainty. (Fraser 1960, 37)

Despite Fraser's significant impact on the discussion on the spread of the Isiac cults and success in challenging the validity of Cumont's imperialistic thesis, his conclusion is alarming on several levels. First, as was presented in this chapter, Fraser's arguments with respect to individual cities in Asia Minor are not historically accurate with respect to assessing the Ptolemaic presence. Second, Fraser declares that evidence of the Isiac cults uncovered in the future in the Ptolemaic cities cannot be used as an indicator of Ptolemaic influence on the spread of the cult, which is a statement completely outside of academic principles. Third, while Fraser recognizes commercial contacts and relationships (such as between Rhodos and Ephesus) as a potential factor of influence, he does not follow this logic in case of political contacts despite the inner mechanisms of these connections might have similar results with respect to the spread of the Isiac cults, that is, facilitate the transmission of a cultural knowledge and practice through mobility of people from one place to another.

Dunand, too, dismisses the validity of the imperialistic theory in case of Asia Minor and argues that there is no evidence exposing a direct and systematic organization of the Isiac cults in the lands belonging to the Ptolemaic possessions outside Egypt (Dunand 1973b: 29). Dunand discusses the same evidence as Fraser and too highlights the potential positive role of Rhodos in the spread of these cults along the western coast of Asia Minor (Dunand 1973b: 1–135). Dunand also provides some additional points. This is the case for the city of Kaunos in Caria that was controlled by the Ptolemies throughout the third century BCE (Hölbl 2001: 19; Cohen 1995: 52; Meadows 2006) where Dunand argues that the evidence for Isiac cults there appears only later, in the second century BCE (Dunand 1973b: 32). However, in 2006, an inscription from Kaunos dedicated to Sarapis, Isis, and the *Theoi Adelphoi* (i.e., the Sibling Gods Ptolemy II and Arsinoe II) dated to ca. 272/1 BCE was published (Marek 2006: 254; RICIS 305/2003). This renders Dunand's claim outdated, and it strengthens the argument that the Isiac cults were affected by Ptolemaic politics. With respect to Myndos, near Halicarnassus, Dunand states that despite the Ptolemaic control over the city from the early third century BCE, the Isiac cults first appeared on the local coinage between the second and first centuries BCE (Dunand 1973b: 35–6). For inland Caria, Dunand argues that although Stratonikeia was among Ptolemaic possessions in the third century BCE, the earliest evidence for the Isiac cults appears there only in the period between the second and first centuries BCE, again on local coinage (Dunand 1973b: 42–4). Here, however, RICIS lists new evidence for Stratonikeia attesting the presence of the temple of Sarapis to the third century BCE (RICIS 305/0501). Therefore, it is important to bear in mind that this stage of the debate represented by the arguments of Fraser and Dunand opposing the imperialistic theory is not only conceptually problematic but also outdated with respect to the archaeological evidence. This being said, there is a crucial milestone related to change in the perception of the Ptolemaic impact on the spread of the Isiac cults present in Dunand's thinking. Particularly when discussing the evidence from Asia Minor, Dunand repeatedly admits that the Ptolemaic political activity must have played a positive, although indirect, role in the spread of the Isiac cults in ancient Asia Minor (Dunand 1973b: 49, 1980: 109). While Dunand stresses that there is no evidence for explicit interest of the Ptolemies in promoting the cult abroad, she presents the situation in Ephesus, where the cult is richly attested since the third century BCE, as a clear example of the positive impact of the long-term Ptolemaic presence on the growth of the Isiac cults abroad.

Laurent Bricault holds a very similar view on the matter as Dunand does and claims that the archaeological evidence indicates that the instalment of these cults abroad was not systematically initiated by the Ptolemaic state. However, Bricault also admits that the political ties between the Ptolemaic dynasty and foreign regions can be considered as favorable conditions in the process of the spread of the Isiac cults (Bricault 2004). Specifically, he names Halicarnassus, Ephesus, Priene, and Stratonikeia as cities where the cults appeared in the context of Ptolemaic military or diplomatic presence (Bricault 2004: 550). Finally, as was already stressed throughout the book, Bricault perceives the process of the spread of the Isiac cults not as homogenous and explainable by one factor but as complex and heterogenous.

5.2 Quantitative Analysis

The spread of the Isiac cults on the west coast of Asia Minor is conceptualized in this book as (a) a long-term transmission of specific cultic practice from one socio-spatial milieu to another and (b) a transmission happening on a transportation network. Such a definition of the process in question allows for the construction of a virtual spatial platform in a geographic information system (GIS) software for the purposes of the quantitative analysis. More specifically, to evaluate the possible impact of political factors on the spread of the Isiac cults on the west coast of Hellenistic Asia Minor, a three-step process was followed: (a) construction of a model of the ancient transportation network; (b) identification, categorization, and geocoding the cities under Ptolemaic influence in the area of interest; and finally, (c) statistical analysis of the spatial relationships between the archaeological evidence related to the Isiac cults from the area of interest and the cities under Ptolemaic influence on the ancient transportation network. Each of these specific methodological steps is elaborated in the following sections.

5.2.1 Transportation Network

In terms of mapping and digitizing transport on the western shores of Asia Minor, similar challenges with respect to the adequate density of the network as in Case Study 1 occurred. Despite the fact that the Stanford geospatial network model of the

Roman world (ORBIS; Scheidel and Meeks n.d.) is a widely recognized tool among historians and archaeologists that allows these researchers to analyze duration and financial expenses for specific routes among major cities and for specific means of travel in antiquity, the scale of the network is large and ORBIS primarily focuses on rendering routes that cover long distances. The scale of ORBIS, as in Case Study 1, did not allow for capturing the mobility between the Ptolemaic Egypt and Asia Minor on the desired level. To construct a more nuanced network on a smaller, regional scale for the purposes of Case Study 2, more detailed and historically accurate datasets needed to be consulted. Moreover, the transportation network of Case Study 1 had only one mode—maritime; in Case Study 2, geocoding mobility needed to incorporate maritime as well as inland modes of travel.

The ancient sailing routes collected and described by Pascal Arnaud in *Les routes de la navigation antique: Itinéraires en Méditerranée* (Arnaud 2005) were considered as an adequate approximation of the edges of the maritime part of the network. After geocoding and redrawing the routes from Arnaud's collection as lines in a GIS environment, the trajectories of the ORBIS network were consulted whether the main routes on the western coast in ORBIS were in accord with the network generated based on Pascal Arnaud's collection. Despite its inadequate density, ORBIS served in this case study as a relevant tool for comparison and validation. Finally, the geometries of the routes were corrected by two spatial buffers around the shores to make them realistic with respect to ancient sailing. One buffer at a distance of 100 meters from the coastline represents the minimum safe distance from the shore for a sailing ship. The value of the second "ideal" buffer was set to 2,000 meters from the shore, which was considered as the distance from which the coast can be seen by sailors allowing them to navigate more accurately but without the risk of entering shallow waters. This buffering method was applied as a consistent rule of correction of the routes in both Case Study 1 and 2.

The inland part of the transportation network was approximated by Roman road network data published by the *Digital Atlas of Roman and Medieval Civilizations* (DARMC; McCormick et al. 2013), which are based on the Roman roads included in Richard Talbert's *Barrington Atlas of the Greek and Roman World* (Talbert 2000). The trajectories and geometries of the road network were checked and validated in GIS software by reconnecting some loose ends of these roads and fixing their occasional misalignment overlooked in the original *DARMC Roman Road Network* dataset. Naturally, the use of Roman roads data in a case study focused on pre-Roman period is anachronistic, which needs to be clarified. There are, however, several reasons why the Roman roads are a suitable approximation for this case study. The major Hellenistic cities on the west coast of Asia Minor identified and analyzed in this case study were with high probability already interconnected by roads that were later used and maintained by the Romans. The argument that Roman roads in Asia Minor overlapped with the pre-Roman roads is also considered as valid in the scholarship on the topic (see e.g., French 1998; Lynch and Matter 2014: 109–10). The Roman roads from the dataset also respect the geographical features such as rivers, valleys, and so forth in the area of interest. For these reasons, it is correct to assume that the main travel flow between the major cities had the same trajectories both in Ptolemaic and Roman times. The Roman roads dataset is thus the most historically realistic proxy applicable in this case study as there are no sufficient data for older periods, and it is more accurate than connecting the cities by direct lines disrespecting the terrain.

After creating the transportation network, a set of nodes representing major Hellenistic ports and settlements was identified for purposes of subsequent analyses on the network. For the maritime part of the network on the west coast of Asia Minor, ancient major ports included in *A Catalogue of Ancient Ports and Harbours* (Graauw 2016) were identified as nodes of the network, and their position and existence in the Hellenistic period were checked using the *Pleiades Database of Ancient Places* (Bagnall et al. 2006). Nodes representing major Hellenistic cities were selected from the *Pleiades* database based on the rule that only those cities that had attributes of "Hellenistic period" and "major settlements" were incorporated. These nodes were considered important because of their prestige and larger population sizes and were incorporated as crucial nodes in the further analyses. The final transportation network utilized as a platform for the quantitative analyses in this case study is depicted in Figure 5.2.

5.2.2 Operationalization of Factors Involved in the Spread

The complete transportation network allowed for attributing further parameters to individual nodes on the network reflecting their qualities with respect to political, religious, or mobility contexts. The spatial relationships between these parameters were then evaluated statistically to reveal potential impact factors in the process of the spread of the Isiac cults. This section focuses on the procedure of identifying appropriate proxies for the nodes' parameters, their collection, and operationalization.

As was already described, the transportation network consisted of maritime and inland portions. The first step with respect to attributing parameters to

Figure 5.2 Transportation network on the west coast of Hellenistic Asia Minor. Base map source: "Natural Earth" n.d.; Data source: Glomb et al. 2020.

individual nodes was to reflect this dual modality. Each node thus received a parameter defining whether they were directly connected to the maritime and/or inland routes. This parameter also helped to overcome one specific problem of maritime connectivity, that is, the major Hellenistic cities in the area of interest were often operating through a close port represented in the network by a different node, and this way it was possible to link the ports with their neighboring cities.

To incorporate parameter of the presence of the Isiac cults to the network, the archaeological evidence related to the Isiac cults from the time and area of interest was geocoded. As in the Case Study 1, Bricault's corpus RICIS (2005b) was used as a dataset to approximate the worship of Isiac cults. The data from

RICIS were categorized into two groups with respect to their type: (1) artifacts (altars, statues, inscriptions, etc.) and (2) temples. This categorization helped to characterize the quality of the cult presence—temples can be considered as indicators of more durable and significant presence than artifacts (Figure 5.3). Furthermore, these data were divided based on their dating in order to capture different phases of the spread with respect to chronology. However, the dates of origins of the Isiac evidence are most often attributable only to a whole century, and the differentiation applied here reflects this, that is, artifacts and temples are categorized based on the estimated century of origin.

Another dataset was collected to approximate the Ptolemaic political activity in the western Asia Minor. This was operationalized by identifying those cities in the region that belonged to the Ptolemaic possessions or were under

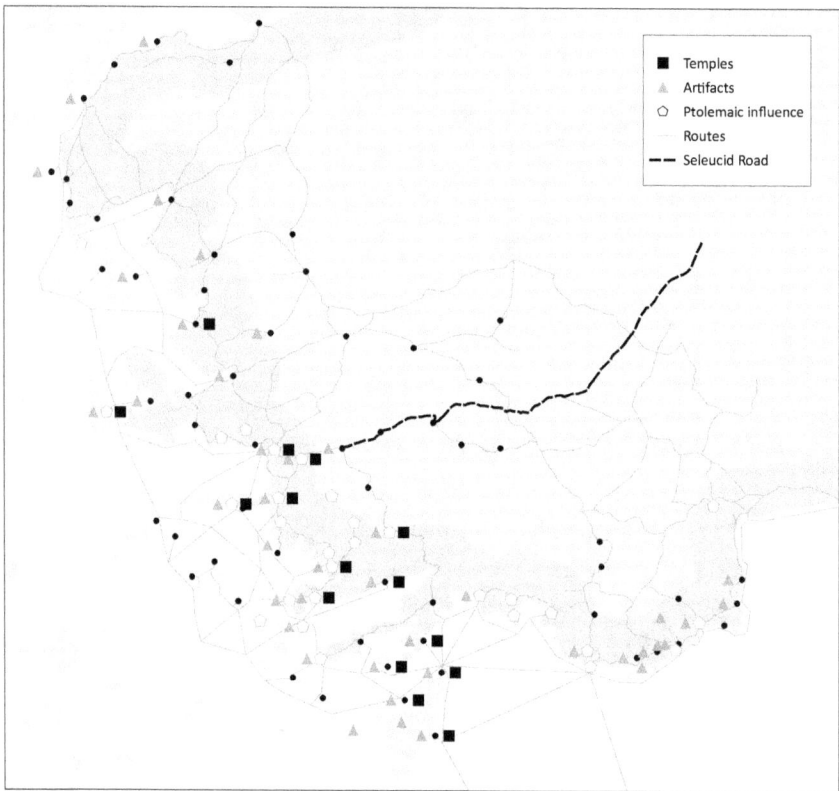

Figure 5.3 Places under the Ptolemaic influence and the evidence of the Isiac cults on the west coast of Hellenistic Asia Minor in the period of interest. Coastline belt in darker shade indicates the distance of 30 km from the coast. Base map source: "Natural Earth" n.d.; Data source: Glomb et al. 2020.

the Ptolemaic influence between the fourth and second centuries BCE. These parameters were attributed in a similar manner as in Case Study 1 based on Bagnall's *The Administration of the Ptolemaic Possessions Outside Egypt* (1976) and checked against other scholarship for consensus on the evidence (e.g., Hölbl 2001; Fischer-Bovet 2014; Chaniotis 2005, 2002; LaBuff 2016; Ma 2002; see Figures 5.3 and A.1 and Appendix for the list and description of these cities). In this literature, the main indicators of the Ptolemaic influence in a city in Asia Minor consist of evidence related to (a) a Ptolemaic garrison in a city; (b) a presence of a high-ranking Ptolemaic official such as *strategos* (i.e., governor); and (c) a civic calendar of a city based on the regnal years of the Ptolemaic kings (i.e., stating time in official documents using formulations such as "in the year 7 of the king Ptolemy"). Although it seems the category of Ptolemaic influence could have been further detailed by differentiating between military and political presence, the nature of the evidence does not allow clear separation. For example, the title of *strategos* went through development in Ptolemaic times leading to a decline in its military role and became more administratively oriented (Hölbl 2001: 59–61). The outcome of this operationalization process was a set of geocoded points representing Hellenistic cities identified in the literature as Ptolemaic possessions or cities under the Ptolemaic influence. For the dataset and tables, see Glomb et al. (2020); for the list of places under Ptolemaic influence, see Appendix.

To evaluate spatial relationships and observe potential patterns among the variables in the final quantitative analysis, it was necessary to measure the distances from each major Hellenistic city to the closest political (Ptolemaic influence) or religious (Isiac temple/artifact) proxy on the transportation network. However, using the simple geographical distance, as was the case in Case Study 1, was not ideal because the conditions for traveling change drastically based on the terrain and mode of transport. In other words, traveling on sea was much faster than on land. To take this factor into account, instead of measuring geographical distances, the quantity of time needed to reach one node from another was implemented as the appropriate definition of a spatial relationship between the nodes. Traveling speeds of ancient ships were approximated based on Lionel Casson's *Ships and Seamanship in the Ancient World* (Casson 1995) to 140km/day, and the speed of pedestrians was determined as 30 km/day based on the values for walking in ancient times defined by the ORBIS project (Scheidel and Meeks n.d.). It needs to be noted that these speed values are rather general estimates, and, in reality, there was significant variability in ship types and speeds; however, with respect to the scale of the analysis, this parameter adequately captures the comparative advantage/disadvantage of the maritime and land transportation network. Furthermore, the time for traveling on land was also adjusted with respect to the terrain using the hiking function formulated by Waldo Tobler (1993). This hiking function defines the speed based on the slope angle. The highest walking speed is at around −2.86 degree slope; to calculate the speed at any other terrain angle is possible using the following formula:

$p = 0.6e^{3.5|m + 0.05|}$, where p is the pace [s/m] and m is the terrain slope gradient [°].

While there are other alternatives to this approach (see e.g., Kondo and Seino n.d.; Ericson and Goldstein 1980), Tobler's method is probably the simplest and most used in archaeological research (see e.g., Herzog 2013). As was noted in the previous paragraph, the speed on sea was constant (140 km/day). This value averages the sailing speed of ancient ships under both favorable and unfavorable wind conditions. Additional external factors as streams, wind directions, or temperature were not taken into consideration as it would be too complex an issue to apply within a relatively small region, and the transparency and interpretability of such complex model would suffer with each added sub-variable. After setting a balanced pace for transportation both on sea and land, it was possible to calculate temporal distances between nodes on the network, that is, durations of the fastest possible trips among them. These distances were the key measurements for exploration of the potential patterns in the dissemination of specific proxies on the network with respect to the process of the local spread of the Isiac cults.

Additionally, network centrality values for each major Hellenistic city on the transportation network were calculated to determine the importance of each node in the network. In the first step, two network metrics were employed: (1) eigenvector centrality as "busyness of harbours" metric employed also in the Case Study 1 (Rivers, Knappett, and Evans 2013: 146), and (2) betweenness centrality for inferring the gateway sites, that is, sites that often serve as a crucial connection point between one section of the network and another (Rivers, Knappett, and Evans 2013). However, because this study focuses on a very specific problem, that is, a cultural spreading process from one direction (Egyptian Alexandria), and the nodes were categorized into qualitative types (crossroad, city, port), another measure that would capture this directionality and mobility was implemented. A simple deterministic agent-based model was constructed where agents (their number being equal to the number of cities on the network) were sent from the port of Alexandria to each city on the network and the agents were programmed to use the fastest possible route. Then, each city on the network had a counter for all agents that used this node as a transition site. This centrality parameter ("number of visits") was an indicator of the potential comparative strategic advantage of each major Hellenistic city on the network with respect to the traffic intensity when traveling from Alexandria (see Figure 5.4). This parameter was then incorporated as one of the factors of impact in the final quantitative statistical analysis. Finally, durations of the fastest trips from the major Hellenistic cities to their nearest port on the network were measured to determine their maritime connectivity and "logistical availability."

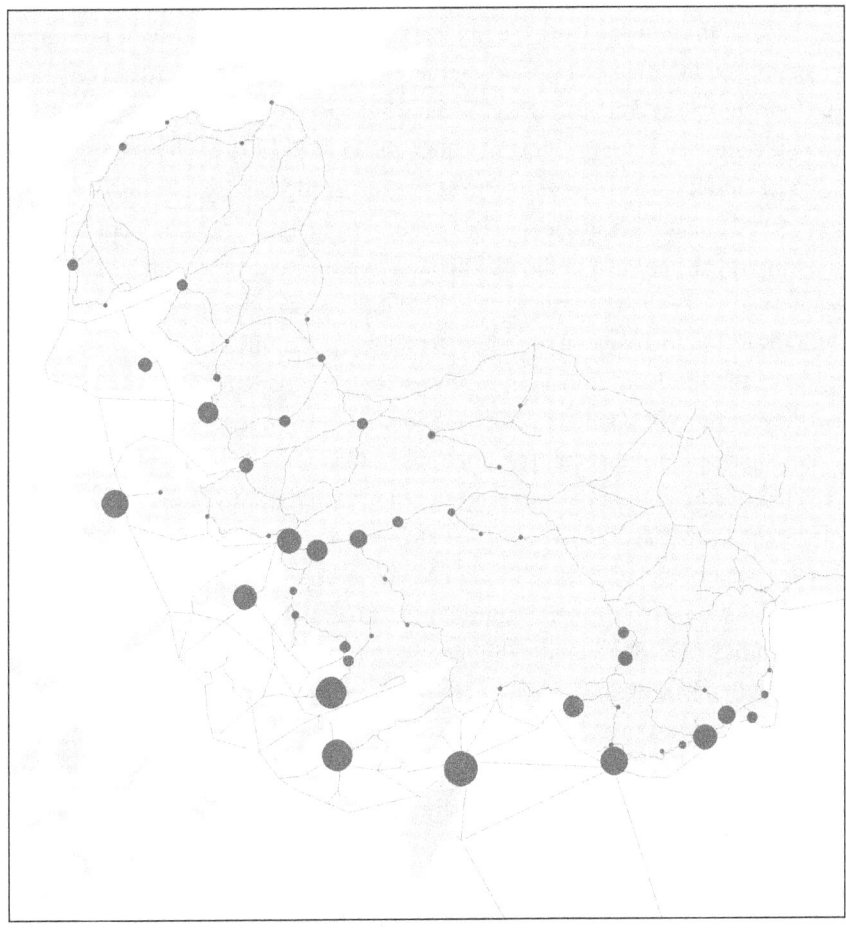

Figure 5.4 Visualization of the "number of visits" parameter on the west coast of Hellenistic Asia Minor. Bigger circles indicate places with a higher number of visits, and smaller circles indicate lower number of visits. Base map source: "Natural Earth" n.d.; Data source: Glomb et al. 2020.

The specific GIS tools and packages that were used for the operationalizations described here can be found in the original published study (Glomb et al. 2020).

5.2.3 Statistical Analysis

The statistical analysis was used to evaluate the correlation among the specific parameters of the nodes on the transportation network on the west coast of Asia Minor and to answer the question of whether the political factor played an important role in the early spread of the Isiac cults in this region. The data obtained in previous steps were organized in a table (Glomb et al. 2020), listing each major Hellenistic city and its centrality values, the duration of the fastest trip (in days) on the network from the city to its closest (i.e., reachable in the minimum possible amount of time): (a) Isiac temple and artifact from the third century BCE; (b) Isiac temple and artifact dated to the whole period of interest (i.e., third and second centuries BCE); (c) Ptolemaic possession or place of Ptolemaic influence; (d) port; and finally, (e) the duration of the fastest trip (in days) from Alexandria in Egypt, the epicenter of the spread, to each city, that is, a measurement defining the traveling distance from Egypt. The next step was to apply a suitable statistical analysis to these data to uncover the potential correlations among these values with respect to their spatial or rather "traveling" proximity.

Since the results of initial descriptive statistics revealed that the variables do not have a normal (Gaussian) distribution, as was the case also in Case Study 1, an appropriate statistical tool, that is, Spearman correlation coefficient, was selected to reveal potential correlations among the data. To repeat the rationale of the Spearman rank correlation coefficient (R_s; always between -1.0, i.e., a perfect negative correlation, and 1.0, i.e., a perfect positive correlation), it ranks the variables based on their values and evaluates the tightness of correlation between the ranked variables. Simply put, this analysis asks same questions for each city, that is, how far (in days) on the network from that location is the nearest political, religious, or other proxy or what is the strategical/centrality value of a city. If these traveling durations and qualities rank similarly, then the correlation is positive. The outcome of the analysis, which correlated each variable to one another, yielded a high amount of statistically significant correlations. To be more precise, the pairwise correlations of all parameters, except centrality values (betweenness and eigenvector centrality), were evaluated as statistically significant.

Furthermore, the Wilcoxon test—a statistical tool that calculates and analyzes the differences between each set of pairs—revealed with high statistical

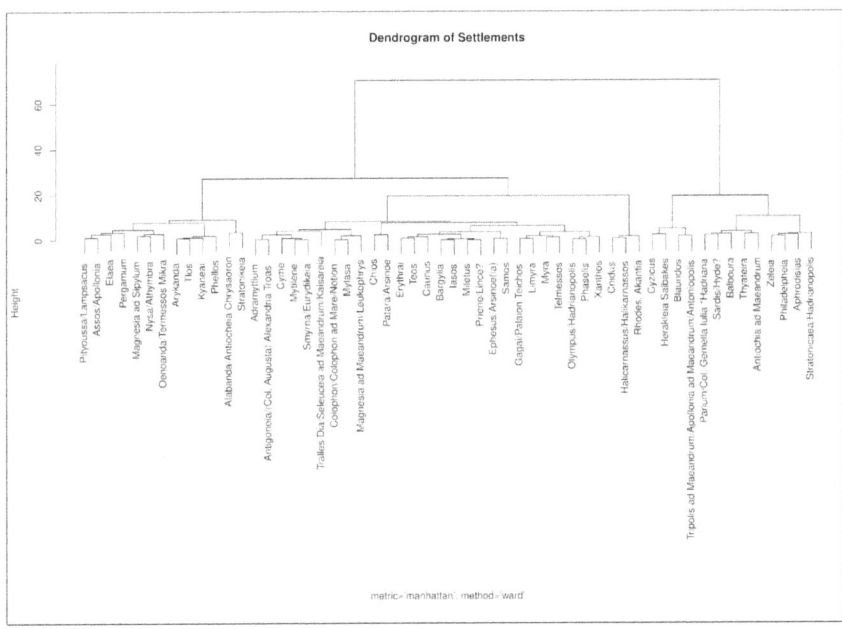

Figure 5.5 Dendrogram with groups of similar cities with respect to their parameters.

significance that the variables differ in cities without a port when compared to cities with a port. Therefore, pairwise correlations for cities with and without a port were also evaluated separately. The results were similar to the ones from the analysis of the whole dataset with the exception that the parameters of cities without a port were not significantly correlated with the amount of traffic in their proximity (i.e., number of visits). The most relevant statistically significant correlations from the whole statistical analysis are interpreted and elaborated in the section 5.2.4, Results.

For a final step, a series of cluster analyses was applied to the dataset to identify cities that are similar with respect to their parameters (Figure 5.5). Here, the group consisting of Knidos, Halicarnassus, and Rhodos stood out in every cluster analysis method applied and therefore deserves further attention.

5.2.4 Results

The statistical analysis applied in this study revealed strong and statistically highly significant correlations among the parameters with the potential impact on the spatial dissemination of the archaeological evidence related to the Isiac cults on the west coast of Hellenistic Asia Minor.

One of the most relevant results is that the correlation between the distance (in days) from major Hellenistic cities to their closest Isiac temple from the third century BCE and to their closest Ptolemaic possession or city under the direct Ptolemaic influence was identified as the strongest ($R_s = 0.946$) with a high statistical significance ($p < 0.001$). This means that when a major Hellenistic city was a Ptolemaic possession (or under Ptolemaic influence) or had one in its proximity, then there was, with high probability, an Isiac temple in the city itself or very close on the transportation network. In other words, based on the analysis, the political proxy plays the role of the predictor for the spatial occurrence of the religious proxy. This very significant spatial dependency between the Isiac temples and Ptolemaic possessions supports the argument that the Ptolemaic political activities on the west coast of Hellenistic Asia Minor had a positive impact on the local spread of the Isiac cults. However, the varying strengths or "tightness" of correlations between the distance (in days) from a city to its closest Ptolemaic possession and the distance to its other proxies related to the closest presence of the Isiac cults such as artifacts from the third century BCE ($R_s = 0.750$, $p < 0.001$) or temples and artifacts from the whole period of interest including the second century BCE (cor. with temples $R_s = 0.882$, $p < 0.001$, with artifacts $R_s = 0.668$, $p < 0.001$) allow for describing the political impact on this cultural transmission in greater detail.

The slightly weaker tightness of the correlation between the traveling distance (in days) from a city to its closest Isiac artifact from the third century BCE and the distance to its closest place of Ptolemaic influence means that the artifacts were in proximity to the Ptolemaic zones, but overall, they were slightly more dispersed than the temples. Here, the results can be interpreted that the temples reflect more durable presence of the cult and reflect the activity of a group of people and that the significant correlation points to a pattern that this cultic activity happened in approachable places with the Ptolemaic presence. With respect to artifacts, the situation could have been very similar because the majority of the evidence spatially overlaps with the temples. However, the presence of a small number of artifacts outside this pattern can reflect the spontaneity of traveling individuals. The results also reveal that this spatial relationship between the presence of the Ptolemaic political activities and the Isiac cults on the west coast of Asia Minor is stronger in the third century BCE than in the second century BCE. This is a logical result since the Ptolemaic firm grip of the area of interest was lost during the second century BCE, and the Isiac temples from the third century could have constituted secondary centers of the spread of these cults. The difference in the results for the third and second centuries BCE supports the argument that the Ptolemaic activity in the area of interest was crucial particularly for the first local instalments of the Isiac cults.

Other factors that correlated significantly with the religious proxies were related to the strategic qualities of the Hellenistic cities on the transportation network. The parameter "number of visits" representing the traffic intensity of people traveling from Egypt is correlated with the distance (in days) from a city to the closest religious proxies (for all temples $R_s = -0.541$, $p < 0.001$, which is highly significant; for all artifacts $R_s = -0.394$, $p < 0.01$ is lower but still highly significant). This means that the cities that were more frequently visited by people traveling from Egypt than others had also the Isiac temples and artifacts in their proximity. However, the results are very different for cities with no ports where the correlation of this pair (number of visits/distance to closest Isiac temple) is only $R_s = -0.194$ with p not being significant. In other words, the relationship between the intensity of traffic of people traveling from Egypt and the presence of the Isiac cults is far stronger in coastal cities than in inland cities. This result is also supported by the correlation tightness between the distance of a city to its closest port and the distance to the closest religious proxy (e.g., for all temples $R_s = 0.822$, $p < 0.001$), where the cities closer to the shore were also closer to the Isiac temples than the cities further inland. Furthermore, the correlation tightness of the pair—distance (in days) of a city to its closest port and the distance to the closest place of Ptolemaic influence—follows the pattern ($R_s = 0.826$, $p < 0.001$). Here, it can be argued that the ports of major Hellenistic cities served as important transition points between the maritime and land transportation network. It is logical that, with their high connectivity for travelers from Egypt traveling elsewhere on the network and because of the cost and time efficiency of supplying them by ships, they served as suitable bases for Ptolemaic campaigns and assumed the role of secondary centers of the spread of the Isiac cults. The statistically insignificant correlations of other centrality values such as betweenness and eigenvector centrality point to the limits of the spatial network analysis rather than to the irrelevance of strategically advantageous positions of the cities with respect to the spread of the Isiac cults. Although the very different topology of the transportation network on the sea when compared to the one on land did not pose a problem when measuring fastest trips among the cities because of the implementation of speed coefficients, it probably affected the consistency and comparability of centrality measurements between the two (sea/land) segments. One example of this topological issue for centrality measurements is that the maritime crossroads are often situated in the open sea, while inland crossroads are often found in a city. The last factor related to strategic qualities of major Hellenistic cities on the west coast of Asia Minor with respect to the spread of the Isiac cults are distances (in days) of these cities to Egyptian Alexandria, that is, the epicenter of the spread on the network. The correlation of the pair—distance (in days) of a city from Alexandria/distance from a city to the closest Isiac temple—is $R_s = 0.653$ and $p < 0.001$, which is highly significant (for all artifacts $R_s = 0.611$, $p < 0.001$). This result, showing that places more distant from Alexandria than others were also more distant from the Isiac temples, is an expected one. The Isiac cults originated in Egypt, and it is logical to assume that the amount of people who carried the cultic practices and artifacts and traveled from Egypt would have been higher in places that are not as far from Alexandria as others.

The statistical evaluation of the pairwise correlations among the parameters attributed to the major Hellenistic cities in the area of interest thus suggests that the traveling distance (in days) to the nearest ports and places of Ptolemaic influence, the distance from Alexandria, and the amount of traffic in coastal areas all contributed to the local spread of the Isiac cults and that the proximity of a Ptolemaic sphere of influence, mainly during the third century BCE, was the most significant factor in this process. These results in combination with the results of the Case Study 1 focusing on the area of the Hellenistic Aegean Sea thus support the hypothesis that the positive impact of the Ptolemaic military and political operations during the third century BCE on the spread of the Isiac cults was a trend occurring in at least two regions of the ancient Mediterranean.

Because the results of the statistical analysis showed that the position of Hellenistic ports correlated strongly with the spatial distribution of Ptolemaic possessions/Ptolemaic influence ($R_s = 0.826$, $p < 0.001$), a spatial visual analysis was conducted to explore the role of the shore in greater detail. The relevant observation in this respect is that all the places of Ptolemaic influence in the region were located within a ca 30-kilometer-wide belt stretching from the coastline (see Figure 5.3). Such spatial consistency is with high probability noncoincidental and can point to the logistical difficulties of the Ptolemaic empire to operate more actively in areas distant from the ports they controlled. The spatial visual analysis also served for evaluation of a potential immunological factor obstructing the spread of the Isiac cults further inland—that is, the presence of Ptolemaic political rival, the Seleucid empire. It was not possible to employ the same spatial network analysis here as in the case of the Ptolemaic possessions because the archaeological evidence of the Isiac cults is absent in the Seleucid territory, and therefore, its spatial distribution and impact of other factors are immeasurable. The ideal scenario here would be to use the spatial visual analysis to measure whether there is a relationship between the spatial distribution of the Isiac cults and the border of the Seleucid empire. However, the western border of the Seleucid empire was not firmly defined and was constantly changing because of the clashes with the Ptolemies on the west coast of Hellenistic Asia Minor. Therefore, the Seleucid main road used by Seleucid armies campaigning to the west coast of Asia Minor from the east in ca. 216, 203, 197, and 190 BCE (Ma 2002: 35, 77) was used as the most suitable proxy for the influence of the Seleucid empire. This spatial visual analysis shows that the spatial dissemination of the archaeological evidence related to the Isiac cults does not overlap with the territory defined by the Seleucid road (Figure 5.3). A relevant observation in this case is that the most eastern artifact on the central-western coast related to the Isiac cults lies in the city of Tralles, which was the most western-border point of the Seleucid road. This result suggests that the Seleucid pressure from the east thus could have potentially constituted an immunological factor limiting the inland spread of the Isiac cults tied to the Ptolemaic dynasty. Also, later, in the Roman times, the Isiac cults did spread inland in the Asia Minor with the Roman presence there (Bricault 2001), which suggests that the barrier in the Ptolemaic times could have been a political one.

The interpretation of the results of the cluster analyses that grouped together Knidos, Halicarnassus, and Rhodos remains open. These locations were recognized as similar with respect to their parameters, and it is possible that they could have played a specific role in the spreading dynamics of the Isiac cults. All three were port cities that were once (ca. 1100–560 BCE) members of the Dorian Hexapolis, a federation of six cities (Knidos, Kos, Halicarnassus, and three cities on the island of Rhodos—Lindos, Kamiros, and Ialysos) sharing the Dorian identity and honoring the cult of Triopian Apollo (Hall 2007: 98). This issue thus invites further debate and research.

To sum up this section, the findings presented in the Case Study 2 reveal a clear spatial and "traveling" dependency between the places of Ptolemaic influence and the Isiac cults on the west coast of Hellenistic Asia Minor. With respect to the academic discussion, these results support the argument that the Ptolemaic dynasty had a positive role in the early spread of the Isiac cults outside Egypt. The nature of the results does not solve the question of whether the instalment of these cults on the west coast of Hellenistic Asia Minor was officially encouraged and directly supported by the Ptolemaic dynasty or if these cults spread there by people from the Ptolemaic social milieu but without the official directive from the upper levels of the state hierarchy. However, this question is tackled again later in this book in Chapter 6, Political Activities of the Ptolemaic Dynasty and Their Impact on the Spread of the Isiac Cults Abroad—a Historical Pattern. However, based on the analysis conducted in the Case Study 1 and 2, it is apparent that the Ptolemaic political activity created specific spatial channels that with high probability facilitated the spreading process.

5.3 Conclusion of the Case Study 2

This study applied the methods of spatial network analysis, statistics, and spatial visual analysis to evaluate the potential impact of the Ptolemaic political activities on the early spread of the Isiac cults on the west coast of Hellenistic Asia Minor. This way, the study also contributed to the bigger question whether the positive role of the Ptolemaic political operations in this cultural transmission, which was revealed in the Case Study 1 focusing on the early spread of the Isiac cults across the islands of the Hellenistic Aegean Sea, was a trend that can be observed in different regions of the ancient Mediterranean.

The results of this study revealed that factors related to mobility and logistics, such as a traveling distance from the nearest port and from Alexandria together with the spatial dissemination of the Ptolemaic possessions and influence, were with high probability beneficial for the successful spread of the Isiac cults on the west coast of Hellenistic Asia Minor. Furthermore, based on the spatial visual analysis, the Case Study 2 reveals the possibility that the activities of the Seleucid empire, a political rival of the Ptolemaic empire, in the region constituted an immunological factor limiting the spread of the Isiac cults further to the eastern inland parts of Asia Minor. Since both Case study 1 and 2 delivered results suggesting the positive role of the Ptolemaic political activities in the spread of the Isiac cults, it is indeed possible to categorize this relationship as a trend in at least two different regions of the ancient Mediterranean. The next step in this book is to interpret these separate results from these case studies together in the context of Ptolemaic political activities in the Mediterranean. The results point to a common factor beneficial for the spread of the Isiac cults in two different regions; it is thus relevant to explore how the Ptolemaic political apparatus as a whole could have provided conditions supporting the cultural transmission.

The results of Case Study 2 demonstrate that the hypotheses on the factors of the spread of the Isiac cults produced by the previous academic debate are too vague in their conceptualization of this dynamic historical process of cultural transmission. Although these hypotheses identify Ptolemaic political activities as possibly relevant in the spread of the Isiac cults and sometimes even speak of combination of factors (e.g., Bricault's view), they are, mainly methodologically, unable to define and unfold the relationships and interplay between the factors of potential influence and the spatial-temporal distribution of these cults. The research presented here thus represents a new way toward the construction of more precise and nuanced hypotheses in the debate.

This study also brings more detail to our understanding of the spread of Hellenistic religions in general. As was demonstrated in both case studies, the political forces of the ancient Mediterranean had significant potential to facilitate cultural transmission, intentionally or not, by having an impact on one of the crucial "epidemiological" conditions, that is, increase in the mobility of people from specific social-cultural milieu outward. In this respect, the argument that the ancient Mediterranean armies played an important role in the cultural transmission due to their mobility and spatial dispersion, which is often illustrated by the evidence from the era of the Roman empire (e.g., Collar 2013; Glomb 2021; Bowden 2010; Van der Ploeg 2018), now finds its support also in the context of the Ptolemaic empire.

Both case studies can also be conceptualized as a methodological contribution to the study of ancient Mediterranean cultures. Results from both case studies demonstrate that the methods of formalized modeling are applicable to different variables and different spatial settings and are a relevant supplement to the methodological portfolio of historiography and therefore represent a very promising path toward the interdisciplinary science of history. It is important to note that this book and its aim to promote the idea of interdisciplinary science of history are built upon specific theoretical developments mainly in historiography and archaeology. Together with the interpretation of the results, the next chapter also explains which theoretical and methodological approaches allowed for synergic combination resulting in the research presented in the Case Study 1 and 2.

6

Political Activities of the Ptolemaic Dynasty and Their Impact on the Spread of the Isiac Cults Abroad: A Historical Pattern

As this is the concluding core chapter that is discussing the theoretical perspectives of this book and interprets the results of the presented research, it is relevant to provide a brief overview of the narrative so far presented in the book.

The early spread of the Isiac cults outside Egypt mainly in the third and second centuries BCE is a fascinating and complicated topic. While the significant amounts of archaeological and literary data provide the answer for the question of where the cults spread, the question of how they spread to those locations is the subject of a very lengthy academic debate. At first, the cults were disseminated on the Aegean Islands and port cities in the ancient Mediterranean. It is thus not controversial to identify the maritime connectivity as one of the factors impacting the spread of these cults. That is not the case for the other potential factors in play. Maritime trade and political activities of the Ptolemaic dynasty were both discussed in the academic debate as potential factors benefiting the cultural transmission of the Isiac cults. The debate, however, struggles to find an agreement on the extent, individual strength, and the degree of mutual interactions of these factors in the process of the spread. The number of variables involved in the spread of the Isiac cults and their mutual interaction increases the complexity of the research problem to a level where it also becomes a mathematical problem. For this reason, the book presents a computational approach that works in synergy with the established methodology of historiography and has the potential to disentangle the problem using the combined strength of both approaches. The spatial analyses and mathematical model applied to the region of the Hellenistic Aegean Sea and western Asia Minor in the two case studies evaluated these factors of potential impact and confirmed their role and interaction in the cultural transmission.

In both case studies, the Ptolemaic presence abroad was identified as the most influential factor in the spread of these cults.

6.1. Theoretical Approaches

6.1.1 Long-Term History

This section introduces the theoretical approaches applied here to the topic of the early spread of the Isiac cults in the ancient Mediterranean. First, it is important to explain how the specific topic is defined in the context of historical "time" and "structure." This will help to translate the approach to the study of history in this book and clarify the aspects of the selected historical phenomenon, which were subjected to analysis. The book conceptualizes the spread of the Isiac cults during the Hellenistic period as a process in which people, carrying specific religious ideas, practices, and artifacts, transmitted them successfully to a new spatio-populational milieu. The dissemination of the archaeological evidence connected to the Isiac cults in the Mediterranean is seen as material evidence of this process. The mobility of people during the Hellenistic period is thus a crucial aspect for this book. The increased mobility of people within the Mediterranean region was a common phenomenon during the Hellenistic period (Prag and Quinn 2013: 47–9). On the other hand, the possibility of travel was significantly restrained by geographical, demographic, economic, and political factors. Geographically, the Mediterranean region is very diverse. People traveling long distances had to avoid wide mountain ranges and often chose to sail across the sea. However, the geographical conditions of the Mediterranean were more or less stable in the course of time, and people could predictably use safe roads and maritime routes with favorable winds or currents. The same cannot be said about the political situation, which is always less predictable and more unstable. After the death of Alexander the Great, the vestiges of his empire were carved up and appropriated by his former generals who then engaged in a number of political clashes and wars. The economic and social levels then reflected these power struggles accordingly. The spread of the Isiac cults outside Egypt can thus be further rephrased as a complex spatio-temporal process involving different, but mutually related, variables.

Such a definition reflects a specific approach to the study of history introduced mainly by the scholars belonging to the Annales school formed in France in 1929 (Burke 2015; Iggers 2012: 51–64). The definition of the spread of the Isiac cults as a complex process is in this aspect inspired especially by the leading scholar of the second generation of the Annales school, Fernand Braudel, who opposed the perception of history as a set of events in chronological order by the elaborate claim that the structure of history is shaped by long-term and diverse processes (Braudel 1995; Wallerstein 2000: 160–9). Braudel poetically wrote that events are "surface disturbances, crests of foam that the tides of history carry on their strong backs" (Braudel 1995: 21). His ultimate goal was to reinstate "la longue durée" (stress on historical duration) as a key epistemological tool for social sciences and to diminish the influence of what Paul Lacombe and Francois Simiand called "l'histoire événementielle" (history of events; Braudel 1995: 21).

In his probably most important book, *The Mediterranean and the Mediterranean World in the Age of Philip II*, Braudel divided historical time, with the emphasis on the "longue durée," into three spheres based on its relationship to groups and individuals (Braudel 1995; Burke 2015: 36–72). In the first sphere, the passage of time in the human interaction with the Mediterranean as a geographical space is, according to Braudel, almost imperceptible. This is history where the change is slow and often repeated in cycles. By distinguishing this sphere or aspect of historical time, Braudel aimed to show that geographical features are part of the history and historical events cannot be fully understood if these features are not taken into consideration. This book takes this assumption seriously because the mobility of people in the ancient Mediterranean crucially depended on the structure of continental and maritime routes shaped by terrain, seasonality, currents, winds, and other geographical, environmental, and meteorological factors. The second sphere of historical time, in Braudel's thinking, is closely connected with social structures of a different scale—economic systems, state societies, or civilizations. Here, the flow of time is perceptible but still very slow when compared to occurring historical events. The changes are happening over the course of generations and centuries, and individuals are only rarely aware of their occurrence. Again, this perception of specific historical time is of importance for this book as was repeatedly demonstrated by taking political and economic activities of Mediterranean states into account. The third historical time is fast and easily perceptible by individuals. This is the theater of historical events, which could be, according to Braudel, interpreted wrongly, if not considered in the context of the previous two historical times. In this book, events such as wars, building of temples, or diplomatic missions are perceived not as independent actions but as parts and results of complex demographic, geographical, political, economic, and cultural processes.

6.1.2 Cliodynamics

The Annales's approach to the study of history continues to have a significant impact on researchers even in the twenty-first century and inspired the formation of cliodynamics—a new transdisciplinary area drawing inspiration from historical macrosociology, economic history, mathematical modeling of long-term social processes, and cultural evolution (Turchin 2008, 2011, 2018). The founder of the term "cliodynamics," Peter Turchin, aims to challenge the Popperian view that there is and will be a qualitative gap between history and natural sciences and proposes the notion of analytical and predictive history, or in general, the science of history (Turchin 2011). There are two main angles that form the weight of Turchin's arguments on why the science of history is a plausible option of scientific endeavor: (a) conceptual possibilities and (b) possibilities opened by technological advances.

With respect to the conceptual possibilities, Turchin identifies scientific prediction as one of the important bridges between history and natural sciences. To define scientific prediction, Turchin explains the category in contrast to forecast and projection (Turchin 2011, 2006). Whereas forecast is a type of prediction where the validity of the underlying theory is accepted and aims to predict what will happen to the observables and a projection examines scenarios based on hypothetical initial conditions and mechanisms, the scientific prediction is, according to Turchin, used to test the validity of scientific theories by working with the observables. In other words, the logic of the scientific prediction is not targeted at "prophesying"; rather it aims to bring "understanding" of the studied phenomena. Although Turchin is an advocate of scientific prediction and claims that it is "the hallmark of a mature science" (Turchin 2006: 2) and that "making forecasts is a useless activity given the current state of development of historical sociology" (Turchin 2006: 2), he is not always able to avoid forecasting, especially when analyzing the topic of current political instability (Turchin 2010).

Another conceptual possibility for Turchin allowing the existence of the science of history is the implementation of mathematical modeling (Turchin 2011, 2008, 2018: 1–7). The first objection toward this idea from the standpoint of a historian might be that historical processes are too complex to be subjected to quantification by mathematical tools. However, Turchin argues that the complexity of history is precisely the reason why mathematical models need to be introduced in the discipline. He claims that it is simply too difficult for the human brain to follow and evaluate interactions among so many variables involved in the historical dynamics (Turchin 2011: 172). The implementation of this mathematical approach in historiography should meet, according to Turchin, the following criteria. The verbal theories should be translated into mathematical models and tested on the empirical material because formalized theories allow for the construction of quantitative testable predictions and thus increase the potential for their falsifiability, transparency, and replicability (Turchin 2011, 2006).

With respect to the possibilities for the science of history opened by technological advances, Turchin focuses particularly on the development of complexity science and nonlinear dynamics (Turchin 2011: 168–72). He points to the fact that we now have adequate tools for analyzing how micro-level interactions lead to the macro-level patterns in history. Specifically, he means stochastic and deterministic mathematical models (or their combination) (Turchin 2011: 182, 2018: 6, 14). A deterministic mathematical model renders always the same result if the initial conditions of the model remain constant. In other words, it is sufficient to run such a model just once for each set of initial conditions, and there are no parameters of probability or any randomness involved (Edwards and Hamson 2001: 69–82). A good example of a deterministic mathematical model is the "find the shortest-path feature" in a GPS navigation system of a car. Based on the current level of traffic, road closures, and, for example, the preference to not use toll roads, the software always shows you the same path as long as these initial parameters do not change. However, if any of the initial conditions changes, for example, if the hypothetical driver chooses to use toll roads, the result might be different. Stochastic models, on the other hand, involve a certain level of randomness and thus can yield different results even if the initial conditions remain the same. While the computing process of a deterministic model is determined by a given set of values, in a stochastic model, the process is impacted by probability distributions (Edwards and Hamson 2001: 69–82). A Susceptible, Infected, and Recovered/or alternatively Removed (SIR) epidemiological agent-based model for analyzing the spread of a disease can serve here as a demonstrative example of a stochastic model (Satsuma et al. 2004). SIR models most commonly involve a defined virtual environment with individuals (agents) who have pre-programmed behavior (e.g., walking randomly in the environment) and initial attributes (e.g., susceptible, infected). The initial conditions of such a model can be as follows: (1) if an infected agent meets a susceptible agent, there is a 30 percent chance that the susceptible agent becomes infected; (2) an infected agent becomes recovered after 50-time units of the model (representing, e.g., a certain amount of days); (3) recovered agents are not susceptible; and (4) initial number of agents in the environment is

1,000. These four conditions can remain unchanged, but, because they involve a certain degree of unpredictability in where, when, and how an agent will interact with another agent, the result, that is, a spread of a disease through the virtual population, will differ in each run of the model. The strength of the stochastic models lies in uncovering patterns and trends despite the randomness involved in historical or real-life scenarios. In the case studies presented in this book, a deterministic model was applied to calculate the intensity of traffic near the cities/islands by counting how many agents, in this case ships, visited certain city/island on their fastest possible path elsewhere.

Another benefit of technological advances for the science of history is, as Turchin claims, the pool of data for testing (Turchin 2011: 182). Indeed, there has been a significant increase in the amount of available datasets suitable for historical analysis. In the twentieth century and before, historians relied mainly on physical archives, corpuses, and atlases. However, now, an increasing portion of these mediums and the data within them are being transformed into a digital form with open access for researchers and are in a suitable format for further exploration and modeling.

Turchin describes the focus of his cliodynamics as follows: "Empires rise and fall, populations and economies boom and bust, world religions spread or wither. ... What are the mechanisms underlying such dynamical processes in history?" (Turchin n.d.). In other words, cliodynamics perceives historical events as products of complex historical processes, and by understanding the mechanisms of these processes, researchers can identify general patterns in history. It is now time to explain how the research presented in his book relates to Turchin's ideas of cliodynamics and the science of history.

The overarching goal of this book is to promote the aforementioned notion of interdisciplinary science of history. The presented research is also an attempt to demonstrate that the benefits of implementing the theoretical and methodological approaches of natural sciences into historiography vastly outweigh the pitfalls. One of the theoretical inspirations from cliodynamics that is present in this book is the conceptualization of the spread of the Isiac cults as a complex historical process from the perspective of complexity science (or complexity theory) (Downey 2018; Brughmans et al. 2019). Complexity science aims to overcome the discrepancy between "irreducible" phenomena such as religious traditions and their methodological reduction to individual parts with unclear ties to the whole. From this perspective, the worship of the Isiac deities can be defined as a complex system consisting of mutually interacting and depending parts culminating in a higher order of emergence. The study of such systems is, in terms of the complexity science, then oriented not only on objects and structures of the phenomena in question but also on analyzing the relationships and processes that form them. In this respect, the research presented here explores how the relationships between political, economic, and geographical (or logistical) aspects of the ancient Mediterranean shaped the spatial level of the worship of the Isiac cults. That the integration of complexity science into historiography and archaeology is already under way can be demonstrated, for example, in "Formal Modelling Approaches to Complexity Science in Roman Studies: A Manifesto" (Brughmans et al. 2019).

The orientation on scientific prediction stressed by Turchin is also resonating within this book. More specifically, both case studies focused on which of the selected factors on political, economic, and geographical/logistical level predicted the historical outcome of the early spread of the Isiac cults outside Egypt and what was their individual impact on the spreading process. The logic of this retrospective prediction is different from prospective predictions in its focus on the process and not the outcome. While epidemiologists analyzing the spread of modern infectious diseases are attempting to predict locations of a possible outbreak and spread based on the known mechanisms of human traveling, here, if we stay in the epidemiological metaphor, the final outcome of the spatial spread of the Isiac cults is known, but the specific process behind the process was unclear. Using the tool of scientific prediction was in this case possible by meeting the requirement of expressing the research problem in formal/quantifiable terms and solving it through a mathematical model. In this respect the spread of the Isiac cults is represented as a set of geocoded locations of archaeological evidence related to these cults. Similarly, the political, economic, and geographical proxies are represented as attributes of geocoded locations (i.e., cities, ports, or islands). The ties between the religious proxies and the political, economic, and geographical ones are then determined by traveling distances or durations between them. This way, the hypotheses on the factors of the early spread of the Isiac cults produced by the established methodological apparatus of historiography were reformulated into predictions testable by mathematical modeling, thus reaching the important benefits common in natural sciences such as the trio of falsifiability, transparency, and replicability.

The implementation of formalized modeling into historiography, however, needs to be considered in a very careful manner because the realm of history has its very significant specifics when compared to the typical subjects of natural sciences' focus such as animal biology or geophysics. One of the most problematic pitfalls related to formalized modeling of history is the limited quality and availability of the data. Historians unfortunately do not have the opportunity to collect data about their subjects in real time and have them proportionately organized based on geographical, social, economic, or other attributes in representative numbers. What historians have in their disposal is a fraction of lived historical reality preserved on objects and structures that somehow resisted the ravages of time. With respect to the problem of data availability, we can differentiate between two main sources of frustration for historians: (a) The subject of research is not well represented in the archaeological or literary evidence since the beginning. A very good example here can be early Christianity, that is, a religious tradition that is archaeologically almost invisible in the first century CE because of the lack of distinguishable iconographic features in its formative phase (Fousek et al. 2018); (b) The subject of research is not representatively captured in material evidence because of the issues related to archaeological excavations such as different agenda to conduct excavations of countries, limited accessibility due to terrain (jungles, ocean bottom, etc.), or destruction of the material because of unexpected events such as war, fire, floods, and so forth. These factors obstruct the unproblematic use of formalized modeling mainly because the outcome of a model could be significantly misleading with this inconsistent data input. However, even if we have available data in representative numbers, the differing quality of the data needs to be addressed before their quantitative evaluation. Mostly, the historical data are of a good quality if they are certain and indisputable indicators of the studied subject. However, more than often, this is not the case in historical research. The Case Study 1 on the spread of the Isiac cults across the Aegean Sea can be used as an example here for dealing with spatial uncertainty. Based on the literary and archaeological evidence, it was not possible to determine which Aegean Islands imported Egyptian grain. A model was introduced to reveal the potential vulnerability to famines of certain islands; these were then recognized as more likely candidates for importing grain from Egypt. Despite overcoming the absence of primary archaeological or literary data, the results of this sub-model are in the realm of "probable" and not "certain" as the inputs of the models are uncertain themselves (e.g., population estimates). It is very important to stress this when presenting such results. There are several options of how to incorporate this awareness into models and their results, but each one should work with clear documenting of the mechanisms of the model to fulfil the requirement of transparency and replicability (Plewe 2002; Shi 2009). If the data are classified properly based on their certainty, for example, as an attribute with a simple rule of 4 degrees where 1 is certain, 2 probable, 3 possible, and 4 unknown, it is possible to model either probable scenarios by including only the most accurate data or more hypothetical scenarios or projections using the uncertain data while maintaining the aforementioned qualities of transparency and replicability. In the Asia Minor case study, only the places with evidence of being in the zone of Ptolemaic influence were incorporated in the model as the focus of the study was on exploring the most probable spatial spread of the Isiac cults. Beside spatial uncertainty of available data, historians have to also deal with temporal uncertainty, mostly related to problematic dating of archaeological or literary evidence. *Terminus ante quem* and *post quem* is a helpful tool for modeling temporal uncertainties because they allow to set clear limits on a timeline, but, even when accounted for, the temporal uncertainties are one of the most painful hindrances in modeling history quantitatively. The archaeological evidence of the Isiac cults is also dated broadly (i.e., in the range of decades or even a century). However, the temporal scale of the accompanying factors was either adequately broad (e.g., long-term political processes) or the factors were not constrained by any relevant timeline (e.g., geographical factors), thus the *post* and *ante quem* dates of origin of the archeological data were sufficient to model, and the outcome can be considered representative.

The research presented in this book applies formalized modeling as a supplementary methodology to the established methods of historiography and by no means as a tool that should supersede the traditional approach of historians. The formalized modeling in historiography has the potential to reveal patterns and trends in data, as is the case here, which could have remained undetected by the eyes of a historian because of the inherent complexity of historical processes. On the other hand, it is not possible to work on the input, construction, and output of such models without expertise in the studied historical problem. Thus, a careful collaboration and learning the language of the collaborating sides in the interdisciplinary research might be a way forward. To sum up the section on cliodynamics and theorizing about the use of formalized modeling in historiography leading ideally to interdisciplinary science of history, I would like to paraphrase statistician George Box who delivers the lesson on this topic very clearly by claiming in his works that all models are wrong but some of them are useful for learning about the world (Box 1976: 792; Box and Luceño 1997: 6). In other words, the idea embroidered in the rhetoric of George Box, cliodynamics, and this book is that the immediate interest of modeling should not be the complex systems themselves but the problems inside them.

6.1.3 Network Theory

A suitable conceptual and methodological framework for following the aforementioned goal of formalizing historiographical research can be found in network theory (Lewis 2009). Recently, the number of researchers assessing the topic of religious change during the Graeco-Roman era from the perspective of network theory has increased significantly (Malkin 2011; Malkin, Constantakopoulou, and Panagopoulou 2013; Collar 2013; Woolf 2016; Eidinow 2011; Fousek et al. 2018; Brughmans, Collar, and Coward 2016a; Seland 2013; Mazzilli 2018). One explanation could be that the network thinking, for example, thinking in terms of relationships between various phenomena, allows these researchers to observe patterns between historical data that previously often remained unnoticed. However, as Carl Knappett explains in his *An Archaeology of Interaction: Network Perspectives on Material Culture and Society* (2011), there is a difference between network thinking and network analysis, where the network thinking is rather a strategy of conceptualizing the problem as described above, while the network analysis involves the specific definitions of the nodes and ties (edges) of the conceptualized network and leads ideally to quantitative analysis (Knappett 2011: 7–9). In this section, the focus will be on both network thinking and network analysis, how they are mutually intertwined, how has been the research in historiography of the ancient Mediterranean progressing from more conceptual uses of network approaches to more technical ones, and finally, how this book follows up on these developments and, more specifically, how exactly the network theory helped to solve the research questions in the topic of the spread of the Isiac cults.

The key aspect of network thinking in historiography is, as was hinted a few sentences earlier, that the subjects of interest are no longer studied as separate units enclosed in their own microcosmos, but instead they are explored in the context of their relationships with other entities. The benefit of such an approach lies in its ability to reveal how the particular object of interest is influenced by these relationships and vice versa how the specific embeddedness of one entity in the studied environment forms the relationships and impacts the other entities. However, to deliver the intended message about the usefulness of the network theory in historiography correctly, it needs to be pointed out that the network theory is a perspective with specific use and should not be conceptualized as a general theoretical framework for each research problem in historiography, which is fittingly explained by Tom Brughmans, Anna Collar, and Fiona Coward in the book *The Connected Past*: "If almost every past phenomenon can be described using loosely defined 'network' concepts we end up seeing networks everywhere, but they will rarely lead to critical insights since it is not clear what advantages they offer over other approaches" (Brughmans, Collar, and Coward 2016b: 9).

An illustrative example of the benefits and pitfalls of network thinking in the historiography of the ancient Mediterranean is the pioneering work of Irad Malkin, *A Small Greek World* (2011). In his book, Malkin employs the concepts of network science to explain the emergence and inner workings of the Greek civilization in the Archaic period. More specifically, he draws inspiration from Mark Granovetter's theory of "strength of weak ties" (Granovetter 1973) but mainly focuses on the mathematical concept of "small world" from Steven Strogatz and Duncan Watts (1998). A small world network has two typical properties: (1) it often contains sub-networks with a high clustering coefficient, that is, a large portion of nodes is only connected to their neighbors within their "local" cluster; and (2) the average shortest-path length between the nodes is small, that is, even a small number of long-distance edges among the nodes are ensuring high connectivity for the entire network. Using these concepts, Malkin argues that the decentralized Greek communities interconnected over long distances were the foundation for the emerging Greek civilization:

> There is no doubt that by the end of the sixth century BCE, we find well-established networks of city-states active in reciprocal exchanges of trade, religion, language, art, literature, and philosophy. They usually followed similar options for social and political organization, a Greek way of doing things, and shared a common orientation toward Panhellenic sanctuaries. The result was a civilization that was undeniably Greek. (Malkin 2011: 24)

Although Malkin provides a theoretical framework for his small Greek world hypothesis and uses the concepts from network science, his model for the emergence of the Greek civilization is still based on qualitative and by no means quantitative approach. While Malkin's contribution deserves praise for being a solid part of the bridge between network theory and historiography of the ancient Mediterranean, the lack of formalization in his argument reduces the chances for its further validability. For example, by remaining in the realm of a relevant network metaphor, Malkin's hypothesis has only limited possibilities of falsifying other network models proposed for the Greek civilization (Horden and Purcell 2000; Morel 1997; Braudel 1995; Mack 2015). However, it needs to be added that Malkin himself is aware of this lack of formalization as he admits that his "network" idea of a small Greek world is a suggestion or an interpretation but with a "high probability of being right" (Malkin 2011: 207).

By providing another example, this time Ester Eidinow's article "Networks and Narratives: A Model for Ancient Greek Religion" (also published in 2011), we can better connect the dots and reveal the key benefit of network thinking for the historiography of the ancient Mediterranean. In her article, Eidinow uses the network theory to tackle the problematic notion of discrepancy between magical practices and *polis* religion imposed by many scholars on the category of ancient Greek religion (Eidinow 2011). By examining two case studies, one focused on creation and use of binding spells (individual activity) and the second on the cultic practices in the worship of Dionysus (group activity), Eidinow explains how the idea of *polis* religion as a separate category standing outside magical practices is unable to encompass nuanced relationships among groups and individuals in Greek communities. She demonstrates that the ties between groups and individuals in Greek communities went frequently beyond the *polis* with respect to both geography and citizenship and points out that the *polis* as a political body probably did not always attempt to take control over each ritual activity but that the relationships toward such practices could have taken the form of ratification, tolerance, or simply ignorance. Both Malkin's and Eidinow's works demonstrate that former models for either Greek civilization or religion were too static and inflexible for grasping dynamic and nuanced processes within these categories, and both scholars showed that the network perspective can overcome these conceptual difficulties by allowing more fluid constructions. Even though Malkin and Eidinow use networks on the level of informalized metaphor, they are still able to conceptually benefit from the close relationship between network theory and complexity science, and Greek civilization and religion undoubtedly can be classified as complex systems (or parts of another complex system).

We can now move on from network thinking to the point where this strategy transforms into formal analysis. This stage of transition in the historiography of the ancient Mediterranean is represented by a very influential work of Anna Collar, *Religious Networks in the Roman Empire: The Spread of New Ideas* (2013). Collar focuses on applying network analysis to understand the diffusion of ancient Mediterranean traditions such as the cult of Jupiter Dolichenus, the cult of Theos Hypsistos, and the Jewish Diaspora. In her work, Collar attempts to identify clusters of communities belonging to these respective traditions and explore their spatial relationships and possible communication routes using proximal point analysis (PPA). PPA is a specific method from the portfolio of network science, which creates a network by connecting each node to the *k* of nearest neighbors, usually to three nearest ones (Evans 2018: 28). In Collar's case, this tool enabled her to reveal cluster patterns in the spatial distribution of epigraphic and archaeological evidence related to the selected traditions. Collar's approach is very innovative in the historiography of ancient Mediterranean religions because it makes the crucial step from network thinking to a more formal approach. However, despite the emphasis on the network analysis in Collar's book, the arguments presented there are mainly developed in synergy with established historiographical tools. There are indications suggesting that Collar's book is representing one of the starting points in the "formalizing" direction with much of the potential of this method being developed in later studies. The edges (i.e., potential communication routes) of Collar's religious PPA networks are created based on geographical proximity between the nodes. The problem is that this approach implicitly conceptualizes the Mediterranean as a homogenous terrain, but in reality, that is not the case. Variability in terrain (e.g., mountains, sea, rivers) constrains human mobility to a significant degree; it influences the trajectories of routes and modes of transport with different speeds of travel (i.e., walking/sailing). This means that the clusters of nodes in Collar's networks can be, in some cases, only seemingly close to each other, but with respect to "traveling approachability," there is a probability that these networks would look different. Nevertheless, Collar's work is of huge importance as it opens the door for a specific innovative way of thinking and, most importantly, analyzing in the study of ancient Mediterranean religions.

Recently, the use of formal network analysis in the historiography of the ancient Mediterranean has become more frequent among scholars, and generally, the idea of interdisciplinary science of history is now even more visible and resonating within the academic debate (Brughmans 2010, 2013; Brughmans and Poblome 2016; Brughmans, Collar, and Coward 2016a; Leidwanger and Knappett 2018; Teigen and Seland 2017). This is attested, for example, by already mentioned "Formal Modelling Approaches to Complexity Science in Roman Studies: A Manifesto" produced in 2019 by sixteen international researchers who declare that the study of complex systems is integral to Roman studies (Brughmans et al. 2019), or by "A Manifesto for the Study of Ancient Mediterranean Maritime Networks" (n.d.) posted on the website of *Antiquity* journal in 2014, encouraging the application of network modeling in the study of seaborn connections in antiquity signed by fifteen scholars from related fields. This trend is also visible in the study of the ancient Mediterranean religions where there are appearing new original research articles utilizing network science to disentangle social, spatial, or semantic relationships tied to specific traditions (Fousek et al. 2018; Glomb et al. 2018, 2020; Da Vela 2019; Czachesz 2016; Glomb 2021; Collar 2013). The main reasons for this increasing use of formal network approach go hand in hand with what was already stated in the section on cliodynamics, that is, the subject of interest is formed or impacted by factors, interactions, and relationships that are too complex to be dealt with using established historiographical methods, and researchers now have increasing amount of available data and technologies at their disposal.

The case studies focusing on the early spread of the Isiac cults outside Egypt presented in this book are a part of this particular stage in the historiography of the ancient Mediterranean where the core of the research arguments is to a significant degree formed by the interpretation of the outcomes of formal analyses. Both case studies attempt to combine network thinking and analysis in a synergic manner where the network thinking is a relevant tool for conceptualizing the research problem in network terms, which is a crucial step toward subsequent formalizations of the problem. Using network thinking, the spread of the Isiac cults is in both case studies conceptualized as a process tied to the human mobility on a network. The nodes represent Hellenistic cities and ports, and the links represent roads or maritime routes, thus forming the formalized environment for modeling the cultural transmission of a specific cultic practice from one socio-spatial milieu to another. Another related task was to divide the formulation of the research problem into three categories—(1) the observed phenomenon, (2) selected factors of influence, and (3) relationships between them—and find out how to define them in a way that allows for their formal analysis in the constructed network environment. Both the observed phenomenon (spatial distribution of the Isiac cults) and the selected factors of influence (e.g., politics, economy, geography, connectivity) were represented as geocoded points in the areas of interest based on their proxies (e.g., archaeological evidence, centrality measurements).

The definition of the quality of the relationships among the data was a crucial task because revealing hidden patterns in these relationships was the intended goal of the research. The rationale behind the definition was the hypothesis that if we frequently find proxies for the factors of potential influence in "traveling" proximity to the archaeological evidence of the Isiac cults, then there is a probability that these factors could have contributed to such spatial distribution of these cults. The quality of these relationships among the data with respect to traveling proximity can be represented in varying measures. They can be, for example, defined by the number of kilometers separating each node (Hellenistic city) from the nearest geocoded proxy for the Isiac cults and from the nearest proxy for the factor of influence on the transportation network, or the distance can be replaced by the duration of the fastest possible trip from node to node if there are data for it. The transportation network in the Case Study 1 on the spread of the Isiac cults across the Hellenistic Aegean Sea consisted of only maritime routes (i.e., with only one mode of transport available—sailing); therefore, the geographical distances (in km) as the units for quality of the relationships among the data were adequate. In the Case Study 2 with the western coast of Hellenistic Asia Minor as the area of interest, the transportation network consisted of both maritime and land traveling options; therefore, the duration of the fastest possible trips among the nodes was used as a suitable measure of quality of the relationships among the data because it can take different speeds of travel into account.

This degree of formalization was considered as adequate for tackling the research problems. Certainly, there is a number of other factors that could have been included on top in the analysis such as population density of the cities, sizes of ancient harbors that could further differentiate their attractivity for Egyptian ships, or transform the entire network model into an agent-based model with dynamic features such as different seasonal parameters for transport, quality of harvest on the Aegean Islands and Egypt, and so forth. However, as was described in the section on complex systems, all models are wrong, but some of them might be useful (Box 1976; Box and Luceño 1997), especially when they model the problem and not the entire system. Model is always a reduction of reality; otherwise it would not be a model. And a useful model picks only those aspects of reality that are relevant for thinking about and solving the problem in question. The more features of reality, or in this case history, the model tries to emulate, the greater is the risk that the model becomes indecipherable. In other words, when a model tries to encompass a big number of inputs, it is very difficult for the researcher to interpret whether the outcome is valid or whether some unaccounted feature or unaccounted interaction among multiple features with disbalanced weights produced that specific result. This is the rationale that stands behind the conceptualization and formalization of the research problems in the presented case studies on the spread of the Isiac cults. But because there might always be a discussion on the adequacy of this particular reduction of reality in the presented models, the attributes of transparency and further falsifiability are incorporated by sharing the data under open access license in their original publications.

To bring some clarity on particular types of network analysis, the last paragraph of this section is dedicated to the question of why the method used in the presented case studies on the spread of the Isiac cults is rather spatial network analysis than social network analysis (SNA; Scott and Carrington 2014). Despite the fact that these studies focus on a social phenomenon (worship of the Isiac deities), the archaeological and other proxies for this phenomenon and for factors influencing it are embedded in geographical space, and the structured geographical space in the form of the transportation network is then defining the relationships between the proxies (see for more Barthélemy 2011). In other words, it is often the case when analyzing the social phenomena of the past that the spatial distribution of specific sites and their attributes are the only available sources for operationalization. Therefore, the SNA in the narrow sense where nodes represent human individuals (or groups) and the edges represent the relationships arising from their social interactions; thus, creating networks embedded in social space is not applicable in this case. It is important that it was mentioned here how the social and physical (or geographical) space and their relationship are articulated in here as there is an ongoing debate in archaeology on the topic of appropriate synthesis between SNA and developments in geospatial modeling and also how the nonhuman agency (i.e., material objects with a role in the network) can be incorporated in SNA (Woolf 2016: 46; Evans 2018: 23; Knappett 2016). These topics are very relevant for historiographers of ancient Mediterranean studying religious traditions because they are often focusing on heterogeneous sociomaterial networks structured by the geographical space, that is, "hybrid" networks beyond the original scope of both SNA and strictly physical geographical analysis.

6.2 Interpretation of the Results

The rationale behind the case studies presented here was to explore and test the ideas, hypotheses, and theories already existing in the academic discussion on the early spread of the Isiac cults and to bring new arguments to the debate by using methods and theoretical perspectives that have the potential to push the limits of what we can determine from the material and literary evidence.

In this regard, the Case Study 1 focusing on the spatial dissemination of the Isiac cults in the Aegean Sea followed Bricault's notion that the spread of these cults was jointly facilitated by several factors (Bricault 2004). Using the theoretical concepts described above, the case study was, among other things, a methodological experiment. On the one hand, it was necessary to quantify the explained variable, that is, the spread of the Isiac cults, to give a mathematically operable structure to the environment where the explained variable was modeled and, finally, to identify the potential factors of influence and quantify and operationalize these as well. On the other hand, as was discussed earlier, one of the main principles of mathematical modeling is to model the problem, not the system. In order to be successful, the experiment needed to have a balance, that is, it had to capture several levels of historical reality in quantitative form to explore the research problem, but at the same time, the model of the portion of the historical reality had to be reductive and simple enough to remain transparent, clearly interpretable, and validatable. Therefore, the model was limited to work with two factors (economic, political) in the context of a third factor (connectivity).

Another experimental layer of the model was the sub-model for determination of potential food shortages for individual islands in the Aegean Sea. This methodological experiment was supposed to offer an innovative way of determining a specific quality in the situation where the primary data for estimating the endangered islands in need of grain import are lacking. The weak spot, with respect to historical certainty, of the sub-model is that the estimated quality, that is, vulnerability to famine, is determined by another estimate; in this case, the ability of an island to support agriculturally its own population is partially established based on the estimated size of the population from a different era. This introduces a portion of historical uncertainty to the analysis and could easily lead to completely virtual exercise divorced from the historical reality. However, if the outcome of the sub-model is incorporated in the whole model in a way that accounts for the estimated nature of the quality, the model can still offer a very relevant insight. Following this rationale, the outcome of the famine vulnerability sub-model was incorporated in the bigger model as a probable ratio indicating which islands were in greater need of importing grain than others, thus significantly limiting the impact of the uncertainty.

The results of the Aegean Sea case study cannot be read as encompassing and explaining all contributing factors of the early spread of the Isiac cults; rather, it tells us the impact balance or ratio between the most discussed factors (economic and political). Although the political factor, that is, Ptolemaic presence in the Aegean Sea, was evaluated as having more weight in the spread than the economic, that is, the need of islands in the Aegean Sea to import Egyptian grain, the results still reveal this cultural transmission as multifactorial. This is providing support for Bricault's conceptualization of this process rather than earlier polarizing views of Fraser and Cumont that promoted only one of the factors and, at the same time, excluded a potential impact of any other factor.

Overall, the methodological experiment of the first case study was successful mainly in two aspects: (1) it revealed a potential pattern in the data that can be the subject of focus in following research and debate and (2) it demonstrated that methodological synergy between traditional historiographical methods and quantitative approaches is a viable option to tackle research problems and provides analytical platforms reusable in research into other topics.

The Case Study 2 on Asia Minor benefited from both these aspects. It explored one of the outcomes of the model from the Aegean Sea case study—a potential relationship between the Ptolemaic influence and the spread of the Isiac cults—in a different spatial milieu. Methodologically, it was largely based on the steps tested in the previous case study mainly with respect to selection of proxies and defining spatial relationships between these proxies by using a transportation network platform. The narrow focus on the political factor helped to reduce the amount of historical uncertainties as the model for Asia Minor was not relying on any sub-model working with population estimates. The only estimate considering numbers was the different speed for sea and land travel on the transportation network; however, more important than the exact number was to capture ratio between the speed of the two modes of travel. The aim of the Case Study 2 was not only to explore the situation in Asia Minor but also to test whether the significant impact of Ptolemaic political activities revealed in the first case study was a historical trend appearing in different regions of the ancient Mediterranean or only a potential pattern in one of them. In this regard, the case studies presented here are in tandem, and they offer their biggest strengths when read together as one contribution. While the Aegean Sea case study comes with an experiment and a result, the Asia Minor study supports the replicability of the method and validates a specific part of the previous result.

In mathematical language, the outcomes of the models applied in the case studies on the Aegean Sea and Asia Minor are noncoincidental statistically significant relationships between the explained variable and the selected factors. The Ptolemaic activities were evaluated as particularly significant for the spread of the Isiac cults in these two regions during the time of the first Ptolemaic rulers. However, the models are not capable of further interpretation, and they need a historian's expertise both in the input and output phases to keep it connected to the actual historical problem. After informing us that there is a trend in the data, it is necessary to put the trend in the frame of historical reality and explain how it could have taken place in the historical environment. And since the spread of the Isiac cults is ultimately a social phenomenon and the most discussed factor facilitating the spread throughout the book is labeled as Ptolemaic political activity, Ptolemaic presence, or influence, the following section discusses which social levels of the Ptolemaic empire in relation to their recognition by people outside Egypt could have played a positive role in this cultural transmission.

On the top of the state hierarchy were Ptolemaic rulers. As described in the section 2.2, Isis and Sarapis under the Ptolemies, their entanglement with the Isiac cults in Egypt is indisputable. There are many traces attesting this positive relationship in Ptolemaic Egypt such as Ptolemy I Soter promoting the cult of Sarapis or incorporating Isis and Sarapis into royal oaths under Ptolemy III Euergetes to building activities of Ptolemy IV Philopator (Pfeiffer 2008: 395; Stambaugh 1972). This link between the royal couples and the Isiac cults was recognized in the third and second centuries BCE abroad as well (e.g., dedications to both Ptolemaic rulers and the Isiac deities and similar co-occurrences in, e.g., Ephesus, Halicarnassus, Thera). By exercising control over foreign territories and by being recognized as politically dominant actors, the Ptolemaic rulers opened a communication channel with these territories that allowed for the cultural transmission as well because in religious sphere, the Isiac cults were seen as patron deities of the dynasty even without the unattested official promotion of these cults abroad. That the channels worked in different directions (not only outward) can be documented, for example, by an inscription from Egyptian Canopus dedicated by a man from Bargylia, a city on the western coast of Asia Minor (SB I 585, translation Oppen de Ruiter 2015: 66): "Artemidorus, the son of Apollonius, from Bargylia, [set this up] to Sarapis, Isis and Nilus, as well as to King Ptolemy (III) and Queen Berenice (II), the Benefactor Gods."

On general level, we know that the influence of the Ptolemaic rule was recognized in foreign regions based on the local calendars using the regnal years of the Ptolemaic kings (Bagnall 1976: 106, 108, 192). But the Ptolemaic empire had also very specific social instruments for exercising this influence or even direct control abroad, which could have further broadened the channels facilitating the spread of the Isiac cults as a by-product of political activities.

One of these instruments is diplomatic activity of Ptolemaic rulers. That this activity was effective with respect to spreading Ptolemaic influence and thus establishing and maintaining connectivity between Egyptian culture and foreign regions as a side effect can be again documented by recognition from abroad in the form of statues erected in honor of Ptolemaic kings, for example, for Ptolemy III in Olympia, Athens, or Delphi, for Ptolemy IV in Rhodos, Oropos (accompanied by a statue of Arsinoe III), or practicing ruler cults as is attested by the priest of Ptolemy I on Cyprus or temenos dedicated to Ptolemy III and Berenice II in Cretan Itanos (Hölbl 2001: 96, 132–3). Various donations, favorable policies, and impactful deeds can be linked to all the early Ptolemaic kings and are in line with the contemporary perception of *basileus*, that is, a kingship where its bearer is expected to be triumphant not only in mythical sphere, as, for example, pharaoh, but be personally engaged and victorious in their historical endeavors such as wars and diplomatic missions (Hölbl 2001: 90–2). The gift of grain to Rhodos to avert catastrophes in time of Ptolemy I and Ptolemy III falls easily within that category. The diplomatic offensive and success of the Ptolemies is also tangible in the Nicuria decree, which is a response of the Nesiotic League of islanders to Ptolemy II Philadelphus who requested their presence at the festival of *Ptolemaia* at Alexandria. We can find following lines honoring Ptolemy I Soter in their reply (translated by Michel Austin in Austin 2006, No. 256): "He freed the cities and gave them back their laws and re-established their ancestral constitution and lightened their tributary payments" and "in fact they had already honoured Soter as a god."

The political recognition was not, however, tied only with the Ptolemaic rulers. The political capabilities of Ptolemaic officials high in the state hierarchy were significant and further disseminated the Ptolemaic influence abroad. The achievements of Sosibios, the priest of Alexander the Great under Ptolemy III Euergetes and the chief minister of Ptolemy IV Philopator, are worth mentioning here. Sosibios was famous and able to maintain international connections from his youth when he was known throughout Greece, was a victor of several games and honored by Delians and Knidians by statues and decrees (Grainger 2010: 190–1). Around 235 BCE, he was attested as the priest of Alexander under Ptolemy III, later became one of the most powerful people as a minister in the Ptolemaic empire, and was highly skilled in court intrigues and political murders. He orchestrated the murder of several members of Ptolemaic family, for example, Magas, the brother of Ptolemy IV; Berenice II, the mother of Ptolemy IV; and Lysimachus, the brother of Ptolemy III, to remove political opposition challenging the rule of Ptolemy IV Philopator (Hölbl 2001: 127–8). According to Polybius (V.65.9; 82.6; 85.9), Sosibios even took personal command of Egyptian troops of 20,000 soldiers. Among his diplomatic activities under Ptolemy IV was to maintain good diplomatic relations with Greece, and recognition of this effort by the Greeks can be documented by the proxeny decree he was granted by the Greek cities of Tanagra and Orchomenus (Hölbl 2001: 132). The Isiac cults appeared in Orchomenus in the third century BCE (RICIS 105/0701) but in Tanagra only later in the beginning of the first century BCE (RICIS 105/0201). Polybius informs us that together with another minister of Ptolemy IV, Agathocles, Sosibios was sending recruiters (*xenologoi*) outside Egypt, and later

Agathocles sent the Ptolemaic general Scopas of Aetolia to Greece for recruiting soldiers (V.63.8–9). According to Christelle Fisher-Bovet, this implies that these Ptolemaic officials utilized for these activities their social connections with politically influential people in the regions abroad (Fischer-Bovet 2014: 169).

Instrumental for gaining and maintaining Ptolemaic footholds outside Egypt in the time of Ptolemaic expansion in the first half of the third century BCE, mainly in the Aegean Sea and western Asia Minor, was Philocles, king of Sidon, serving under Ptolemy I and II (Hauben 1987b, 2004); Ptolemaic *strategos* (general, but in this case rather supreme commander) Patroclus of Macedon; and *nauarchos* (admiral) Callicrates of Samos serving under Ptolemy II (Hauben 2013). Philocles, a Phoenician who assumed the title king of Sidon, became a Ptolemaic general (*strategos*) with significant authority and power. Between ca. 310 and 280s/270s BCE, he played a major part in realizing Ptolemy I's and II's plans for expansion and organized the Ptolemaic rule over the Aegean and Asia Minor (Hauben 1987b, 2004; Hölbl 2001: 23, 38). Patroclus and Callicrates were both tied closely to the ruling couple as priests of Alexander and the *Theoi Adelphoi* (the deified royal couple of Ptolemy II and Arsinoe II). While Patroclus, as was already discussed in section 4.2, was profiled as a military leader with significant accomplishments with respect to garrisoning crucial islands in the Aegean Sea, Callicrates is more known for his successes in cultural and political spheres. One of his main acts in connection to religion is the establishment of the cult of Arsinoe-Aphrodite Euploia Zephyritis, in proximity to Canopus, thus elevating the Ptolemaic queen to a patron deity of seafarers (Hauben 2013: 47). He also dedicated to Zeus statues of Ptolemy II and Arsinoe II in Olympia and built a shrine in the name of this Ptolemaic royal couple to Isis and Anubis in Canopus, Egypt (Hauben 2013: 49–50; Oppen de Ruiter 2015: 71, 160). His promotion of the Isiac cults manifesting in Egypt is not attested abroad, and it is not the point of the argument here since we are talking about creation and maintenance of socio-spatial connections between Ptolemaic Egypt and foreign regions that could have increased chances for cultural transmission between them. Callicrates's diplomatic activities were recognized in various corners of the Mediterranean. He was held in high regard in his homeland, the island of Samos, which was one of the key Ptolemaic naval bases in the third century BCE. Samians erected statues in his honor, one in the temple of *Theoi Soteres* (deified royal couple of Ptolemy I and Berenice I) and a second one later rendering Callicrates as their Benefactor (Hauben 2013: 49). He was honored by the Island League on Delos and had statue in Cyprian Paphos (Hauben 2013: 49).

These loyal Ptolemaic high naval officials were acting as the extended hand of the Ptolemaic rulers over the thalassocracy in the Aegean Sea. Furthermore, between the rule of Ptolemy II and Ptolemy IV, the ways of controlling foreign regions were continuously being developed and relied on other more regionally focused officials and institutions (Hölbl 2001: 58–61; Bagnall 1976: 213–51). For example, in the time of Philocles, there was a *nesiarch* Bacchon acting as a royal appointee of Ptolemy II handling the matters of the Island League (Meadows 2013). From the reign of Ptolemy II is also attested a *pamphyliarch* appointed by the Ptolemaic king in Pamphylia (however, the nature of this office remains unclear) (Hölbl 2001: 60; Meadows and Thonemann 2013). In the time of Ptolemy II and III, there were *strategoi* acting as local/provincial governors in the southwestern Asia Minor, and under Ptolemy IV, there is also a *strategos* attested for Syria and Phoenicia (Hölbl 2001: 59–60).

Finally, there were Ptolemaic soldiers and their officers (such as *phrourarchos*—garrison commander, see Bremen 2017: 7; Robert and Robert 1983, 124-7) stationed in the Ptolemaic garrisons on the coast of Asia Minor and in the Aegean Sea (Bagnall 1976: 220–4) who can be conceptualized as successful agents of cultural transmission between Ptolemaic Egypt and places of their foreign residence. The term "successful" instead of "potential" can be used here with ease as there is the evidence for direct spread and interest in Isiac cults from the Ptolemaic soldiers stationed at Thera, which were discussed in detail in Chapter 4. Another layer unfolding on the level of the individual soldiers is that in their minds, the Isiac cults and the higher Ptolemaic hierarchy are not disconnected phenomena, quite on the contrary. This is the already discussed case in Thera in the third century BCE where Diokles, one of the devotees of the Ptolemaic royal cult (*basilistai*), dedicated to the Isiac cults, or the former Ptolemaic officer Artemidorus who restored the Isiac temple there in the name of Ptolemy III (Chaniotis 2005: 152).

The paragraphs above present how rich administrative and social apparatus the Ptolemaic dynasty utilized for spreading and maintaining their presence and influence abroad and how were the channels of contact between the Ptolemies and foreign lands being operated on a different scale. This apparatus only increased the chances of the Isiac cults being transmitted. To illustrate the epidemiologically advantageous effect of this Ptolemaic political activity for the Isiac cults, we can turn to the description of the process of garrisoning the Aegean Islands by the Ptolemies by Hans Hauben (2013: 40): "In order to establish and preserve such a thalassocracy, a number of requirements had to be fulfilled. It was necessary to control a sufficient number of well-situated islands and coastal areas, with advantageous factors like geographical spread, strategic value and economic strength prevailing over territorial size." In other words, the Ptolemies successfully occupied the transportation network in the Aegean Sea by capturing verry connective nodes with respect to the flow of people, goods, and information, thus significantly increasing the amount of Ptolemaic elements being communicated and distributed on the network, which is only beneficial for the spread of the Isiac cults. Such spread had then favorable conditions even without any official royal promotion and could have spread spontaneously by these channels that were opened and maintained by the Ptolemaic representatives. Same principles then work for other territories where, as was demonstrated above, Ptolemaic influence was present and, importantly, recognized, which is an indicator of a successful contact channel between the place of origin of the Ptolemaic element and the foreign region. The joint dedications to the Ptolemaic family and the Isiac one from different locations are, in this context, a logical spontaneous outcome. The models of the case studies provide supporting evidence for this mechanism as they primarily reveal that the places under the Ptolemaic influence indeed were frequently in traveling proximity to the evidence of the Isiac cults.

6.3 Implications for the Academic Discussion

The research presented in this book provides several arguments that relate not only to the past but also to the future of the academic discussion on the topic of the spread of the Isiac cults. One key moment and hypothesis that needs to be addressed is Cumont's imperialistic theory. Cumont's view that the early spread of the Isiac cults was successful because of the official promotion abroad and propaganda by Ptolemaic rulers impacted the discussion in such intensity that the scholarship discussing the topic of the spread that followed was to a significant extent oriented on disproving Cumont's thesis. This is particularly tangible in Fraser's arguments, and Dunand dedicated a lot of words in this direction as well. Although Cumont's work is from the beginning of the twentieth century and Fraser wrote on this account mainly in the 1960s and 1970s, the imperialistic theory and the discussion revolving round it are still debated in more recent works on the Isiac cults (Bricault 2004; Lefebvre 2008). Indeed, Fraser successfully exposed the weaknesses of the imperialistic theory by pointing to the reality that the cult outside Egypt was, in majority of cases, initially private and not public and therefore only hardly resulting from the official propaganda for which there is no evidence also. However, Fraser in his effort to disprove the imperialistic theory swayed the argumentation and the discussion too far to the opposite limit by claiming that the Ptolemaic influence was almost never impacting the spread of the Isiac cults and that it cannot be argued that it was, even in case of new evidence revealed in the future. Such polarization of the scholarship naturally aggregating at the two limits did not allow for some time a more delicate conceptualization of the spread of the Isiac cults as a complex historical process impacted by several factors, which was only recently more elaborately realized by Bricault.

One of the most difficult obstacles Cumont and Fraser created with respect to the conceptualization of the problem of the factors behind the spread was to build argumentation exclusively around the topic of direct Ptolemaic involvement and propaganda of these cults abroad while omitting completely the possibility of indirect Ptolemaic influence. Fortunately, Dunand was able to hint at the potential of indirect Ptolemaic impact on the spread relatively early after Fraser, but still even in recent discussion and in this book, the conceptual obstacle is present, and the arguments that are trying to capture this cultural transmission as multifactorial process usually start at these opposite limits and work its way somewhere inside the spectrum of possibilities of impact from there (e.g., Versluys 2006: 9; Bricault 2004).

Although one of the key results presented in this book is the significant connection between Ptolemaic influence and the early spread of the Isiac cults, it needs to be stressed that these results do not support Cumont's imperialistic theory. As was demonstrated on many examples and argued throughout the book, the Ptolemies created favorable conditions for the spread of the Isiac cults by opening several highly connective channels for social contacts between Ptolemaic Egypt and foreign regions. The creation and maintenance of these channels relied on multilayered and multimodal administrative apparatus, ranging from political acts of Ptolemaic rulers themselves, diplomatic missions, and controlling regions by means of specific Ptolemaic officials to soldiers residing in garrisons. Artifacts, practices, or information in any form related to the Isiac cults then could have been spontaneously transmitted via these channels benefiting from the reality that these cults were one of the most celebrated in Ptolemaic Egypt, and additionally, they were theologically linked to Ptolemaic royals. In other words, we can agree on the significance of Ptolemaic politics in this process but, at the same time, deny that there was any official promotion of these cults outside Egypt. Furthermore, as was demonstrated in the Aegean Sea case study, the political impact was not the only factor of potential influence, and it was demonstrated that several factors contributed together with different intensities of impact and with different mutual entanglements. It is easy to notice how far on the spectrum this argument is from both Cumont's and Fraser's views on the matter. It is one of the aims of this book to contribute to the formation or solidification of a consensus that the spread of the Isiac cults was a complex and a long-term historical process. Such a consensus would allow future scholars to avoid starting their argumentation on the topic by overcoming repeatedly the pitfalls of these two big "monochromatic" and polarizing theories.

Another correction to the discussion that this book aims to introduce is also rooted in perceiving the spread of the Isiac cults as a long-term process. Fraser argues that the evidence of the Isiac cults appearing in the second century BCE outside Egypt is of no value to the discussion about the Ptolemaic influence on the spread of these cults since the Ptolemies were no longer in control of the Aegean Sea at that time (Fraser 1960: 45). Putting aside the fact that the last Ptolemaic troops were withdrawn from Thera, Itanos, and Methana in 145 BCE (Hölbl 2001: 195), there is again a conceptual issue, that is, the hidden assumption that the material evidence for a cult appears instantaneously after being introduced or carried elsewhere. The varying time gap between existence of a cult at some place and its visibility in material culture, however, is a common aspect, and when compared to epidemiology of infectious diseases, the cultural representations have much longer life, and therefore, the window for successful transmission is significantly wider than in the case of viruses. Again, the early Christianity can be a good example, that, despite its earlier existence, it can be archaeologically recognized only after centuries after its origins. If we stay with the Isiac cults, the story of Artemidorus of Perge is another example of this process. It was after his long career in the Ptolemaic forces that he settled on the island of Thera and restored the temple of the Isiac deities there (Chaniotis 2005: 152–3). In other words, the conceptualization proposed in this book allows us to observe the spread of the Isiac cults in macro-perspective but, at the same time, opens door for more historically nuanced debate than before.

One of the innovations for the future discussion on the spread of the Isiac cults this book proposes is to widen the scope of data that can be utilized to tackle this topic and aim for further collaboration with natural sciences. This is again related to the call for study of the Isiac cults from macro-perspective and as a part of the complex history of the ancient Mediterranean. By now, it is apparent that such an approach, for example, to the study of Roman history is fruitful, and the application of insights from climatology, osteology, zooarchaeology, archaeobotany, demography, economy, or biomolecular archaeology enriched our understanding of the Roman world itself and in the context of the long-term microhistory and macrohistory (Scheidel 2019). This is certainly a viable path for the study of the Isiac cults as well, and the case studies presented here demonstrate its potential. Both case studies, for example, demonstrated how important was transportation network (and its modes) for cultural spread, and the Aegean Sea case study successfully employed data from geology and climatology to deal with the research problem on the level of sub-model.

Finally, the proposal for widening the scope of the data used in the research on the spread of the Isiac cults goes hand in hand with introducing interdisciplinary methodological approaches to it. The methodological synthesis between quantitatively oriented approaches and established tools of historiography could gradually lead to a solidification of discussion that (1) provides hypotheses, (2) tests hypotheses, and (3) results in transparent, reproducible, and cumulative research.

6.4 Future Directions

The research presented in this book is demonstrating the potential of applying formal modeling to the study of the spread of the Isiac cults. However, it focuses on a specific spatio-temporal portion of this historical process and is not, by any means, exhaustive in employing the wide array of relevant formal methods and in the selection of all potential contributing factors. This section will propose possible future directions that can elaborate and enrich the contribution of this research.

An obvious way forward is to exploit the potential of replicability of the presented methodology and apply the models from the two case studies in some form to the study of the spread of the Isiac cults in other regions and different times to procedurally, step by step, add tiles to the mosaic of this historical process and to observe, with each added piece, the continuities and breaks in spatial and temporal trends related to the factors of the spread. The potential regions that would fit the time frame of the early spread of the Isiac cults are continental Greece, Syria, or northern Africa. With respect to later waves of the spread, the method can be applied to explore the spatial dissemination of the evidence for the Isiac cults from the first century BCE in connection to already-established cult sites at that time as secondary centers of the spread. For times of the Roman empire, the models could again operate in a similar fashion; for example, instead of Ptolemaic garrisons, the variable of military influence could be approximated by Roman military fortresses and legion bases in the provinces. If we stay in the frame of the Roman empire, patterns in the perception of the Isiac cults by Roman emperors deserve further exploration. A preliminary exploration of the *Online Coins of the Roman Empire* (OCRE) database shows not only times with increased or decreased popularity of Isiac iconography on Roman coinage but also significant differences in the emphasis either on Sarapis or Isis in different centuries. While Isis and Sarapis are a divine couple, it would be relevant to further ask what these emperors could have conveyed to Roman population by issuing coins depicting only one deity of the two.

Outside the applicability of the models used in the two case studies but still within the methods of formal modeling would be the focus on social aspect (group level) of the spread of the Isiac cults from the perspective of network theory. It would certainly bring more clarity to the research problem to analyze the spatial and social ties between activities of members of voluntary associations dedicated to the worship of the Isiac cults such as *Sarapiastai* or *Isiastai*, or politically oriented groups loyal to the Ptolemies attested worshipping the Isiac deities (e.g., *basilistai*), and focus on how these activities explain some of the patterns of the spread spatially, socially, and also with respect to the question of why Isis appeared in some places more frequently than Sarapis and vice versa.

Another viable approach to the topic, in this case allowing for more dynamic exploration of the spread developing in time, would be agent-based modeling (ABM), that is, a simulation approach using predefined agents (e.g., ships, soldiers, or merchants) with specific behavior in a predefined virtual environment (transportation network of the ancient Mediterranean). A deterministic variant of ABM was already successfully applied in the Asia Minor case study to simulate the traffic of ships on the western coast of Hellenistic Asia Minor traveling from Ptolemaic Alexandria.

So far, the discussion has been mainly focusing on the factors favorable for the spread of the Isiac cults, that is, epidemiology of the Isiac cults, as Bricault (2013: 144–5) labeled it according to Dan Sperber's concept of epidemiology of representations used in the cognitive science of religions (Sperber 1996). However, at a certain point, we should turn our attention to the immunological part of this historical process, that is, start to answer the question of why the Isiac cults did not spread to some of the locations with favorable conditions or in proximity to the already-established cult. This way, this cultural transmission can be understood not only as one-directional process but rather as a dynamic phenomenon benefiting from specific conditions, on one hand, and being hindered by different conditions, on the other. The concept of immunological factor obstructing further spatial dissemination of the Isiac cults was incorporated to the Case Study 2 focusing on Asia Minor in the form of spatial barrier defined by the transportation network used by the Seleucid empire to campaign against the Ptolemies. This was, however, included in a simple and static fashion, and the topic deserves to be explored in greater detail. While the Seleucid opposition potentially limited the spread of the Isiac cults further inland from the western coast of Asia Minor, this does not constitute a rule for the relationship between the Seleucid empire and the Isiac cults in different regions or different times. This argument can be supported, for example, by the evidence, although scarce, of the Isiac cults in Seleucid Syria or by changes in the relationship between the two empires, which was not, at times, completely hostile, for example, when Antiochus II married the daughter of Ptolemy II, Berenice (Hölbl 2001: 48). Furthermore, the Seleucid role in the not-yet-explored dynamic between epidemiological and immunological factors in the spread of the Isiac cults is clearly only one potential factor of many others. This can be illustrated by the inscription mentioned from Amphipolis dedicated to Isis, Sarapis, and Philip (V) dated to the end of the third century BCE (RICIS 113/0902), which places Isiac cults together with a political figure who actively weakened Ptolemaic positions on the western coast of Asia Minor. In this context, a political force that is expected to impact the process of the spread as an immunological factor had, in this case and indirectly, a positive influence, thus revealing another layer of complexity related to the cultural transmission of the Isiac cults, a complexity that deserves to be further explored by researchers.

Appendix

Places under Ptolemaic Influence

Itanos

The commander of the Ptolemaic forces, Patroclus, most probably stationed a garrison in Cretan Itanos during his voyage to Attica at the beginning of the Chremonidean War (267–261 BCE). The year 267/6 BCE could thus be established as a *terminus post quem* for the Ptolemaic garrison in Itanos. The end of this garrison is definitely related to the year 145 BCE when Ptolemy VI died, and the Ptolemaic troops retreated from the eastern Crete. It should be noted that there is a possibility that the Ptolemaic forces were already withdrawn from Itanos during the rule of Ptolemy V (204–181 BCE) or Ptolemy VI (180–145 BCE); however, Ptolemy VI answered the request of Itanos for help and garrisoned the city again. According to Roger S. Bagnall, the renewal of the Ptolemaic garrison in Itanos happened around or after the year 163 BCE during the general reassertion of the royal power abroad after Ptolemy VI Philometor's return to Egypt (Bagnall 1976: 117–22; Hölbl 2001: 40–3; Fischer-Bovet 2014: 60–2; Chaniotis 2005: 11, 88–9). For the map of the locations under Ptolemaic influence, see Figure A.1.

Thera

As with Itanos, Patroclus stationed a garrison on the island of Thera in 267/6 BCE on his way to Attica leading Ptolemaic forces to Chremonidean War. Patroclus also appointed a certain Apollodotus as the commander of the base. After Ptolemy VIII acceded to the throne in 145 BCE, he withdrew the Ptolemaic forces from Thera (Bagnall 1976: 123–34; Hölbl 2001: 40–3; Chaniotis 2005: 89, 149–54; Fischer-Bovet 2014: 60–2).

Methana

The Ptolemaic military base in the Arsinoe-Methana peninsula was also established in the course of the Chremonidean War (267–261 BCE). Garrisoning the peninsula was strategically advantageous because of its proximity to Attica, and it offered suitable port facilities. Under the Ptolemaic influence, the peninsula of Methana was renamed to Arsinoe, the name of the very popular queen and sister-wife of Ptolemy II. The garrisons in Itanos, Thera, and Arsinoe-Methana were a single administrative unit and eventually shared the same fate. They were all abandoned in the year 145 BCE after the death of Ptolemy VI (Bagnall 1976: 135–6; Hölbl 2001: 40–3; Fischer-Bovet 2014: 60).

Keos

The island of Keos was involved in the diplomatic relations with the Ptolemies even before the Chremonidean War (267–261 BCE); however, Patroclus made the port of Koresia (also named Arsinoe) a major military base during this conflict. We do not know the exact date of the withdrawal of the Ptolemaic troops from the garrison. It is speculated that it happened at the end of the third century BCE when the name of the city Arsinoe changed back to Koresia (Bagnall 1976: 141–5; Hölbl 2001: 40–3; Fischer-Bovet 2014: 60; Chaniotis 2005: 90).

Ephesus

Ephesus came under the Ptolemaic control in ca. 262 BCE. However, only a few years later, the Ptolemaic fleet was defeated at the battle of Ephesus by the Rhodians, who exceptionally sided with Antiochus II and the city was taken. Inscriptions attest Seleucid presence in Ephesus in 254/3 BCE. In about 246 BCE, the Seleucid commander deserted the city, and the Ptolemies could retake it again. According to Polybius (V.35.2), Ephesus was still garrisoned by the Ptolemaic forces in 221 BCE, and it remained that way until 197 BCE when Antiochus III seized the city (Fischer-Bovet 2014: 61, 65, 73–4; Chaniotis 2002, 2005: 89; Bagnall 1976: 170–1; Hölbl 2001: 50).

Samos

In 280/79 the Island League gathered on Samos, the new Ptolemaic possession, and negotiated the character of the Greek festival *Ptolemaia*. Samos was an important naval base for the Ptolemies until 201 BCE when Philip V of Macedon conquered the island (Polybius III.2.8; XVI.2.9; Livy XXXI.31.4). However, the Ptolemaic forces took back Samos around the year 197 BCE. Shortly after that, the island regained its freedom (Bagnall 1976: 80–8; Hölbl 2001: 38; Fischer-Bovet 2014: 55–65).

Iasos

The harbor city of Iasos came under Ptolemaic control around 309 BCE during the campaign of Ptolemy I to Lycia and Caria. The Ptolemaic influence and the presence of Ptolemaic soldiers are documented by a treaty between Ptolemy I, his commanders, and the city of Iasos. It is possible that around 215 BCE, Iasos was already independent from the Ptolemaic empire. At that time, the city faced local political pressures and turned to Rhodos for help instead of the Ptolemies. Although the Seleucid empire led a campaign in 203 BCE to western Asia Minor resulting in territorial gains of former Ptolemaic cities, cities on the Carian coast were taken later, in 201 BCE, by Philip V (Cohen 1995: 52; Bremen 2017; Chaniotis 2002: 104; Meadows 2006: 468; LaBuff 2016: 33; Ma 2002: 40–68).

Mylasa

The city of Mylasa was situated in the inland part of Caria, and the Ptolemaic control there is attested to 267 BCE by a decree found in the shrine of Zeus Labraundios at Labraunda, mentioning the qualities of a certain Apollonios, an *oikonomos* appointed by Ptolemy II. However, Mylasa did not stay under Ptolemaic influence for a long time. Around 246 BCE, the successor of Antiochus II, Seleucus II, gave the city its independence from a Seleucid rule, and the academic debate therefore places the Seleucid control of the city already in the time of Antiochus II who ruled between 261 and 246 BCE (Bremen 2003, 2017; Le Rider 1990; Cohen 1995: 53; Chrubasik 2016: 58; Ma 2002: 40–68; Hölbl 2001: 68).

Stratonikeia

Another city under Ptolemaic influence in inland Caria was Stratonikeia. The city was acquired by Ptolemy II as a result of the so-called Syrian War of Succession (280/279 BCE) that followed the ascension of Antiochus I Soter into Seleucid throne after the death of Seleucus I Nicator. A sale contract from Stratonikeia attests the control of Ptolemy II over the city by a formula that dates the text to the ninth ruling year of Ptolemy II, which is identified as the year 274 BCE by Bagnall but 277/6 BCE by Hölbl (2001, 68). Similarly as Mylasa, the city was taken by the Seleucids during the reign of Antiochus II and, at that time, probably received the name Stratonikeia after Antiochus's mother. The city was then given by the Seleucids to Rhodians (probably by Seleucus II who ruled between 246 and 225 BCE). Rhodians briefly lost the city to Philip V in 201 BCE, but it was again under the control of Rhodos not much later than 197 BCE (Bremen 2017, 2003; Robert 1989: 449–568; Ma 2002: 40–85; LaBuff 2016: 35–40; Meadows 2006: 467).

Amyzon

Amyzon was another Carian city acquired by Ptolemy II in the Syrian War of Succession (280/279 BCE). For 278/7 BCE, there is a document honoring the Ptolemaic *strategos* Margos in Amyzon attesting local institutional administration by the Ptolemies. In 203 BCE, Antiochus III was able to take over several Carian cities from the Ptolemies, Amyzon among them. Antiochus was able to do so without any significant opposition because of the internal political problems in Egypt following the death of Ptolemy IV in 204 BCE with Ptolemy V inheriting the throne in the age of five and co-ruling with the regent Agathocles (Bremen 2003, 2017; Meadows and Thonemann 2013; Cohen 1995: 246–8; Grainger 2017: 61–2; Dmitriev 2005: 294–5; Meadows 2006; LaBuff 2016: 35–8; Ma 2002: 40–68; Robert and Robert 1983: 127f).

Halicarnassus

The earliest testimony for Ptolemaic influence over Halicarnassus is a decree of Samos in honor of judges from Myndos from ca. 280 BCE attesting relationship between Philocles of Sidon, a Ptolemaic military commander, and the judges from Halicarnassus (Austin 2006, No.155; Hauben 1987b, 2004). The city thus can be listed among the Ptolemaic acquisitions from the Syrian War of Succession. Ptolemaic garrison in the city can be dated to 270/269 BCE based on the date of the decree of Athens in honor of Kallias of Sphettos (Shear 1978), who was a commander of mercenary soldiers under the Ptolemies and is mentioned to being stationed by Ptolemy II to Halicarnassus in the text. The city was in Ptolemaic hands for decades until 197 BCE. In that year, the Seleucid king Antiochus III launched a campaign to Asia Minor to capture Ptolemaic possessions. Antiochus was successful in Cilicia, Lycia, and Ephesus in Ionia. However, Rhodians intervened in Caria and negotiated freedom for Halicarnassus (Hölbl 2001: 38; Bagnall 1976: 94–8; Ma 2002: 40, 84; LaBuff 2016: 35–42; Meadows 2006).

Miletus

Although in 280/79 BCE Antiochus I was still recognized as *stephanophoros* in Miletus, the allegiance shifted shortly after (in 279 BCE) when Ptolemy II donated land to the city. Between 267 and 261 BCE, the Ptolemies were engaged in the Chremonidean War in the Aegean. Later in this time frame, the son and co-regent of Ptolemy II called by historians as Ptolemy "the son" took military command and consolidated Ptolemaic influence in Ionia. In this context around 262/1 BCE, Ptolemy II wrote a letter to the Milesians (translation by Michel Austin in Austin 2006, No. 259):

> And now, as you have preserved dutifully your city and your friendship and alliance with us—for my son and Callicrates and my other "friends" who are with you have written about the display / you have made of your goodwill towards us—we acknowledge this and give you unstinted praise, and we shall try to repay the people with benefactions, and we urge you to preserve for the future the same favourable attitude to us, so that we may show even greater care for your city in the light of your good dispositions.

The western coast of Asia Minor was however very unstable and was eventually consumed by the Second Syrian War (260–253 BCE). The difficulties for the Ptolemies appeared on two levels. First, a new Seleucid ruler, Antiochus II, made an agreement with the Antigonid ruler, Antigonus II Gonatas, which helped Antiochus to lead a campaign against Ptolemaic outposts in Asia

Minor. Second, Ptolemy "the son" revolted against his father, and the Aetolian mercenary commander Timarchos joined him and proclaimed himself the tyrant of Miletus. This revolt was, however, short-lived, and since 259 BCE, Ptolemy "the son" was missing from the Egyptian dating formula, which implies his definitive end in the Ptolemaic hierarchy. In 259/8 BCE, Antiochus II seized Miletus and managed to hold it even after the peace between the Ptolemies and the Seleucids was negotiated in 253 BCE. New successions both in the Ptolemaic empire (Ptolemy III) and the Seleucid empire (Seleucus II) led to a Third Syrian War (246–241 BCE), resulting in extensive territorial gains for Ptolemy III in Asia Minor, including Miletus. Finally, Miletus was lost to Ptolemies after Philip V of Macedon captured it in 201 BCE, and later, the city gained its independence (Ma 2002: 41–94; Hölbl 2001: 38–44, 138; LaBuff 2016: 35–43; Grainger 2017: 58, 79–81, 2010: 114, 119–252; Kosmin 2018: 18, 85; Dmitriev 2005: 64–76; Fischer-Bovet 2014: 61).

Myndos

Myndos was acquired already in 309 BCE as a result of the expedition of Ptolemy I in Asia Minor in Lycia and Caria. The Myndian judges honored in the decree of Samos dated to ca. 280 BCE were directed by Philocles of Sidon, a high Ptolemaic official (Austin 2006, No. 155; Hauben 1987b, 2004). The end of Ptolemaic control of Myndos is tied with the year 197 BCE when Rhodians negotiated freedom for the city, similarly as in the case of Kaunos and Halicarnassus (Hölbl 2001: 19, 38, 138; LaBuff 2016: 35–41; Ma 2002: 40; Kosmin 2018: 301; Dmitriev 2005: 96; Meadows 2006: 459).

Kaunos

Kaunos was a Carian city on the southwestern coast and was in the sphere of Ptolemaic influence already in 309 BCE after the campaign of Ptolemy I in the region. Similarly as Myndos, the city was not taken by Antiochus III as other Ptolemaic possessions in Asia Minor in 197 BCE, but Rhodians managed to buy freedom for the city for 200 talents (Hölbl 2001: 19, 138; Ma 2002: 40, 89; Cohen 1995: 52; LaBuff 2016: 35–42; Meadows 2006).

Knidos

With Knidos, it is important to nuance the difference between Ptolemaic control and influence. There is no direct evidence of Ptolemaic control over this city in Caria. However, at an uncertain date, although Bagnall suggests the reign of Ptolemy III or IV, the diplomatically cunning Ptolemaic minister under these rulers and a priest of Alexander, Sosibios, was honored by a statue erected in Knidos by an Alexandrian. While the Ptolemaic influence is tangible, it cannot be perceived as evidence that Knidos was a Ptolemaic possession (LaBuff 2016: 35–54; Bagnall 1976: 98; Hölbl 2001: 127; Shear 1978: 24; Eckstein 2008: 162).

Kalynda

For the city of Kalynda in Caria, there is evidence for Ptolemaic administration in time of Ptolemy II. A papyrus documenting a transaction related to supplying wine to the yearly festival at Kalynda attests that the farmer and supplier Theopropos was discontent with the process by being paid insufficiently and appealed to the Ptolemaic *strategos* Motes. The papyrus is dated to the 38th year of Ptolemy II, which Bagnall dates to 248/7 BCE. The time of the end of Ptolemaic influence in the city is uncertain; however, John Ma points out that the nearby city of Daidala was besieged by the Seleucid empire in 190 BCE, and it is probably safe to assume that at the latest, the city was not under Ptolemaic influence after the campaigns of Antiochus III in Caria around 197 BCE (Campbell 1925, No. 59341; Bagnall 1976: 99–102; Ma 2002: 155).

Kos

The island of Kos located in the proximity of the Halicarnassus peninsula has a specific place in relationship to Ptolemaic family. In 309/308 BCE, Ptolemy I with his family stayed over winter on the island, and in 308 BCE, Berenice delivered a son who later became the king Ptolemy II. Although Ptolemaic control of the island is not attested, Ptolemaic relations with Kos are documented. In the decree of Naxos in honor of the Ptolemaic *nesiarch* (i.e., administrative head of the Island League) Bacchon dated to ca. 280 BCE, the nesiarch was instructed by Ptolemy II to visit Kos and send judges from Kos to Naxos to settle a contract dispute

(Austin 2006, No. 257). Ptolemy II himself sponsored the temple of Asclepius on the island. Politically, Kos was an independent state. For the *homopoliteia* agreement between Kos and Kalymna in relation to king Ptolemy, see Kalymna below (Bremen 2017: 11; Hölbl 2001: 19, 24, 98; Eckstein 2008: 156–9; LaBuff 2016: 33–54; Bagnall 1976: 103–5).

Kalymna

As in the case of Kos, there is no clear evidence for direct Ptolemaic control over the island. However, diplomatic ties and Ptolemaic influence are attested by an inscription from Kalymna, which informs us that "King Ptolemy" was responsible for sending a judge to Kalymna (Segre 1952, No. 17). Mario Segre, who published *Tituli Calymmnii*, identified the King Ptolemy as Ptolemy II (ruled 284–246 BCE), which is also Bagnall's inclination (Bagnall 1976: 104). The island of Kalymna is located in proximity to Kos and was politically a part of Kos in the late third century BCE (ca. 205–201 BCE) by an agreement (*homopoliteia*). The agreement itself did not survive; however, an inscription bearing the oath to uphold this agreement survived. Part of the oath is as follows (translated by Michel Austin in Austin 2006, No. 153): "I will abide by / the established democracy, the restoration of the *homopoliteia*, the ancestral laws of Cos, the resolutions of the assembly and the provisions of the *homopoliteia*; I will also abide by the friendship and alliance with King Ptolemy and the treaties / ratified by the people with the allies." The king Ptolemy mentioned is identified by Bagnall as Ptolemy IV (Bagnall 1976: 105), but Austin lists Ptolemy V (Austin 2006, No. 153). The friendship and alliance with King Ptolemy mentioned in the oath then imply strong political relationship with the Ptolemies (Bremen 2017: 11; LaBuff 2016: 35–54; Eckstein 2008: 163; Bagnall 1976: 103–5).

Lissa

Lissa was a city located to the south of the western coast of Asia Minor, in Lycia. For Lissa, the Ptolemaic control is documented by regnal years of Ptolemaic rulers in decrees. There are two decrees bearing the dating formula for the second and eighth ruling year of Ptolemy II. This attests that the city was a Ptolemaic possession between 280 and 270 BCE. Further, there is a decree dated to the second year of Ptolemy III, which would be ca. 245/4 BCE. It could show continuity in Ptolemaic control; however, it is also possible that Ptolemy III regained the city from the Seleucid hands (Bagnall 1976: 106; Ma 2002: 40,158; Meadows 2006: 467).

Telmessos

Ptolemaic control of Lycia is attested to the years of Ptolemy II and was the subject of Ptolemaic interest already in the campaigns of Ptolemy I Soter. Ptolemy II is praised by Telmessos in a decree from 279 BCE (Austin 2006: 469; Wörrle 1978). Later, a decree from 240 BCE states that Ptolemy III gave the rule over the city to Ptolemy, son of Lysimachus, and he served there as a client king/official under the Ptolemies (Austin 2006, No. 270). The city was taken by the Seleucid empire in the campaigns of Antiochus III (197 BCE), and this transition is reflected also in the allegiances of the successors of Ptolemy of Telmessos. The son of this Ptolemy was named Lysimachus, and his son was then again Ptolemy—this second-generation Ptolemy, son of Lysimachus, is mentioned in a document from 193 BCE as a relative of Antiochus III (Bagnall 1976: 106–10; Ma 2002: 40–8, 84–94; Hölbl 2001: 38, 138; Marquaille 2008: 46, 63; Oneil 2008: 67, 88; Grainger 2017: 59, 2010: 129; Meadows 2006: 467).

Xanthos

Located in Lycia on the southern coast, Xanthos was won over to Ptolemy I during his campaigns to Lycia and Caria in 309/8 BCE. In the reign of Ptolemy II, there is a decree from Xanthos dated to 260/59 BCE honoring Pandaros, a *phrourarchos*, that is, a military commander of the local garrison sent by Ptolemy II (Pleket and Stroud 1983). Xanthos thus was of military importance to the Ptolemies. There is a continuity of control attested to the reign of Ptolemy III by a letter that he sent to Xanthos in 242 BCE where he praised the people of the city for maintaining the bond (*hairesis*) toward the Ptolemaic king (which is a frequent motive in letters of Hellenistic rulers to their possessions) (Pleket and Stroud 1986; Bousquet 1986). Xanthos was captured by Antiochus III in 197 BCE as part of the Seleucid reconquest of Asia Minor (Chaniotis 2002, 2005: 89–90; Ma 2002: 40, 84, 110; Hölbl 2001: 19–138; Grainger 2017: 80; Bremen 2017: 14; Bagnall 1976: 108–10).

Patara, Andriake, and Limyra

The dominance of the first Ptolemies in Lycia is richly attested by inscriptions, and the cities on the coast and river valleys such as Patara, Andriake, and Limyra were part of this Ptolemaic achievement. On the southwestern tip of Asia Minor of Lycia was the city of Patara. That Patara was a Ptolemaic possession is recognizable by the fact that Ptolemy II renamed the city after his sister-wife Arsinoe II. As was the case for many Ptolemaic possessions around the year of 197 BCE, Patara too passed to Seleucid hands during the campaign of Antiochus III. Andriake followed similar trajectory, and the end of Ptolemaic control is dated to 197 BCE when the city was captured by Antiochus III. For Limyra, the situation was not significantly different, and the end of Ptolemaic administration in the city is again tied with Antiochus III; however, there is evidence providing further detail for the Ptolemaic presence. There is a decree from Limyra honoring two Ptolemaic *oikonomoi* with the dating formula of 36th year of the reign of King Ptolemy (Pleket and Stroud 1977). This was generally accepted as the 36th year of Ptolemy I, with 288/7 BCE as the year of the decree. This was however recently challenged by Andrew Meadows who claims that the broader historical political context is more in favor of Ptolemy II as the king mentioned, and he proposes the year 249 BCE as the date of origin of the decree (Meadows 2006). Also from Limyra, there is a document revealing Ptolemaic administration in the form of *prostagma* concerning abuses in the levying of taxes dated to 250 BCE or possibly to 277/6 BCE (both dates are in the reign of Ptolemy II) (Chaniotis et al. 2010). Finally, Hölbl and others suggest that a podium structure in Limyra should be dated to the reign of Ptolemy II and identified as *Ptolemaion* (Hölbl 2001: 96; Borchhardt 1991). For further reading, see (Hölbl 2001: 138; Ma 2002: 40, 84; Grainger 2010: 267).

Termessos

Termessos was a city on the border between Pamphylia and Pisidia on the south of Asia Minor. A *Pamphyliarch* (i.e., a Ptolemaic governor of Pamphylia) is honored in Termessos by a decree dated to the end of 278 BCE in the reign of Ptolemy II (Robert 1966: 53–8). Meadows offers a different interpretation and reconstruction of the decree changing the office from *Pamphyliarch* to a *strategos* (Meadows and Thonemann 2013). The acquisition of possessions in

Pamphylia by the Ptolemies thus can be attributed to the spoils of the so-called Syrian War of Succession where Ptolemy II conducted a successful campaign against Antiochus I (280/279 BCE). Pamphylia became Seleucid after the peace between the Ptolemaic empire and Antiochus II. However, in 243 BCE, Ptolemy III was in control of Pamphylia but lost the region still during his reign. We do not possess information about the situation in Pamphylia in the time of the campaign in Asia Minor of Antiochus III (197 BCE), but it is safe to assume that it was already Seleucid at that time (Ma 2002: 40; Meadows 2006: 467; Bagnall 1976: 111–14).

Methymna

From Methymna on the island of Lesbos, we have several pieces of evidence attesting Ptolemaic influence. One of them is a plague bearing the name of Arsinoe Philadelphus, the sister-wife of Ptolemy II, dated to 260s BCE. A decree of the *koinon* of the *Proteoi* from Methymna honoring certain Praxikles, son of Philinos, is dated by the year of Ptolemy IV, however, without specifying the year (thus, dated to ca. 221–205 BCE). There is also a document attesting a priest of the Ptolemaic royal cult (usually dated to the reign of Ptolemy II). Thus, the Ptolemaic impact on Lesbos is thorough as it encompasses not only political but also cultural aspects. The end of the Ptolemaic dominance on Lesbos coincided with the reign of Ptolemy V (between 240 and 180 BCE) (Brun 1991; Bagnall 1976: 159–68; Ma 2002: 158; Marquaille 2008: 49).

Chios

From Chios, the evidence is scarce. However, there is a decree from Chios honoring Appollophanes who was sent by king Ptolemy (Woodhead 1963). The text does not specify which Ptolemy, but Bagnall suggests dating to the period 278–270 in the reign of Ptolemy II based on the fact that the votive formula mentions the sovereigns in the plural, which could be perhaps linked to the royal couple of Ptolemy II and Arsinoe II (Bagnall 1976: 168–9). At least some degree of administrative influence by the Ptolemies is therefore tangible on Chios (Bagnall 1976: 168–9; Grainger 2010: 114; LaBuff 2016: 53).

Lebedos

It is not possible to identify when the city came under Ptolemaic control for the first time, but around 266 BCE the city honored Antiochus I. The city of Lebedos on the Ionian coast was taken by Ptolemy III (243 BCE) during the Third Syrian War (246–241 BCE) and, at some point, renamed Ptolemais also probably by Ptolemy III. For the ultimate end of Ptolemaic control, Ma speculates that if nearby Teos fell into Seleucid hands in 204 or 203 BCE, then the same may apply to Lebedos, which could have been taken by Antiochus III at that time. While in the end of the third century BCE, a Magnesian inscription mentioned that "Ptolemaians who were previously called Lebedians," in the beginning of the second century BCE, an inscription from Samos records decree of "Lebedians," which only adds to the probable suspicion that the name Ptolemais did not survive long after 197 BCE when Antiochus III captured many Ptolemaic possessions, including those in Ionia (Fischer-Bovet 2014: 65; Hölbl 2001: 72; Gauthier 2003: 479; Ma 2002: 45, 72; Cohen 1995: 188–92).

Kolophon

As in the case of Lebedos, Kolophon was most probably retaken by Ptolemy III in the context of the Third Syrian War (246–241 BCE). A trace of Ptolemaic administration in Kolophon is provided by a Kolophonian decree in honor of Sosias, son of Sokrates, who was a Ptolemaic official. The text was discovered in 1959 in Claros and briefly mentioned by Louis Robert but was not published for some time. For example, both Ma and Bagnall report this decree and its content only as being mentioned by Robert (Bagnall 1976: 175; Ma 2002: 45). However, in 2003, the decree was published by Philippe Gauthier who suggests that the king Ptolemy mentioned is most probably Ptolemy III (as also Robert claimed) and should be dated to 240–220 BCE (Gauthier 2003). In 218 BCE, the ruler of Pergamon Attalos I led a campaign to regain his former territories in the Seleucid Asia Minor and took Kolophon. However, it is not entirely certain whether Kolophon was still Ptolemaic at that time or if the city changed its allegiances or gained independence before Attalos captured it (Gauthier 2003; Chrubasik 2016: 74–83; Cohen 1995: 183–7).

Magnesia ad Maeandrum

Magnesia on the river Maiandros was an inland city in Ionia with strategic placement on the crossroads between Priene, Ephesus, and Tralles. The evidence for Ptolemaic influence is very scarce. However, Porphyry writes that Ptolemy III sent troops to Magnesia to help the usurper of the Seleucid throne Antiochus Hierax against his older brother Seleucus II (so-called Brothers' War, ca. 239–236 BCE), probably to weaken the overall power of the Seleucid empire. However, Ptolemy was partially restrained from more significant actions by peace he made with Seleucus II at the end of the Third Syrian War (246–241 BCE) (Ma 2002: 44–5; Grainger 2010: 179; Hölbl 2001: 53–4; Chrubasik 2016: 250–2).

Priene

Priene in Ionia is lacking any substantial evidence for Ptolemaic control. However, some Ptolemaic influence can be attested by an inscription from Priene (early second century BCE) concerning the decision of Rhodian judges on the territorial dispute between Samos and Priene that mentions an official Antiochus, "appointed by king Ptolemy" (Hiller von Gaertringen 1906, No. 37). (See also Fischer-Bovet 2014: 65; Ma 2002: 45.)

Bargylia

There is a consensus among historians that Bargylia in Caria was falling under Ptolemaic and Seleucid control in the third century BCE (probably taken by Antiochus II during the Second Syrian War; 260–253 BCE). The Ptolemaic hold of the city however could not have lasted after the campaigns of Philip V of Macedon into Asia Minor where he spent the winter of 201/0 BCE in Bargylia trapped by fleets of Rhodos and Pergamon. An inscription from Bargylia dated to 195–185 BCE and published in 2000 informs us also about nearby cities going under Seleucid control after the campaigns of Philip V and after "war arose between King Antiochus and the King Ptolemy"—the kings in this temporal context are Antiochus III and Ptolemy V and the war is the Fifth Syrian War

(202–195 BCE) (Blumel 2000). (Further reading: Eckstein 2008: 156; Bremen 2003; Bresson 2012; Grainger 2010: 253, 2017: 180; Ma 2002: 68, 77).

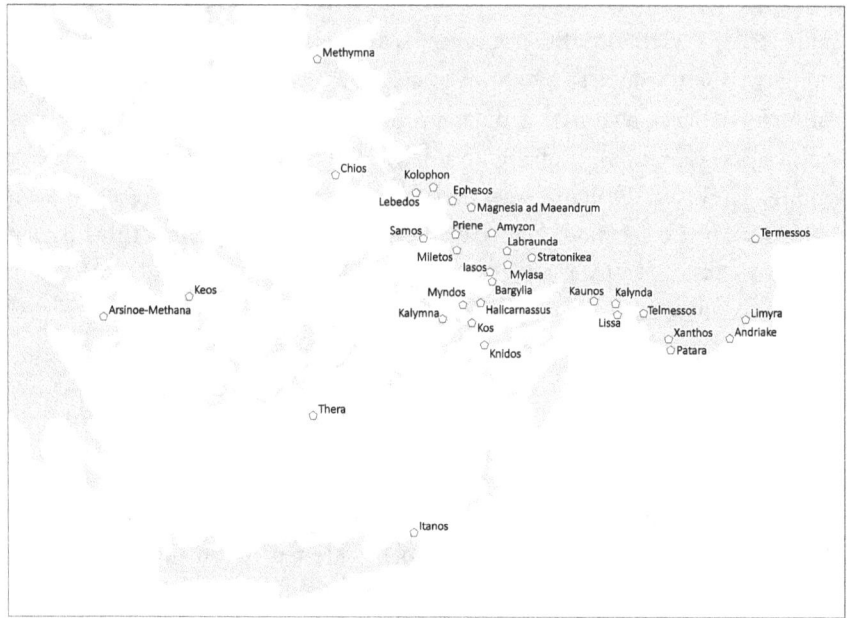

Figure A.1 Ptolemaic garrisons and places under Ptolemaic influence incorporated in case studies 1 and 2. Base map source: "Natural Earth" n.d.; Data source: Glomb et al. 2018, 2020.

References

Allen, James P. 2015. *Ancient Egyptian Pyramid Texts*. Atlanta: SBL Press.
"Ancient World Mapping Center." n.d. http://awmc.unc.edu/wordpress/map-files/. Accessed September 21, 2021.
Anson, Edward. 1996. "The 'Ephemerides' of Alexander the Great." *Historia: Zeitschrift für Alte Geschichte* 45 (4): 501–4.
Anson, Edward. 2014. *Alexander's Heirs: The Age of the Successors*. Malden: Wiley Blackwell.
Apuleius, and Sarah Ruden. 2012. *The Golden Ass*. New Haven: Yale University Press.
Archibald, Zofia H. 2007. "Contacts between the Ptolemaic Kingdom and the Black Sea in the Early Hellenistic Age." In *The Black Sea in Antiquity: Regional and Interregional Economic Exchanges*, edited by Vincent Gabrielsen and John Lund, 153–271. Aarhus: Aarhus University Press.
Arnaoutoglou, Ilias. 2013. "Group and Individuals in IRhamnous 59 (SEG 49.161)." In *Individus, groupes et politique à Athènes de Solon à Mithridate*, edited by Jean-Christophe Couvenhes and Silvia Milanezi, 315–37. Perspectives Historiques. Tours: Presses universitaires François-Rabelais.
Arnaoutoglou, Ilias. 2018. "Isiastai Sarapiastai: Isiac Cult Associations in the Eastern Mediterranean*." In *Individuals and Materials in the Greco-Roman Cults of Isis*, edited by Valentino Gasparini and Richard Veymiers, 248–79. Leiden: Brill.
Arnaud, Pascal. 2005. *Les routes de la navigation antique: Itinéraires en Méditerranée*. Paris: Editions Errance.
Arnon, Itzhak. 1972. *Crop Production in Dry Regions*. London: Leonard Hill.
Austin, Michel. 2006. *The Hellenistic World from Alexander to the Roman Conquest: A Selection of Ancient Sources in Translation*. Cambridge: Cambridge University Press.
Bagnall, Roger S. 1976. *The Administration of the Ptolemaic Possessions Outside Egypt*. Leiden: Brill.
Bagnall, Roger S., Richard J. A. Talbert, Sarah Bond, Jeffrey Becker, Tom Elliott, Sean Gillies, Ryan Horne, et al. 2006. "Pleiades: A Community-Built Gazetteer and Graph of Ancient Places." Collection. http://pleiades.stoa.org. Accessed January 1, 2017.
Barthélemy, Marc. 2011. "Spatial Networks." *Physics Reports* 499 (1–3): 1–101.
Basch, Lucien. 1985. "The Isis of Ptolemy II Philadelphus." *Mariner's Mirror* 71 (2): 129–51.
Beloch, Karl J. 1886. *Die Bevölkerung der griechisch-römischen Welt*. Leipzig: Duncker & Humblot.

Bernand, Étienne. 2001. *Inscriptions grecques d'Alexandrie ptolémaïque*. Le Caire: Institut français d'archéologie orientale.
Bissa, Erietta. 2009. *Governmental Intervention in Foreign Trade in Archaic and Classical Greece*. Leiden: Brill.
Blumel, Wolfgang. 2000. "Ein rhodisches Dekret aus Bargylia." *Epigraphica Anatolica* 32: 94–6.
Bøgh, Birgitte. 2013. "The Graeco-Roman Cult of Isis." In *The Handbook of Religions in Ancient Europe*, edited by David A. Warburton, Lisbeth B. Christensen, and Olav Hammer, 228–41. London: Routledge.
Bonnet, Corinne. 2006. "Les 'religions orientales' au laboratoire de l'hellénisme. II: Franz Cumont." *Archiv für Religionsgeschichte* 8 (1): 181–205.
Booth, Charles D. G., and Isabelle B. Booth. 1928. *Italy's Aegean Possessions*. London: Arrowsmith.
Borchhardt, Jürgen. 1991. "Ein Ptolemaion in Limyra." *Revue Archéologique* 2: 309–22.
Borgeaud, Philippe, and Youri Volokhine. 2000. "La formation de la légende de Sarapis: Une approche transculturelle." *Archiv Für Religionsgeschichte* (2): 37–76.
Bosworth, Albert B. 1988. *From Arrian to Alexander: Studies in Historical Interpretation*. Oxford: Oxford University Press.
Bousquet, Jean. 1986. "Lettre de Ptolémée Evergète III à Xanthos de Lycie." *Revue Des Études Grecques* 99 (470/471): 22–32.
Bowden, Hugh. 2010. *Mystery Cults of the Ancient World*. Princeton: Princeton University Press.
Box, George E. P. 1976. "Science and Models." *Journal of the American Statistical Association* 71 (356): 791–9.
Box, George E. P., and Alberto Luceño. 1997. *Statistical Control by Monitoring and Feedback Adjustment*. New York: John Wiley & Sons.
Brady, Thomas A., Fordyce Mitchell, and Charles F. Mullett. 1978. *Sarapis & Isis: Collected Essays*. Chicago: Ares Publishers.
Braudel, Fernand. 1995. *The Mediterranean and the Mediterranean World in the Age of Philip II*. Berkeley: University of California Press.
Braund, David. 2018. *Greek Religion and Cults in the Black Sea Region: Goddesses in the Bosporan Kingdom from the Archaic Period to the Byzantine Era*. Cambridge: Cambridge University Press.
Bremen, Riet van. 2003. "Ptolemy at Panamara." *Epigraphica Anatolica* 35: 9–14.
Bremen, Riet van. 2017. "Labraunda and the Ptolemies: A Reinterpretation of Three Documents from the Sanctuary of Zeus (I.Labraunda 51, 45 and 44)." *Studi Ellenistici* 31: 223–59.
Bremmer, Jan N. 2014. *Initiation into the Mysteries of the Ancient World*. Berlin: De Gruyter.
Bresson, Alain. 2012. "Bargylia." In *The Encyclopedia of Ancient History*. Wiley Online Library.

Bricault, Laurent. 1997. "Les cultes isiaques en Grèce centrale et occidentale." *Zeitschrift für Papyrologie und Epigraphik* 119: 117–22.

Bricault, Laurent. 1999. "Sarapis et Isis Sauveurs de Ptolémée IV à Raphia." *Chronique d'Egypte; Bulletin Periodique de La Fondation Egyptologique Reine Elisabeth* 74 (148): 334–43.

Bricault, Laurent. 2001. *Atlas de la diffusion des cultes isiaques (IVe s. av. J.-C.—IVe s. apr. J.-C.)*. Paris: Diffusion de Boccard.

Bricault, Laurent. 2004. "La diffusion isiaque: une esquisse." *Fremdheit-Eigenheit. Ägypten, Griechenland und Rom. Austausch und Verständnis* 19: 548–56.

Bricault, Laurent. 2005a. "Les dieux de l'Orient en Afrique romaine." *Pallas* (68): 289–309.

Bricault, Laurent. 2005b. *Recueil des inscriptions concernant les cultes isiaques: RICIS*. Paris: Diffusion de Boccard.

Bricault, Laurent. 2006. *Isis, Dame des flots*. Aegyptiaca Ieodiensia. Vol. 7. Liège: C.I.P.L.

Bricault, Laurent. 2011. "Isis à Rome." In *De Cybèle à Isis*, edited by Jean-Pierre Montesino, 137–51. Paris: Éd. Cybèle.

Bricault, Laurent. 2013. *Les cultes isiaques dans le monde gréco-romain*. Paris: Belles Lettres.

Bricault, Laurent. 2014. "Les Sarapiastes." In *Le myrte et la rose: mélanges offerts à Françoise Dunand par ses élèves, collègues et amis*. Vol. 1, edited by Françoise Dunand and G. Tallet, 41–9. Montpellier: Équipe "Égypte Nilotique et Mediterranéenne" de l'UMR 5140, "Archéologie des Sociétés Méditerranénnes" (Cnrs—Univ. Paul Valéry—Montpellier III).

Bricault, Laurent. 2015. "The 'Gens Isiaca' in Graeco-Roman Coinage." *The Numismatic Chronicle (1966–)* 175: 83–102.

Bricault, Laurent. 2018. "Traveling Gods: The Cults of Isis in the Roman Empire." In *Beyond the Nile: Egypt and the Classical World*, edited by Jeffrey Spier, Timothy Potts, and Sara E. Cole, 226–31. Los Angeles: The J. Paul Getty Museum.

Bricault, Laurent. 2019. "Isis, Sarapis et Rome: Jeux d'échelles et de pouvoirs." In *Religion et Pouvoir: Monde Romain 218 av. J.-C.—235 ap. J.-C.*, edited by Catherine Wolff and Marie-Odile Laforge-Charles, 195–228. Paris: Atlande.

Bricault, Laurent. 2020. *Isis Pelagia: Images, Names and Cults of a Goddess of the Seas*. Leiden: Brill.

Bricault, Laurent, and Miguel J. Versluys. 2014. "Isis and Empires." In *Power, Politics and the Cults of Isis: Proceedings of the 5. International Conference of Isis Studies, Boulogne-Sur-Mer, October 13–15, 2011: Organised in Cooperation with Jean-Louis Podvin*, edited by Laurent Bricault and Miguel J. Versluys, 1–35. Leiden; Boston: Brill.

Bricault, Laurent, Yann Le Bohec, and Jean-Louis Podvin. 2004. "Cultes isiaques en Proconsulaire." In *Isis en Occident: Actes du IIème Colloque international sur les études isiaques, Lyon III 16–17 mai 2002*, edited by Laurent Bricault, 221–41. Leiden: Brill.

Broodbank, Cyprian. 2000. *An Island Archaeology of the Early Cyclades*. Cambridge: Cambridge University Press.

Brughmans, Tom. 2010. "Connecting the Dots: Towards Archaeological Network Analysis." *Oxford Journal of Archaeology* 29 (3): 277–303.

Brughmans, Tom. 2013. "Thinking through Networks: A Review of Formal Network Methods in Archaeology." *Journal of Archaeological Method and Theory* 20 (4): 623–62.

Brughmans, Tom, Anna Collar, and Fiona Coward, eds. 2016a. *The Connected Past: Challenges to Network Studies in Archaeology and History*. Oxford: Oxford University Press.

Brughmans, Tom, Anna Collar, and Fiona Coward. 2016b. "Network Perspectives on the Past: Tackling the Challenges." In *The Connected Past: Challenges to Network Studies in Archaeology and History*, edited by Tom Brughmans, Anna Collar, and Fiona Coward, 1–19. Oxford: Oxford University Press.

Brughmans, Tom, and Jeroen Poblome. 2016. "MERCURY: An Agent-Based Model of Tableware Trade in the Roman East." *Journal of Artificial Societies and Social Simulation* 19 (1): 1–3.

Brughmans, Tom, John William Hanson, Matthew J. Mandich, Iza Romanowska, Xavier Rubio-Campillo, Simon Carrignon, Stephen Collins-Elliott, Katherine Crawford, Dries Daems, Francesca Fulminante, Tymon de Haas, Paul Kelly, Maria del Carmen Moreno Escobar, Eleftheria Paliou, Luce Prignano, and Manuela Ritondale. 2019. "Formal Modelling Approaches to Complexity Science in Roman Studies: A Manifesto." *Theoretical Roman Archaeology Journal* 2 (1): 4.

Brun, Patrice. 1991. "Les Lagides à Lesbos: Essai de chronologie." *Zeitschrift für Papyrologie und Epigraphik* 85: 99–113.

Bruneau, Philippe. 1970. *Recherches sur les cultes de Délos à l'époque hellénistique et à l'époque impériale*. Paris: De Boccard.

Bruneau, Philippe. 1975. *Le sanctuaire et le culte des divinités égyptiennes à Érétrie*. Leiden: Brill.

Buraselis, Kostas. 2008. "The Problem of the Ptolemaic Sibling Marriage: A Case of Dynastic Acculturation?" In *Ptolemy II Philadelphus and His World*, edited by P. McKechnie and P. Guillaume, 291–302. Leiden: Brill.

Buraselis, Kostas. 2013. "Ptolemaic Grain, Seaways and Power." In *The Ptolemies, the Sea and the Nile*, edited by K. Buraselis, M. Stefanou, and D. J. Thompson, 97–107. Cambridge: Cambridge University Press.

Burke, Peter. 2015. *The French Historical Revolution: The Annales School, 1929-2014*. Cambridge: Polity.

Burkert, Walter. 1987. *Ancient Mystery Cults*. Cambridge: Harvard University Press.

Campbell, Edgar C. 1925. *Catalogue général des antiquités égyptiennes du Musée du Caire: Zenon Papyri, 4 Vols*. Le Caire: Institut français d'archéologie orientale.

Carney, Elizabeth D. 2013. *Arsinoë of Egypt and Macedon a Royal Life*. New York: Oxford University Press.

Cassius Dio, Cocceianus, Earnest Cary, and Herbert B. Foster. 1987. *Dio's Roman History*. Vol. 4. Cambridge: Harvard University Press.

Casson, Lionel. 1954. "The Grain Trade of the Hellenistic World." *Transactions and Proceedings of the American Philological Association* 85: 168.

Casson, Lionel. 1995. *Sea and Seamanship in the Ancient World*. Baltimore: Johns Hopkins University Press.

Chaniotis, Angelos. 2002. "Foreign Soldiers—Native Girls? Constructing and Crossing Boundaries in Hellenistic Cities with Foreign Garrisons." In *Army and Power in the Ancient World*, edited by P. Ducrey and A. Chaniotis, 99–113. Stuttgart: Steiner.

Chaniotis, Angelos. 2005. *War in the Hellenistic World: A Social and Cultural History*. Malden: Blackwell Publishing.

Chaniotis, Angelos. 2011. "The Ithyphallic Hymn for Demetrios Poliorketes and Hellenistic Religious Mentality." In *More than Men, Less than Gods: Studies on Royal Cult and Imperial Worship; Proceedings of the International Colloquium Organized by the Belgian School at Athens (November 1–2, 2007)*, edited by P. P. Iossif, A. S. Chankowski, and C. C. Lorber, *Studia Hellenistica* 51: 157–95. Leuven: Peeters.

Chaniotis, Angelos, Thomas Corsten, Nikolaos Papazarkadas, and Rolf A. Tybout. 2010. "SEG 60-1536. Limyra. Ptolemaic Prostagma Concerning Abuses in the Levying of Taxes, ca. 250 B.C., Possibly 277/276 B.C." Supplementum Epigraphicum Graecum. Brill. http://dx.doi.org/10.1163/1874-6772_seg_a60_1536.

Christodoulou, Perikles. 2015. "Sarapis, Isis and the Emperor." In *Romanising Oriental Gods? Religious Transformations in the Balkan Provinces in the Roman Period. New Finds and Novel Perspectives. Proceedings of the International Symposium, Skopje, 18–21 September 2013*, edited by Aleksandra Nikoloska and Sander Müskens, 167–211. Skopkje: Macedonian Academy of Sciences and Arts and University of Leiden.

Chrubasik, Boris. 2016. *Kings and Usurpers in the Seleukid Empire: The Men Who Would Be King*. Oxford: Oxford University Press.

Chugg, Andrew. 2005. "The Journal of Alexander the Great." *Ancient History Bulletin* 19 (3–4): 155–75.

Cohen, Getzel M. 1995. *The Hellenistic Settlements in Europe, the Islands and Asia Minor*. Berkeley: University of California Press.

Collar, Anna. 2013. *Religious Networks in the Roman Empire*. New York: Cambridge University Press.

Constantakopoulou, Christy. 2012. "Identity and Resistance: The Islanders' League, the Aegean Islands and the Hellenistic Kings." *Mediterranean Historical Review* 27 (1): 51–72.

Constantakopoulou, Christy. 2017. *Aegean Interactions: Delos and Its Networks in the Third Century*. Oxford: Oxford University Press.

"Corine Land Cover 2006 Seamless Vector Data V17." n.d. https://www.eea.europa.eu/data-and-maps/data/clc-2006-vector-data-version-3. Accessed July 27, 2017.

Cumont, Franz. 1911. *The Oriental Religions in Roman Paganism*. Chicago: Open Court.

"The Curse of Artemisia." n.d. World Digital Library. https://www.wdl.org/en/item/4310/. Accessed January 3, 2018.

Czachesz, István. 2016. "Network Analysis of Biblical Texts." *Journal of Cognitive Historiography* 3 (1–2): 43–67.

Da Vela, Raffaella. 2019. "Interlocking Networks and the Sacred Landscape of Hellenistic Northern Etruria: Capturing Social and Geographic Entanglement through Social Network Analysis." *Open Archaeology* 5 (1): 505–18.

Dmitriev, Sviatoslav. 2005. *City Government in Hellenistic and Roman Asia Minor*. New York: Oxford University Press.

Downey, Allen B. 2018. *Think Complexity: Complexity Science and Computational Modeling (Second Edition)*. Sebastopol: O'Reilly.

Dunand, Françoise. 1973a. *Le culte d'Isis dans le bassin oriental de la Méditerranée. 2, Le culte d'Isis en Grèce*. Leiden: E. J. Brill.

Dunand, Françoise. 1973b. *Le culte d'Isis dans le bassin oriental de la Méditerranée. 3, Le culte d'Isis en Asie Mineure*. Leiden: E. J. Brill.

Dunand, Françoise. 1980. "Cultes égyptiens hors d'Égypte, Essai d'analyse des conditions de leur diffusion." In *Religions, Pouvoir, Rapports Sociaux*, edited by P. Briant, 71–148. Paris: Les belles lettres.

Dunand, Françoise. 2007. "The Religious System at Alexandria." In *A Companion to Greek Religion*, edited by D. Ogden, 253–63. Oxford: Blackwell.

Eckstein, Arthur M. 2008. *Rome Enters the Greek East: From Anarchy to Hierarchy in the Hellenistic Mediterranean, 230–170 B.C.* Malden: Blackwell.

Edwards, Dilwyn, and Mike Hamson. 2001. *Guide to Mathematical Modelling*. Basingstoke: Palgrave.

Eidinow, Esther. 2011. "Networks and Narratives: A Model for Ancient Greek Religion." *Kernos* (24): 9–38.

Ericson, Jonathon E., and R. Goldstein. 1980. "Work Space: A New Approach to the Analysis of Energy Expenditure." *Anthropology UCLA* 10: 21–30.

"European Soil Database." n.d. http://esdac.jrc.ec.europa.eu/content/european-soil-database-derived-data. Accessed January 1, 2017.

Evans, Tim. 2018. "Robust Spatial Network Analysis*." In *Maritime Networks in the Ancient Mediterranean World*, edited by Carl Knappett and Justin Leidwanger, 22–38. Cambridge: Cambridge University Press.

Fassa, Eleni. 2015. "Sarapis, Isis, and the Ptolemies in Private Dedications." *Kernos* (28): 133–53.

Fischer-Bovet, Christelle. 2014. *Army and Society in Ptolemaic Egypt*. Cambridge: Cambridge University Press.

Fontana, Federica, and Emanuela Murgia. 2010. *I culti isiaci nell'Italia settentrionale*. Trieste, Italy: EUT Edizioni Università di Trieste.

Fousek, Jan, Vojtěch Kaše, Adam Mertel, Eva Výtvarová, and Aleš Chalupa. 2018. "Spatial Constraints on the Diffusion of Religious Innovations: The Case of Early Christianity in the Roman Empire." *PLOS One* 13 (12): e0208744.

Foxhall, Lin, and Hamish A. Forbes. 1982. *Sitometreia: The Role of Grain as a Staple Food in Classical Antiquity*. Munchen: C. H. Beck.
Fraser, Peter M. 1960. "Two Studies on the Cult of Sarapis in the Hellenistic World." *Opuscula Atheniensia* 3: 1–54.
Fraser, Peter M. 1967. "Current Problems Concerning the Early History of the Cult of Sarapis." *Opuscula Atheniensia* 7: 23–45.
Fraser, Peter M. 1972. *Ptolemaic Alexandria I*. Oxford: Clarendon Press.
French, David. 1998. "Pre-and Early-Roman Roads of Asia Minor." *Iran* 36 (1): 15–43.
Gabrielsen, Vincent. 2013. "Rhodes and the Ptolemaic Kingdom: The Commercial Infrastructure." In *The Ptolemies, the Sea and the Nile: Studies in Waterborne Power*, edited by K. Buraselis, M. Stefanou, and D. J. Thompson, 66–81. Cambridge: Cambridge University Press.
Gasparini, Valentino, and Richard L. Gordon. 2018. "Egyptianism: Appropriating 'Egypt' in the 'Isiac Cults' of the Graeco-Roman World." *Acta Antiqua Academiae Scientiarum Hungaricae* 58 (1–4): 571–606.
Gauthier, Philippe. 2003. "Deux décrets hellénistiques de Colophon-sur-Mer." *Revue des Études Grecques* 116 (2): 470–93.
Glomb, Tomáš. 2021. "The Spread of the Cult of Asclepius in the Context of the Roman Army Benefited from the Presence of Physicians: A Spatial Proximity Analysis." *PLOS One* 16 (8): e0256356.
Glomb, Tomáš, Adam Mertel, Zdeněk Pospíšil, and Aleš Chalupa. 2020. "Ptolemaic Political Activities on the West Coast of Hellenistic Asia Minor Had a Significant Impact on the Local Spread of the Isiac Cults: A Spatial Network Analysis." *PLOS One* 15 (4): e0230733.
Glomb, Tomáš, Adam Mertel, Zdeněk Pospíšil, Zdeněk Stachoň, and Aleš Chalupa. 2018. "Ptolemaic Military Operations Were a Dominant Factor in the Spread of Egyptian Cults across the Early Hellenistic Aegean Sea." *PLOS One* 13 (3): e0193786.
Gordon, Richard L. 1975. "Franz Cumont and the Doctrine of Mithraism." In *Mithraic Studies I*, edited by J. Hinnells, 215–48. Manchester: Manchester University Press.
Gordon, Richard L. 2003. *Image and Value in the Graeco-Roman World: Studies in Mithraism and Religious Art*. Aldershot: Ashgate Variorum.
Graauw, Arthur de. 2016. "Catalogue of Ancient Ports Antiques." http://www.ancientportsantiques.com/. Accessed January 1, 2017.
Grach, Nonna. 1984. "Otkrytiye Novogo Istoricheskogo Istochnika v Nimfeye." *Vestnik Drevnej Istorii* 167 (1): 81–8.
Grainger, John D. 2010. *The Syrian Wars*. Leiden: Brill.
Grainger, John D. 2017. *Great Power Diplomacy in the Hellenistic World*. London: Routledge.
Granovetter, Mark S. 1973. "The Strength of Weak Ties." *American Journal of Sociology* 78 (6): 1360–80.
Grimm, Günter. 1998. *Alexandria: die erste Königsstadt der Hellenistischen Welt: Bilder aus der Nilmetropole von Alexander dem Großen bis Kleopatra VII*. Mainz am Rhein: Von Zabern.

Gygax, Marc D. 2005. "Change and Continuity in the Administration of Ptolemaic Lycia: A Note on P. Tebt. I 8." *The Bulletin of the American Society of Papyrologists* 42 (1/4): 45–50.

Habicht, Christian. 1989. "The Seleucids and Their Rivals." In *The Cambridge Ancient History*, 2nd ed., edited by A. Astin, F. Walbank, M. Frederiksen, and R. Ogilvie: 324–87. The Cambridge Ancient History. Cambridge: Cambridge University Press.

Hall, Jonathan M. 2007. "International Relations." In *The Cambridge History of Greek and Roman Warfare. Vol. 1, Greece, the Hellenistic World and the Rise of Rome*, edited by Philip Sabin, Hans van Wees, and Michael Whitby, 85–107. Cambridge: Cambridge University Press.

Hammond, Nicholas G. L. 1988. "The Royal Journal of Alexander." *Historia: Zeitschrift für Alte Geschichte* 37 (2): 129–50.

Hansen, Mogens H. 2006. *The Shotgun Method: The Demography of the Ancient Greek City-State Culture*. London: University of Missouri Press.

Harland, Philip A. 2003. *Associations, Synagogues, and Congregations: Claiming a Place in Ancient Mediterranean Society*. Minneapolis: Fortress Press.

Harland, Philip A. n.d.a. "Decrees Regarding a Kitian Temple for the Syrian Aphrodite (333/332 BCE)." Associations in the Greco-Roman World, An Expanding Collection of Inscriptions, Papyri, and Other Sources in Translation. http://philipharland.com/greco-roman-associations/10-decrees-regarding-a-kitian-temple-for-the-syrian-aphrodite/. Accessed January 4, 2018.

Harland, Philip A. n.d.b. "Dedication of an Offering Receptacle by the Royalists (270-250 BCE)." Associations in the Greco-Roman World, An Expanding Collection of Inscriptions, Papyri, and Other Sources in Translation. http://philipharland.com/greco-roman-associations/dedication-of-a-offering-receptacle-by-the-royalists/. Accessed January 4, 2018.

Harland, Philip A. n.d.c. "Honors by Fellow-Banqueters for Procurator Panopaios (161-169 CE)." Associations in the Greco-Roman World, An Expanding Collection of Inscriptions, Papyri, and Other Sources in Translation. http://philipharland.com/greco-roman-associations/honors-by-fellow-banqueters-for-p-aelius-panopaios-161-169-ce/. Accessed September 22, 2021.

Harland, Philip A. n.d.d. "Honors by Sarapiasts for Apollodoros (after 216/215 BCE)." Associations in the Greco-Roman World, An Expanding Collection of Inscriptions, Papyri, and Other Sources in Translation. http://philipharland.com/greco-roman-associations/honors-by-sarapiasts-for-a-benefactor-after-216215-bce/. Accessed October 14, 2021.

Harper, Kyle, and Michael McCormick. 2018. "Reconstructing the Roman Climate." In *The Science of Roman History: Biology, Climate, and the Future of the Past*, edited by W. Scheidel, 11–52. Princeton: Princeton University Press.

Hauben, Hans. 1987a. "Cyprus and the Ptolemaic Navy." *Report of the Department of Antiquities Cyprus*, 213–26.

Hauben, Hans. 1987b. "Philocles, King of the Sidonians and General of the Ptolemies." In *Phoenicia and the East Mediterranean in the First Millennium BC. Proceedings of the Conference Held in Leuven from the 14th to the 16th of November 1985*, edited by Edward Lipiński, 413–27. Studia Phoenicia 5. Leuven: Peeters.

Hauben, Hans. 2004. "A Phoenician King in the Service of the Ptolemies: Philocles of Sidon Revisited." *Ancient Society* 34: 27–44.

Hauben, Hans. 2013. "Callicrates of Samos and Patroclus of Macedon, Champions of Ptolemaic Thalassocracy." In *The Ptolemies, the Sea and the Nile: Studies in Waterborne Power*, edited by Dorothy J. Thompson, Kostas Buraselis, and Mary Stefanou, 39–65. Cambridge: Cambridge University Press.

Hayne, Leonie. 1992. "Isis and Republican Politics." *Acta Classica: Proceedings of the Classical Association of South Africa* 35 (1): 143–9.

Hekster, Olivier J. 2002. *Commodus: An Emperor at the Crossroads*. Amsterdam: J.C. Gieben.

Herzog, Irmela. 2013. "Theory and Practice of Cost Functions." In *Proceedings of the 38th Annual Conference on Computer Applications and Quantitative Methods in Archaeology, CAA 2010*, edited by Francisco Conteras, Mercedes Farjas, and Javier Melero, 375–82. Granada, Spain. Oxford: Archaeopress.

Heyob, Sharon Kelly. 1975. *The Cult of Isis among Women in the Graeco-Roman World*. Leiden: Brill.

Hiller von Gaertringen, Friedrich. 1906. *Inschriften von Priene*. Berlin: G. Reimer.

Hölbl, Günther. 2001. *A History of the Ptolemaic Empire*. New York: Routledge.

Horden, Peregrine, and Nicholas Purcell. 2000. *The Corrupting Sea: A Study of Mediterranean History*. Oxford: Blackwell.

Iggers, Georg G. 2012. *Historiography in the Twentieth Century: From Scientific Objectivity to the Postmodern Challenge*. Middletown: Wesleyan University Press.

Isager, Signe, and Jens E. Skydsgaard. 1995. *Ancient Greek Agriculture: An Introduction*. London: Routledge.

Karpat, Kemal H. 1985. *Ottoman Population, 1830–1914: Demographic and Social Characteristics*. London: University of Wisconsin Press.

Kloppenborg, John S., and Richard S. Ascough. 2011. *Greco-Roman Associations: Texts, Translations, and Commentary, Vol. 1 Attica, Central Greece, Macedonia, Thrace*. Berlin: De Gruyter.

Knappett, Carl. 2011. *An Archaeology of Interaction: Network Perspectives on Material Culture and Society*. Oxford: Oxford University Press.

Knappett, Carl. 2016. "Networks in Archaeology: Between Scientific Method and Humanistic Metaphor." In *The Connected Past: Challenges to Network Studies in Archaeology and History*, edited by Tom Brughmans, Anna Collar, and Fiona Coward, 21–33. Oxford: Oxford University Press.

Kondo, Yasuhisa, and Yoichi Seino. n.d. "GPS-Aided Walking Experiments and Data-Driven Travel Cost Modeling on the Historical Road of Nakasendō-Kisoji (Central Highland Japan)." In *Making History Interactive. Computer*

Applications and Quantitative Methods in Archaeology (CAA). Proceedings of the 37th International Conference, Williamsburg, Virginia, USA, March 22–26, 2009, edited by L. Fischer, B. Frischer, and S. Wells, BAR International Series 2079, 158–65. https://proceedings.caaconference.org/paper/21_kondo_seino_caa2009/. Accessed October 9, 2019.

Kosmin, Paul J. 2018. *The Land of the Elephant Kings: Space, Territory, and Ideology in the Seleucid Empire.* Cambridge: Harvard University Press.

LaBuff, Jeremy. 2016. *Polis Expansion and Elite Power in Hellenistic Karia.* Lanham: Lexington Books.

Launey, Marcel. 1987. *Recherches sur les armées hellénistiques.* Paris: De Boccard.

Le Rider, Georges. 1990. "Antiochos II à Mylasa." *Bulletin de Correspondance Hellénique* 114 (1): 543–51.

Lefebvre, Ludovic. 2008. "La diffusion du culte de Sarapis en Grèce continentale et dans les îles de l'Égée au IIIe siècle avant J.-C." *Revue d'Histoire et de Philosophie religieuses* 88 (4): 451–67.

Legras, Bernard. 2014. "Sarapis, Isis et le pouvoir lagide." In *Power, Politics and the Cults of Isis: Proceedings of the 5. International Conference of Isis Studies, Boulogne-Sur-Mer, October 13–15, 2011: Organised in Cooperation with Jean-Louis Podvin,* edited by Miguel J. Versluys and Laurent Bricault, 95–115. Leiden: Brill.

Leidwanger, Justin, and Carl Knappett, eds. 2018. *Maritime Networks in the Ancient Mediterranean World.* Cambridge: Cambridge University Press.

Levick, Barbara. 2020. *Vespasian.* London: Routledge.

Lewis, Theodor G. 2009. *Network Science: Theory and Applications.* Hoboken, NJ: Wiley.

Lipinski, Edward. 1995. *Dieux et déesses de l'univers phénicien et punique.* Leuven: Peeters.

Lipka, Michael. 2009. *Roman Gods: A Conceptual Approach.* Leiden: Brill.

Loyd, Alan B. 2011. "From Satrapy to Hellenistic Kingdom: The Case of Egypt." In *Creating a Hellenistic World,* edited by A. Erskine and L. Llewellyn-Jones, 83–105. Swansea: The Classical Press of Wales.

Łukaszewicz, Adam. 1998. *Antoninus Philosarapis: Observations on Caracalla's Visit to the Sarapeum of Alexandria (A.D. 215–216).* Warszawa: Uniwersytet Warszawski, Instytut Archeologii, Zakład Papirologii.

Lynch, Kathleen, and Stephen Matter. 2014. "Trade of Athenian Figured Pottery and the Effects of Connectivity." In *Athenian Potters and Painters.* Vol. 3, edited by John H. Oakley, 107–15. Oxford: Oxbow books.

Ma, John. 2002. *Antiochos III and the Cities of Western Asia Minor.* Oxford: Oxford University Press.

Ma, John. 2014. "Les cultes isiaques dans l'espace séleucide." In *Power, Politics and the Cults of Isis,* edited by Laurent Bricault and Miguel J. Versluys, 116–34. Proceedings of the Vth International Conference of Isis Studies, Boulogne-Sur-Mer, October 13–15, 2011. Leiden: Brill.

Mack, William. 2015. *Proxeny and Polis: Institutional Networks in the Ancient Greek World*. Oxford Studies in Ancient Documents. Oxford: Oxford University Press.

MacMullen, Ramsay. 1983. *Paganism in the Roman Empire*. London: Yale University Press.

Magie, David. 1953. "Egyptian Deities in Asia Minor in Inscriptions and on Coins." *American Journal of Archaeology* 57 (3): 163–87.

Magie, David. 2014. *Historia Augusta*. Cambridge: Harvard University Press.

Malaise, Michel. 1972. *Les conditions de pénétration et de diffusion des cultes égyptiens en Italie*. Leiden: E.J. Brill.

Malek, Jaromir. 2014. "The Old Kingdom (c.2686-2160 BC)." In *Oxford History of Ancient Egypt*, edited by I. Shaw, 83–107. Oxford: Oxford University Press.

Malkin, Irad. 2011. *A Small Greek World: Networks in the Ancient Mediterranean*. Oxford: Oxford University Press.

Malkin, Irad, Christy Constantakopoulou, and Katerina Panagopoulou. 2013. *Greek and Roman Networks in the Mediterranean*. London: Routledge.

Manders, Erika. 2012. *Coining of Images of Power. Patterns in the Representation of Roman Emperors on Imperial Coinage, A.D. 193–284*. Leiden: Brill.

"A Manifesto for the Study of Ancient Mediterranean Maritime Networks—Research—Aarhus University." n.d. http://journal.antiquity.ac.uk/projgall/leidwanger342. Accessed September 21, 2021.

Manolaraki, Eleni. 2013. *Noscendi Nilum Cupido Imagining Egypt from Lucan to Philostratus*. Berlin: De Gruyter.

Marek, Christian. 2006. *Die Inschriften von Kaunos*. Munich: C. H. Beck.

Marquaille, Céline. 2008. "The Foreign Policy of Ptolemy II." In *Ptolemy II Philadelphus and His World*, edited by P. McKechnie and P. Guillaume, 39–64. Leiden: Brill.

Martzavou, Paraskevi. 2010. "Les cultes isiaques et les Italiens entre Délos, Thessalonique et l'Eubée." *Pallas. Revue d'études antiques* 84 (December): 181–205.

Mazzilli, Francesca. 2018. *Rural Cult Centres in the Hauran: Part of the Broader Network of the Near East (100 BC–AD 300)*. Oxford: Archaeopress Publishing Ltd.

McCormick, Michael, Guoping Huang, Giovanni Zambotti, and Jessica Lavash. 2013. "Roman Road Network (Version 2008)." Harvard Dataverse.

McGing, Brian C. 1986. *The Foreign Policy of Mithridates VI Eupator King of Pontus*. Leiden: Brill.

Meadows, Andrew. 2006. "The Ptolemaic Annexation of Lycia: SEG 27.929." In *Proceedings of the Third International Lycia Congress. Symposion Proceedings 2*, edited by Kayhan Dörtlük, Burhan Varkivanç, Tarkan Kahya, Jacques des Courtils, Meltem Doğan Alparslan, and Remziye Boyraz, 459–70. Antalya: AKMED.

Meadows, Andrew. 2013. "The Ptolemaic League of Islanders." In *The Ptolemies, the Sea and the Nile*, edited by K. Buraselis, M. Stefanou, and D. J. Thompson, 19–38. Cambridge: Cambridge University Press.

Meadows, Andrew, and Peter Thonemann. 2013. "The Ptolemaic Administration of Pamphylia." *Zeitschrift für Papyrologie und Epigraphik* 186: 223–6.

Menander, and W. Geoffrey Arnott. 1979. *Aspis. Georgos. Dis Exapaton. Dyskolos. Encheiridion. Epitrepontes.* Loeb classical library 132. Cambridge: Harvard University Press.

Meritt, Benjamin D., Henry T. Wade-Gery, and Malcolm F. McGregor. 1939. *The Athenian Tribute Lists.* Princeton: American school of classical studies at Athens.

"Ministry of Interior: Resultats statistiques du recensement de la population de 5–6 October 1896." n.d. http://dlib.statistics.gr/Book/GRESYE_02_0101_00003.pdf. Accessed January 1, 2017.

Mojsov, Bojana. 2005. *Osiris: Death and Afterlife of a God.* Oxford: Blackwell Publishing.

Morel, Jean-Paul. 1997. "Problématique de la colonisation grecque en Méditerranée occidentale: L'exemple des réseaux." In *Il dinamismo della colonizzazione greca: Atti della tavola rotonda "Espansione e colonizzazione greca d'età arcaica: metodologie e problemi a confronto*, edited by Claudia Antonetti, 59–70. Naples: Loffredo.

Morgan, Gwyn. 2007. *69 A.D.: The Year of Four Emperors.* New York: Oxford University Press.

Morrison, John S. 1996. *Greek and Roman Oared Warships 399–30 B.C.* Oxford: Oxbow Books.

Moyer, Ian S. 2008. "Notes on Re-Reading the Delian Aretalogy of Sarapis ('IG' XI.4 1299)." *Zeitschrift für Papyrologie und Epigraphik* 166: 101–7.

Moyer, Ian S. 2011. *Egypt and the limits of Hellenism.* Cambridge: Cambridge University Press.

Münster, Maria. 1968. *Untersuchungen zur Göttin Isis: vom Alten Reich bis zum Ende des Neuen Reiches. Mit hieroglyphischem Textanhang.* Berlin: B. Hessling.

Nagel, Svenja. 2012. "The Cult of Isis and Sarapis in North Africa: Local Shifts of an Egyptian Cult under the Influence of Different Cultural Traditions." In *Egyptian Gods in the Hellenistic and Roman Mediterranean: Image and Reality between Local and Global*, edited by Laurent Bricault and Miguel J. Versluys, 67–92. Proceedings of the IInd International PhD Workshop on Isis Studies, Leiden University, January 26, 2011. Caltanissetta: Salvatore Sciascia Editore.

"Natural Earth." n.d. http://www.naturalearthdata.com. Accessed November 13, 2021.

Oliver, Graham J. 2007. *War, Food, and Politics in Early Hellenistic Athens.* Oxford: Oxford University Press.

Oneil, James L. 2008. "A Re-Examination of the Chremonidean War." In *Ptolemy II Philadelphus and his World*, edited by P. McKechnie and P. Guillaume, 65–90. Leiden: Brill.

Oppen de Ruiter, Branko Fredde van. 2015. *Berenice II Euergetis: Essays in Early Hellenistic Queenship.* New York: Palgrave Macmillan.

Orlin, Eric M. 2008. "Octavian and Egyptian Cults: Redrawing the Boundaries of Romanness." *The American Journal of Philology* 129 (2): 231–53.

Pachis, Panayotis. 2010. *Religion and Politics in the Graeco-Roman World: Redescribing the Isis-Sarapis Cult.* Thessaloniki: Barbounakis Publications.

Pachis, Panayotis. 2014. "Data from Dead Minds? Dream and Healing in the Isis / Sarapis Cult during the Graeco-Roman Age." *Journal of Cognitive Historiography* 1 (1): 52–71.

Pailler, Jean-Marie. 1989. "Les religions orientales, troisième époque." *Pallas* 35 (1): 95–113.

Parker, Robert. 2017. *Greek Gods Abroad: Names, Natures, and Transformations. Greek Gods Abroad*. Oakland: University of California Press.

Pearson, Lionel. 1955. "The Diary and the Letters of Alexander the Great." *Historia: Zeitschrift für Alte Geschichte* 3 (4): 429–55.

Pfeiffer, Stefan. 2008. "The God Serapis, His Cult and the Beginnings of the Ruler Cult in Ptolemaic Egypt." In *Ptolemy II Philadelphus and His World*, edited by P. McKechnie and P. Guillaume, 387–408. Leiden: Brill.

Pinch, Geraldine. 2002. *Handbook of Egyptian Mythology*. Santa Barbara: ABC-CLIO.

Pleket, Henry W., and Ronald S. Stroud. 1977. "SEG 27-929. Limyra. Honorary Decree for Two Caunians, 288–287 B.C." Supplementum Epigraphicum Graecum. Brill. http://dx.doi.org/10.1163/1874-6772_seg_a27_929.

Pleket, Henry W., and Ronald S. Stroud. 1983. "SEG 33-1183. Xanthos. Honorary Decree for the Phrourarchos Pandaros, 260-259 B.C." Supplementum Epigraphicum Graecum. Brill. http://dx.doi.org/10.1163/1874-6772_seg_a33_1183.

Pleket, Henry W., and Ronald S. Stroud. 1986. "SEG 36-1218. Xanthos. Letter of Ptolemy III Euergetes, 243–242 B.C." Supplementum Epigraphicum Graecum. Brill. http://dx.doi.org/10.1163/1874-6772_seg_a36_1218.

Plewe, Brandon. 2002. "The Nature of Uncertainty in Historical Geographic Information." *Transactions in GIS* 6 (4): 431–56.

Plutarch. 1936. *Moralia, with an English Translation by Frank Cole Babbitt*. Cambridge: Harvard University Press.

Podvin, Jean-Louis. 2014. "Le tropisme isiaque des Sévères: une acmé reconsidérée?" In *Power, Politics and the Cults of Isis: Proceedings of the 5. International Conference of Isis Studies, Boulogne-Sur-Mer, October 13–15, 2011: Organised in Cooperation with Jean-Louis Podvin*, edited by Miguel J. Versluys and Laurent Bricault, 300–25. Leiden: Brill.

Prag, Jonathan R. W., and Josephine C. Quinn. 2013. *The Hellenistic West: Rethinking the Ancient Mediterranean*. Cambridge: Cambridge University Press.

Quaegebeur, Jan. 1971. "Documents concerning a Cult of Arsinoe Philadelphos at Memphis." *Journal of Near Eastern Studies* 30 (4): 239–70.

Quaegebeur, Jan. 1998. "Documents égyptiens anciens et nouveaux relatifs à Arsinoé Philadelphe." In *Le culte du souverain dans l'Egypte ptolémaïque au IIIe siècle avant notre ère: actes du colloque international, Bruxelles, 10 mai 1995*, edited by H. Melaerts, 73–108. Leuven: Peeters.

Reed, Charles M. 2003. *Maritime Traders in the Ancient Greek World*. Cambridge: Cambridge University Press.

Reger, Gary. 1994a. "The Political History of the Kyklades 260-200 B.C." *Historia: Zeitschrift für Alte Geschichte* 43 (1): 32–69.

Reger, Gary. 1994b. *Regionalism and Change in the Economy of Independent Delos, 314–167 B.C.* Berkeley: University of California Press.

Reinach, Adolphe J. 1911. "Inscriptions d'Itanos." *Revue des Études Grecques* 24 (110): 377–425.

Rivers, Ray, Carl Knappett, and Tim Evans. 2013. "What Makes a Site Important? Centrality, Gateways, and Gravity." In *Network Analysis in Archaeology*, edited by C. Knappett, 125–50. Oxford: Oxford University Press.

Robert, Jeanne, and Louis Robert. 1983. *Fouilles d'Amyzon en Carie I.* Paris: Diffusion De Boccard.

Robert, Louis. 1966. *Documents de l'Asie Mineure Méridionale.* Paris: Droz.

Robert, Louis. 1989. *Opera minora selecta: épigraphie et antiquités grecques.* Vol. 5. Amsterdam: Adolf M. Hakkert.

Roberts, Alexander, James Donaldson, and A. Cleveland Coxe. 1993. *The Ante-Nicene Fathers. Translations of The Writings of the Fathers down to A.D. 325: Latin Christianity, Its Founder Tertullian: I. Apologetic, II. Anti-Marcion, III. Ethical Vol. 3.* Edinburgh: T&T Clark.

Roebuck, Carl. 1950. "The Grain Trade between Greece and Egypt." *Classical Philology* 45 (4): 236–47.

Roullet, Anne. 1972. *The Egyptian and Egyptianizing Monuments of Imperial Rome.* Leiden: Brill.

Rowe, Alan. 1946. *Discovery of the Famous Temple and Enclosure of Serapis at Alexandria.* Supplément aux Annales du Service des Antiquités, Cahier No. 2. Le Caire: Impr. de l'Institut français d'archéologie orientale.

Rowlandson, Jane, and Roger S. Bagnall. 1998. *Women and Society in Greek and Roman Egypt: A Sourcebook.* Cambridge: Cambridge University Press.

Ruschenbusch, Eberhard. 1983. "Tribut und Bürgerzahl im ersten athenischen Seebund." *Zeitschrift für Papyrologie und Epigraphik* 53: 125–43.

Ruschenbusch, Eberhard. 1984a. "Die Bevölkerungszahl Griechenlands im 5. und 4. Jh. v. Chr." *Zeitschrift Papyrologie Epigraphik* 56: 55–7.

Ruschenbusch, Eberhard. 1984b. "Modell Amorgos." In *Aux origines de l'hellénisme: la Crète et la Grèce. Hommage à Henri van Effenterre*, edited by Centre Gustave Glotz (Paris), 265–9. Paris: Publications de la Sorbonne.

Ruschenbusch, Eberhard. 1988. "Getreideerträge in Griechenland in der Zeit von 1921 bis 1938 n. Chr. als Massstab für die Antike." *Zeitschrift Papyrologie Epigraphik* 72: 141–53.

Rutishauser, Brian. 2012. *Athens and the Cyclades: Economic Strategies 540–314 BC.* Oxford: Oxford University Press.

Samuel, Alan E. 1986. "The Earliest Elements in the Alexander Romance." *Historia: Zeitschrift für Alte Geschichte* 35 (4): 427–37.

Satsuma, Junkichi, Ralph Willox, Alfred Ramani, Basile Grammaticos, and Adrian S. Carstea. 2004. "Extending the SIR Epidemic Model." *Physica A: Statistical Mechanics and Its Applications* 336 (3): 369–75.

Scheid, John. 2009. "Le statut du culte d'Isis à Rome sous le Haut-Empire." In *Les religions orientales dans le monde grec et romain: cent ans après Cumont (1906–2006): bilan historique et historiographique*, edited by Corinne Bonnet, Vinciane Pirenne-Delforge, and Danny Praet, 173–86. Brussels: Institut Historique Belge de Rome.

Scheid, John. 2016. *The Gods, the State, and the Individual: Reflections on Civic Religion in Rome*. Philadelphia: University of Pennsylvania Press.

Scheidel, Walter, ed. 2019. *The Science of Roman History: Biology, Climate, and the Future of the Past*. Princeton: Princeton University Press.

Scheidel, Walter, and Elijah Meeks. n.d. "Stanford Geospatial Network Model of the Roman World (ORBIS)." http://orbis.stanford.edu/. Accessed January 1, 2021.

Scott, John, and Peter Carrington, eds. 2014. *The SAGE Handbook of Social Network Analysis*. London: SAGE.

Segre, Mario. 1952. *Tituli Calymnii*. Bergamo: Istituto italiano d'arti grafiche.

Seland, Eivind H. 2013. "Networks and Social Cohesion in Ancient Indian Ocean Trade: Geography, Ethnicity, Religion." *Journal of Global History* 8 (3): 373–90.

Shear, Theodore L. 1978. *Kallias of Sphettos and the Revolt of Athens in 286 B.C.* Princeton, NJ: American School of Classical Studies at Athens.

Shi, Wenzhong. 2009. *Principles of Modeling Uncertainties in Spatial Data and Spatial Analyses*. New York: CRC press

Siculus, Diodorus, and Charles H. Oldfather. 1989. *Diodorus of Sicily in Twelve Volumes with an English Translation by C. H. Oldfather*. Vols. 4–8. Cambridge: Harvard University Press.

Skeat, Theodore C. 1974. *Greek Papyri in the British Museum 7. The Zenon Archive*. London: British Museum for the British Library Board.

Sperber, Dan. 1996. *Explaining Culture: Naturalistic Approach*. Oxford: Blackwell.

Spyridakis, Stylianos V. 1969. "The Itanian Cult of Tyche Protogeneia." *Historia: Zeitschrift für Alte Geschichte* 18 (1): 42–8.

Stambaugh, John E. 1972. *Sarapis Under the Early Ptolemies*. Leiden: E. J. Brill.

Stroumsa, Gedaliahu G. 2009. "Ex oriente lumen: From Orientalism to Oriental Religions." In *Les religions orientales dans le monde grec et romain: cent ans après Cumont (1906–2006): bilan historique et historiographique*, edited by C. Bonnet, V. Pirenne Delforge, and D. Praet, 91–103. Bruxelles: Institut Historique Belge de Rome.

Tacitus, Alfred J. Church, William J. Brodribb, and Sara Bryant. 1942. *Complete Works of Tacitus*. New York: Random House.

Takács, Sarolta A. 1995. *Isis and Sarapis in the Roman World*. Leiden: Brill.

Talbert, Richard J. A. 2000. *Barrington Atlas of the Greek and Roman World: Map-by-Map Directory*. Princeton: Princeton University Press.

Teigen, Håkon Fiane, and Eivind Heldaas Seland, eds. 2017. *Sinews of Empire: Networks in the Roman Near East and Beyond*. Oxford: Oxbow Books.

Theocritus, and Richard L. Hunter. 2003. *Encomium of Ptolemy Philadelphus*. Berkeley: University of California Press.

Thompson, Dorothy J. 1987. "Ptolemaios and the 'Lighthouse': Greek Culture in the Memphite Serapeum." *Proceedings of the Cambridge Philological Society* 33: 105–21.

Thompson, Dorothy J. 2012. *Memphis under the Ptolemies*. Princeton: Princeton University Press.

Tobler, Waldo. 1993. *Three Presentations on Geographical Analysis and Modeling: Non-Isotropic Geographic Modeling; Speculations on the Geometry of Geography; and Global Spatial Analysis (93-1)*. Santa Barbara: University of California.

Turchin, Peter. 2006. "Scientific Prediction in Historical Sociology: Ibn Khaldun Meets Al Saud." In *History and Mathematics: Historical Dynamics and Development of Complex Societies*, edited by Peter Turchin, Leonid Grinin, Andrey Korotayev, and Victor C. de Munck, 9–38. Moscow: URSS.

Turchin, Peter. 2008. "Arise 'Cliodynamics.'" *Nature* 454 (7200): 34–5.

Turchin, Peter. 2010. "Political Instability May Be a Contributor in the Coming Decade." *Nature* 463 (7281): 608.

Turchin, Peter. 2011. "Toward Cliodynamics—an Analytical, Predictive Science of History." *Cliodynamics* 2: 167–86.

Turchin, Peter. 2018. *Historical Dynamics Why States Rise and Fall*. Princeton: Princeton University Press.

Turchin, Peter. n.d. "Cliodynamics: History as Science." Peterturchin.Com. http://peterturchin.com/cliodynamics/. Accessed August 21, 2020.

Van der Ploeg, Ghislaine E. 2018. *The Impact of the Roman Empire on the Cult of Asclepius*. Leiden: Brill.

Versluys, Miguel J. 2002. *Aegyptiaca Romana: Nilotic Scenes and the Roman Views of Egypt*. Leiden: Brill.

Versluys, Miguel J. 2004. "Isis Capitolina and the Egyptian Cults in Late Republican Rome." In *Isis en Occident: Actes du IIème Colloque international sur les études isiaques, Lyon III 16-17 mai 2002*, edited by Laurent Bricault, 421–48. Leiden: Brill.

Versluys, Miguel J. 2006. "Aegyptiaca Romana: The Widening Debate." In *Nile into Tiber: Egypt in the Roman World: Proceedings of the 3rd International Conference of Isis Studies, Leiden, May 11-14 2005*, edited by Laurent Bricault, Miguel John Versluys, and Paul G. P. Meyboom, 1–14. Leiden: Brill.

Veymiers, Richard. 2009. "Les cultes isiaques à Amphipolis. Membra disjecta (IIIe s. av. J.-C.—IIIe s. apr. J.-C.)." *Bulletin de Correspondance Hellénique* 133 (1): 471–520.

Veymiers, Richard. 2018. "Agents, Images, Practices*." In *Individuals and Materials in the Greco-Roman Cults of Isis*, edited by Valentino Gasparini and Richard Veymiers, 1–58. Leiden: Brill.

Vos, Marietta de. 1996. "Iseum Metellinum." In *Lexicon Topographicum Urbis Romae,* Vol. 3, edited by Margareta Steinby, 110–12. Rome: Quasar.

Wallerstein, Immanuel M. 2000. *The Essential Wallerstein.* New York: New Press.

Watts, Duncan J., and Steven H. Strogatz. 1998. "Collective Dynamics of 'Small-World' Networks." *Nature* 393 (6684): 440–2.

Welles, Charles B. 1962. "The Discovery of Sarapis and the Foundation of Alexandria." *Historia: Zeitschrift für Alte Geschichte* 11 (3): 271–98.

Wilcken, Ulrich. 1927. *Urkunden der Ptolemäerzeit I (ältere Funde): Papyri aus Unterägypten.* Berlin: De Gruyter.

Will, Édouard. 1982. *Histoire politique du monde hellénistique (323–30 av. J.-C.), 2. Des avènements d'Antiochos III et de Philippe V à la fin des Lagides.* 2nd ed. Nancy: Presses universitaires de Nancy.

Witt, Reginald E. 1997. *Isis in the Ancient World.* Baltimore: Johns Hopkins University Press.

Woodhead, A. Geoffrey. 1963. "SEG 19-569. Chios (in Museo, Inv. n. 997). Honores Apollophanis, c. Med. s. IIIa." Supplementum Epigraphicum Graecum. Brill. http://dx.doi.org/10.1163/1874-6772_seg_a19_569.

Woolf, Greg. 2016. "Only Connect? Network Analysis and Religious Change in the Roman World." *Hélade* 2 (2): 43–58.

"WorldClim 1.4: Current Conditions." n.d. http://www.worldclim.org/current. Accessed January 1, 2017.

Wörrle, Michael. 1978. "Epigraphische Forschungen zur Geschichte Lykiens II: Ptolemaios II. und Telmessos." *Chiron* 8: 201–46.

Worthington, Ian. 2016. *Ptolemy I: King and Pharaoh of Egypt.* Oxford: Oxford University Press.

Index

Abydos 45
Aegean Islands 3, 55, 57, 59, 62, 66, 70, 73–8, 115, 122, 129, 136
Africa 42, 43
Agathocles 92, 134, 135, 146
agricultural fertility 8, 67, 73
agricultural vulnerability 74, 75, 79, 81, 82, 122, 131
Aigion 38
Ainos 38
Alexander the Great 1, 10, 12, 14–17, 20, 28, 29, 50, 66, 67, 116
Alexandria 2, 10, 12, 14–17, 20, 22, 23, 27, 38, 40, 44, 50–3, 56, 57, 66, 71, 72, 80, 86, 92, 101, 104–6, 110, 112, 134, 141, 149
Amathous 42
Ambracia 37
Ammon 8, 14
Amorgos 33, 58, 59, 63, 75
Amphipolis 36, 142
Amyzon 90, 146
Andriake 152
Andros 58, 67, 74, 75
Annales school 5, 116–18
Antigonid dynasty 37, 41, 47, 66, 67, 91, 92, 147
   Antigonus I Monophthalmus 67, 89
   Antigonus II Gonatas 68, 91, 147
   Demetrius I of Macedon (Poliorcetes) 29, 41, 47, 66–8, 89, 90
   Philip V of Macedon 36, 92, 95, 142, 145, 146, 148, 155
Antoninus Pius 51
Anubis 13, 16, 17, 25, 27, 33, 36, 48, 51, 86, 95, 135
Aphrodite 12, 15, 19, 20, 24, 29, 30
   Aphrodite-Arsinoe 15
Apis 9, 11
Apollo 42, 93, 111
   Apollo-Horus 60

Apollonia Salbace 39
Arsinoe-Methana 68, 90, 139, 144
Artemidorus of Perge 16, 27, 86, 139
Artemisia 11
Asclepius (Aesculapius) 9, 12, 150
Astypalaia 33, 60, 63
Athens 14, 16, 20, 24–6, 33, 35, 47, 56, 59, 62, 65, 67, 68, 77, 133, 147
   Athenians 29, 35, 65, 67, 77
   Athenian citizens 24–6

Babylon 10, 14, 91
Bargylia 38, 94, 95, 133, 155
barley 75, 76
basilistai 15, 16, 58, 136, 141
Beroia 36
Black Sea 37, 38, 43, 45, 66
Boeotia 35, 36
Bosporan kingdom 43–5, 158
Bricault, Laurent 2, 20, 29–31, 52, 55, 56, 60, 61, 64, 72, 85, 89, 98, 101, 113, 130, 131, 138, 141

Callicrates of Samos 90, 135, 147
Canopus 27, 41, 60, 133, 135
Caracalla 52
Caria 38, 57, 77, 89, 91, 93–7, 145–9, 151, 155
Carpasia 42
Carthage 42, 46
Cassius Dio 49, 51, 52
centrality 71, 79, 81–4, 104–6, 109, 110, 128
Chaironeia 20, 36
Chalcis 36
Chersonesos 53
Chios 59, 60, 153, 173
Chremonidean war 59, 61, 67, 68, 143, 144, 147
Christianity 21, 53, 122
Cilicia 39, 40, 91, 147
Cleomenes 66

cliodynamics 6, 118, 120, 123
coins 14, 17, 51, 52, 141
commercial 4, 22, 26, 30, 31, 53, 57, 59, 60, 63–6, 85, 86, 89, 93, 96
Commodus 51, 52
complexity 118–21, 123, 126, 127, 142
Corinth 38
Crete 27, 33, 54, 61, 63, 64, 143
Cumont, Franz 1, 4, 21–5, 28, 29, 53, 58, 59, 62, 64, 86, 92, 96, 131, 137–9
Cyclades 16, 24, 31–3, 47, 58, 59, 64, 67, 70, 74
Cyprus 10, 38, 41, 42, 65, 89, 133
Cyrene 42

Daulis 36
Delos 16, 24–7, 30, 31, 33, 47, 48, 53, 56–9, 61, 65, 72, 93, 135
 Delians 26, 134
Demeter 8, 12
demographic estimates 73, 76–8
Demosthenes 65, 66
diadochi 1, 28, 67, 90
Diodorus Siculus 8, 14, 66, 77
Diokles 16, 25, 27, 58, 85, 136
Dionysus 8, 9, 12, 126
Dunand, Françoise 13, 26–30, 62–4, 94, 97, 98, 137, 138

Egyptians 13, 15, 17, 20, 22–4, 26, 30, 32, 35
eigenvector 71, 104, 109
Ephesus 27, 38, 54, 68, 91, 96, 98, 133, 144, 147, 155
epidemiology 30, 64, 113, 119, 121, 136, 139, 141, 142
Epirus 37, 74
Euboea 20, 35

Faustina 51
Flavian dynasty 31, 50, 51
Fraser, Peter M. 4, 11, 12, 22–7, 29, 33, 58–64, 92–7, 131, 137–9

Galerius 52
grain trade 4, 32, 41, 46, 57, 60, 65–7, 72–5, 78, 79, 84, 86, 122, 131, 134

Hadrian 51
Halicarnassus 20, 38, 90, 94, 97, 98, 107, 111, 133, 146–9
Harpocrates 13, 17
Hellenomemphites 11, 12
Hellespont 38, 91
Horus 8, 13, 42
Hyampolis 36
Hypata 36
Hyrcania 41

Iasos 77, 90, 145
immunological factor 41, 110–12, 142
imperialistic theory 22, 24, 25, 27, 29, 53, 54, 58–63, 86, 92, 96, 97, 137, 138
Ionia 37, 38, 91, 93, 95, 96, 147, 154, 155
Ios 58
Island League 27, 32, 56–8, 63, 65, 67, 68, 134–6, 145, 149
Istrus 38
Italy 3, 45, 47, 48
Itanos 61, 68, 90, 133, 139, 143, 144

Jupiter 9
 Dolichenus 21, 126
 Helipolitanus 21

Kallias of Sphettos 65, 67, 147
Kalymna 150
Kalynda 149
Kamiros 39, 111
Kaunos 54, 90, 97, 148
Keos 16, 26, 33, 58, 59, 63, 68, 144
Keramos 20
Knidos 95, 107, 111, 134, 149
Kolophon 154
Kos 16, 111, 149, 150

Labraunda 145
League of islanders (*see* Island League)
Lebedos 154
Lesbos 59, 60, 153
Limyra 16, 40, 152
Lindos 39, 111
Lissa 150
longue durée 117
Lycia 40, 57, 89, 91, 145, 147, 148, 150–2

Lysimachus
  brother of Ptolemy III 134
  the diadoch 67, 68

Macedonia 36, 66–8
  Macedonian 1, 24, 28, 29, 68
Magnesia ad Maeandrum 95, 96, 155
Marcus Aurelius 51
maritime travel
  network 5, 31, 41, 44, 53, 69, 70, 79, 84, 86
  routes 32, 33, 38, 70, 72, 86, 116, 117, 128, 129
  sailing 70, 99, 104, 127, 129
  sailors 8, 22, 38, 44, 70, 71, 73, 99
  trade 4, 65, 115
Maroneia 38
mathematical model 5, 6, 69, 79, 82, 84–6, 115, 118, 119, 121
  deterministic 104, 119, 120, 141
  stochastic 119, 120
Memphis 9, 11, 12, 14, 23, 27
mercenaries 11, 33, 61, 64, 91, 147, 148
merchants 14, 18–20, 22, 25, 32, 47, 48, 66, 84, 86, 141
Mesembria 38
Methymna 153
Miletus 91, 93, 95, 147, 148
Mithra 21
Mithridates 30, 31, 48, 56
  Mithridatic wars 31, 48
mobility 38, 68, 97, 99, 100, 104, 112, 113, 116, 117, 127, 128
Moesia 37, 38
Mylasa 90, 95, 145, 146
Myndos 17, 97, 146, 148
Myra 40
Mytilene 60

nauarchos 135
Naupactus 36
naval base 26, 59, 63, 135, 145
Naxos 149
nesiarch 136, 149
Nesiotic League (*see* Island League)
network theory 6, 79, 81, 104, 124–7, 141
Nile 8, 41, 51, 133
Nymphaeum 43, 44

Olympia 133, 135
Orchomenus 20, 36, 134
Osiris 7–9, 11, 13, 15, 17, 22, 93, 94
  Osiris-Apis 9, 11–13, 52

Paerisades 44, 45
Pamphylia 39, 91, 136, 152, 153
pamphyliarch 136, 152
Parium 45
Patara 152
Patroclus of Macedon 61, 68, 90, 135, 143, 144
Pausanias 14, 30
Pellene 38
Peloponnese 28, 38, 74
Perinthus 38
pharaoh 1, 14, 50, 134
Philocles of Sidon 90, 135, 136, 147, 148
Phocis 36
Phoenicia 42, 89, 92, 135, 136
phrourarchos 136, 151
Piraeus 14, 18, 19, 30, 33, 35, 53, 56, 67
Pisidia 40, 152
Plutarch 7–10, 15, 31
Pluto 8, 9, 11, 12
Polybius 66, 134, 144, 145
precipitation 74
Priene 38, 95, 96, 98, 155
Pseudo-Callisthenes 10, 12
Ptolemaia 14, 24, 47, 134, 145
Ptolemaic dynasty
  Arsinoe II 15, 16, 25, 59, 94, 97, 135, 152, 153
  Arsinoe III 17, 36, 59, 133
  Berenice I 135, 149
  Berenice II 16, 42, 133, 134
  Egypt 20, 26, 29, 31, 44–6, 60, 63, 64, 66, 67, 133
  garrisons 17, 25, 27, 31, 32, 35, 41, 58, 59, 61, 63, 68, 72, 73, 79, 82, 84–6, 90, 103, 136, 138, 140, 143, 144, 147, 151, 156
  officials and administration 16, 26, 27, 31, 44, 59, 63, 86, 90, 96, 103, 134–6, 138, 148, 149, 152, 154
  propaganda 4, 22, 25, 62, 93, 94, 137, 138

Ptolemy I Soter 1, 8–10, 12–15, 22–4, 41, 47, 50, 56, 60, 65–7, 89, 90, 133–5, 145, 148, 149, 151, 152
Ptolemy II Philadelphus 14–16, 44, 59, 65, 68, 90, 91, 94–7, 134–6, 142, 144–7, 149–53
Ptolemy III Euergetes 9, 16, 24, 27, 38, 41, 42, 60, 66, 86, 91, 96, 133, 134, 136, 148, 149, 151, 153–5
Ptolemy IV Philopator 16, 17, 23, 27, 36, 59, 61, 92, 95, 133, 134, 136, 146, 150, 153
Ptolemy V Epiphanes 92, 143, 146, 150, 153, 155
Ptolemy VI Philometor 61, 90, 143, 144
troops 16, 25, 26, 32, 33, 41, 54, 64, 67, 68, 84, 86, 87, 136, 139, 143–5
Puteoli 47, 53
Pyrrhus of Epirus 67, 68

rainfall (*see* precipitation)
Rhacotis 9, 23
Rhamnous 20, 33–5
Rhodos 16, 20, 25, 31, 38, 53, 56, 57, 60, 62, 64–6, 72, 96, 97, 107, 111, 133, 134, 144–8, 155
roads 69, 78, 99, 100, 102, 111, 116, 128
Rome 46–50, 52, 53, 56, 57
  Roman empire 1, 21, 31, 33, 39, 40, 42, 50, 52, 53, 55, 69, 126, 140, 141
  Roman influence 1, 36, 46, 57
  Roman republic 30, 49
  Roman roads 99, 100

Samos 59, 60, 63, 68, 90, 91, 135, 145, 146, 148, 154, 155
Sarapiastai 24, 35, 59, 63, 141
Sarapieion (*see* Serapeum)
Seleucia in Pieria 91, 92
Seleucid dynasty 41, 90–5, 102, 110–12, 142, 144–9, 151–5
  Antiochus I Soter 41, 90, 91, 93, 146, 147, 153, 154
  Antiochus II Theos 91, 142, 144–8, 153, 155
  Antiochus III the Great 92, 144, 146–9, 151–55

Seleucus I Nicator 90, 93, 146
Seleucus II 91, 145, 146, 148, 155
Serapeum 10, 11, 15–17, 23, 26, 47, 50–53, 95
Severan dynasty 52
Sicily 45, 46
Sicyon 38
Sinope 8
Sosibios 36, 92, 95, 134, 149
strategos 41, 61, 68, 103, 135, 136, 146, 149, 152
Stratonikeia 20, 90, 95, 97, 98, 146
Syracuse 45, 46
Syria 9, 21, 41, 53, 89–91, 136, 140, 142

Tacitus 8, 9, 15
Tanagra 36, 134
Telmessos 151
Tenos 33, 58, 74
Teos 154
Termessos 152
Tertullian 48, 170
Theoi Adelphoi 15, 97, 135
Thera 16, 17, 25, 27, 33, 54, 58, 59, 62, 63, 68, 85, 133, 136, 139, 143, 144
Thessalonica 20, 36, 52
Thracia 37, 38
Timarchos 91, 148
trade 4, 25, 47, 53, 54, 62, 65, 66, 75, 81, 83, 84, 115
Tralles 39, 111, 155
transportation network 69, 70, 72, 73, 81, 86, 98–101, 103, 104, 106, 108, 109, 129, 130, 132, 140
Troad 45
Turchin, Peter 118–21
Tyche 61
Tyras 45
Tyrus 41

Vespasian 31, 50

Xanthos 40, 151

Zenon 44, 45, 59, 95
Zeus 8, 12, 14, 15, 135, 145

www.ingramcontent.com/pod-product-compliance
Lightning Source LLC
Chambersburg PA
CBHW061834300426
44115CB00013B/2378